Inspired Action

Create More Purpose, Productivity,
And Peace in Your Life

Erin Elizabeth Wells, M.Div.

Inspired Action
Create More Purpose, Productivity, & Peace in Your Life

Chosen Course Press
ISBN 978-0-9968615-0-2

Contact:
Erin Elizabeth Wells
(978) 238-8211
2 ½ Becket Street, Salem, MA 01970

Info@ChosenCourse.com
www.ChosenCourse.com

Printed in the United States of America

We are what we repeatedly do.
Excellence, then, is not an act but a habit.
—Aristotle

Dear Sue,

For all your years of encouragement, love, support, and hugs... I can never thank you enough. You lifted me up, guided me through, and brought me joy. You will always be both my dear friend and my extra Mom. I Love You.

Be Well,

Erin

Contents

Acknowledgments

When a book takes you over five years to complete there are inevitably many people to thank for their encouragement and support.

First, I want to thank my clients for their inspiration, stories, and for giving me the opportunity to learn beside them over the past twelve years.

My colleagues for their enthusiasm and encouragement including particularly the members of my Living Peace Team, My POmies, Wendy Buglio, Lisa Wessan, & Lisa Montanaro.

Nikki Bruno Clapper & Claudia Gere for their editing and book finishing prowess as they midwifed this project over the finish line.

Marcia Wochner & Emily Weinstock Straub for the illustrations included in the book.

Niurka & the SIIA Tribe for their energy and enthusiasm and for allowing me to continue to learn and grow along side them.

My best friends Marti Newland, Rebecca Turkel Marangos, & Jade Goodhue for the many, long phone calls.

David Allen, Julie Morgenstern, Charles Duhigg, Tony Schwartz, Stephen Covey, Leo Babauta, Tim Ferriss, Jack Canfield, Marie Forleo and many others who influenced me.

And, most importantly my wonderful husband, Brian, and my Mom and Dean. ILY as big as the universe. No words can encompass my gratitude for having your love and support in my life.

Introduction: How to Use This Book

Imagine that you are the captain of your own life's ship. You have a hull beneath you and a choice before you. You can simply float along through life, or you can define your course, refine your rigging, and set sail. How will you make your journey memorable and intentional?

Have you found yourself wishing there were an instruction manual for life? Something that could help you create more clarity, not only on your calendar and your kitchen counter, but also in your mind and heart? This book aims to accomplish that mammoth task, with a direct, action-oriented approach.

You could read *Inspired Action* like a devotional. Starting at the beginning, you could read one chapter each week, and then reflect and act on its contents during the week that follows. Each of the nine parts builds upon the next and guides you from a deep reflection on your life's core purpose to its full manifestation in your daily life. Reading this way the fifty chapters would lead you through a year of transformation.

Or, you could read this book like a fix-it manual. This would mean going directly to the chapter that addresses your greatest challenge and implementing the appropriate resolutions from there. You can visit additional chapters as new frustrations arise. Below, I offer suggestions for which chapters will help you resolve some common challenges.

Personally, I like to think of this book as one of the Choose Your Own Adventure children's novels that were popular in the 1970s and 80s. In many ways, this book is best approached as a self-guided journey into improving your everyday life in all its modern messiness. Many chapters lead to and reference each other, and some will bring you to www.InspiredActionBook.com/Resources, where further resources are available. So, if you start with the chapter that calls loudest to you, you will likely be drawn quickly to another chapter that is closely related. In this way, you can customize your journey for your needs.

Our lives are not straight lines. Most of us don't have the persistence to read a book such as this from cover to cover. So, I give you permission to encounter this book in bursts…hopefully switching from bursts of reflection to bursts of action as you create valuable improvements in your everyday life.

To help you move quickly to the areas that will support you most in *your* life's challenges, here are a few possible road maps:

- If you feel like you're floating through life aimlessly, then start with Chapters 1 to 6, which make up Part 1 (Destination: Defining Your Purpose).
- If you're frequently forgetting what you said you'd get done, read Chapter 19: Carrying a Capture Tool and Chapter 21: Task-Management Tools (a.k.a. To-Do Lists). Then read Part 5 (Your Helm & Rudder: Task-Management Essentials).
- If every day feels like a race to exhaustion, then Chapters 11 to 15 (Mending Your Sails: Energy Management) are for you.
- If your world is a chaos of papers and general "stuff," then Chapters 16 to 22 (Rigging and Spars: Tools and Systems to Get Organized) may hold valuable keys.
- If your days are missing a spark of meaning or fun, get started on your route to joy in Chapters 7 to 10 (The Route: Passion, Dreams, and Lifestyle). Then see Chapters 40 to 45 (The Journey: Everyday Meaning) for tips to create more depth in your everyday life.
- If everything feels persistently overwhelming, then start with Chapters 29 to 33 (Ballast Overboard: Simplifying). Then go

back to Chapters 11 to 15 (Mending Your Sails: Energy Management).

- ✧ If you feel alone, unsupported, or bogged down by unclear communication with people in your life, then Chapters 34 to 39 (Your Crew: Leveraging Your Team) might be your entryway into this work.
- ✧ If you're looking for more rhythm and structure to manage the flow of your day-to-day life, then Chapters 46 to 50 (Course Correcting: Knowing Where You Are) may give you the necessary insights.

Wherever you begin, may this book be an insightful guide to filling your everyday life with inspired action by bringing more meaning into the mundane, and may it help you develop the methods that keep you on course for a beautiful, intentional life.

Part 1

The Destination: Defining Your Purpose

—1—

Dowsing for Purpose

Take a look at this conversation. Does it sound familiar?

Someone you know: "Hey, how are you doing?"

You: "Oh, busy busy."

"Crazy busy"... "Really busy"... "Keepin' busy"... "Really overwhelmed."

These have become our pat answers to the common question, "How are you doing?"

The problem is that we have a confusing relationship with the term busy. On the one hand, we believe it's good to be busy because we've been taught that busy equals productive: we're getting a lot done. On the other hand, we often feel as if life were a roller coaster about to careen off its track or a hamster wheel in which we run superfast but never seem to get anywhere significant. We go, go, go, go...and where exactly do we end up?

Simply being busy hasn't necessarily improved our effectiveness at getting to a meaningful or purposeful destination. In other words, busy doesn't usually equal productive. Because life isn't a race for how much we can get done, but rather are the right things getting done to make your life fulfilling, meaningful, and joyful to you and those you impact.

What would happen if we paused, breathed, and stepped back from being busy? What if we chose to shift this unfulfilling pattern of activity? What if we stopped doing more and more, and asked the question that is most fundamental to our existence: why?

Asking "Why?"

"Why?" is the simplest and yet most challenging question you can ask yourself. In fact, it's so challenging to answer that most people avoid it or default to an answer that requires no thought. It's easy to generalize or to give the answers you were taught: "We are all here to love each other." "We are here because God put us here." "We just *are;* there is no reason."

Since you picked up a book about bringing more meaning to your life, I'm going to guess that you disagree with that last pat answer: "There is no reason." Certainly, your purpose can be drawn from spirituality, but it can also be viewed as defining your legacy. What will be the impact of your existence here? Whether you believe in God or any supreme power who might have a purpose for you, *you* have the power to create your own meaning and sense of purpose. You can define your own legacy, your purpose, *your* reason for being here. Which leads back to your original question: Why am I here?

Why are *you,* specifically, on this planet? What do you want to create with your life's time? What will be your legacy? What is your purpose?

If you remember when you were about five years old—or if you've spent time with a five-year-old—you know that the favorite question about every new thing is "Why?" Through a child's eyes everything seems strange and unusual, and that natural inquisitiveness brings forth the question to parents, siblings, and everyone nearby: "Why do I have to go to bed? Why is the sky blue? Why do birds fly? Why do turtles hide their heads in their shells? Why, why, why?"

In childhood, we ask this question quite easily and naturally, but as adults we frequently stop. Perhaps the question and answers start feeling too big and insurmountable. Maybe you spent too much time in that college philosophy class studying Descartes, Kant, and Nietzsche and came to feel that the answers you want are unknowable.

Today is the day to reclaim your power to *create* an answer. This is *your* life, your purpose, and you have all the answers you need available to you right here and now.

Own Your Journey

On your journey to create more meaning in your life, the first step is to recognize that *you* are the creator of your life. You may prefer to see yourself as a co-creator with God or the Universe, but either way, you do have the power to direct the focus, energy, and intentions for your life. Niurka, one of my teachers, explains this state as being *at cause* rather than *in effect*. It refers to a state of mind in which you own and recognize both your power to choose and your responsibility for whatever unfolds in your life. Your choices create your experiences and results. You are the cause of your life, not the victim of perpetually uncontrollable circumstances.

I often think of my role in life's journey as that of a ship's captain. I currently live within two blocks of the ocean in Massachusetts, and although I grew up in Ohio, I have discovered a love and passion for the sea. My relationship with large bodies of water is rather complex, since for many years I suffered from a fear of swimming in them. This fear held me back. I would stand on the shore and listen to the waves, but I would feel no desire to go into the water, even on the hottest of summer days.

On the other hand, I grew up around boats. My father was deeply involved in the sport of rowing, and I spent many hours of my childhood on motorboats with the officials for various regattas. I loved being out on the water and feeling the wind in my hair. But when as an adult, I discovered the quiet joy of sailing, the sea began to sing to my heart.

I am still a novice sailor, but I have discovered that sailing is a perfect metaphor for life. We sail in partnership with the wind and the waves; they blow and roll, but we can learn how to leverage them. In sailing, if you set your course and sails correctly, your boat can speed you toward another shore. In your life's journey the same is true; if you learn how to rig your boat and sail it properly, then you can end up in places you can barely imagine. But, you have to be willing to dare. As author and Nobel Prize winner André Gide said, we "cannot discover new oceans unless [we] have the courage to lose sight of shore."

To me, Gide's statement means that, in order to create the life we want, we must begin to take complete responsibility for everything that happens to us. If we have the courage to leave shore, then it is our action or inaction that might land us into the drink. We can choose to journey, to create, to grow, and to reach for our dreams—or simply to remain in place and feel the wind whip against our face on the shore. If we choose to act, to move, to seek our purpose, then we are part of moving humanity forward. We who choose to journey are the force that invents the new, creates the beautiful, and solves all our current problems. As we become ever more awake and enlightened to our own power—to our light, as Marianne Williamson calls it—we own our capacity to change ourselves and our world.

According to the Law of Attraction, our energy and vibrations bring toward us those experiences and outcomes that are in harmony with our thoughts, feelings, and actions. This means that, consciously or unconsciously, you are manifesting whatever you frequently think or feel. We have the power to create through our thoughts and feelings as well as through our decisions and actions. We attract both what we want and what we fear. For example, as I learned to overcome my fear of water, I discovered that the more I feared and resisted it, the more I ended up wet.

We are creators of such power that our journey is one of both outward creation and inward development, which allows us to release the fears that may have held us in place in the past. To quote William Ernest Henley's poem "Invictus," "I am the master of my fate: I am the captain of my soul." Are you ready to own your journey?

Where to Start

On the journey to seek your purpose, each reader of this book will begin in a different place. It's the perfect place for you right now because we all begin where we are. You begin from where you are to chart your own course, both in life and your course through this book.

That's why your first step is to consider which type of seeker you are, and then continue along the appropriate path for you.

I find that virtually everyone lands in one of the following four groups when it comes to the question of purpose.

Manifesters

These folks know their purpose clearly and consciously. They are in a constant state of exploring how they can live that purpose better and more fully. If this is you, then congratulations! You are on your journey, and this book will help you move forward even more intentionally. You may want to jump to Chapter 2: Show Me the Energy.

Resisters

These are the folks who have a semiconscious awareness of their purpose. It's been rattling around in the back of their head, but they have been resisting or ignoring it. The people in this group are often waiting for the perfect opportunity to let their life purpose come out. If this is you, then you might want to continue your journey through this book with Chapter 3: Dissolving Resistance before returning to Chapter 2: Show Me the Energy.

Doubters

These folks have spent some time asking themselves, "What is my purpose?" but feel doubtful, confused, or dissatisfied with their answers. Thus, their purpose is still unknown or unclear. If this is you, then you will want to keep reading this chapter because it provides strategies to become clearer, and you almost certainly want to spend some time with Chapter 2: Show Me the Energy, because doubt often comes from either resistance (see "Resisters," above) or lack of clarity.

Drifters

"Purpose? Meaning? Huh? I just get up, go to work each day, and go home." Drifters have allowed themselves to become adrift from any sense of intention or direction in their lives. They float aimlessly from job to job, activity to activity, and group to group with no clarity and little energy for any specific goal. They are disconnected, and often living more "in effect" than "at cause" in their lives as we discussed earlier. If this is you, then you are in exactly the right place. Keep reading, because it's time to make a big change in your life!

Necessary Presuppositions

If you are a Drifter or a Doubter who is ready to establish a clear purpose, then we need to begin by agreeing on two things:

1. You are the creator of your life. We started the chapter with this essential idea, and it cannot be repeated enough: you have the power to make decisions, to take action, and to change what you do each and every day. If you want a road out of monotony and drifting, then you are the only one who can build it, so you have to make the decision to change. If you're struggling to accept this presupposition, then pretend that you've just walked into a parallel dimension in which you do have creative power, and act accordingly. If you behave from that mind space, eventually you may notice how much creative power you have simply by claiming it. For example, this evening after work, you get to decide what you want to do: watch TV, read this book, or call a friend. These options represent your power to choose, your power to create the life experience you want. Whether it's what you do with a day, an evening, an hour, or this very minute, you are in control of that decision.

2. Having a purpose is good for you. To accept this presupposition, we can start by acknowledging the opposite: living without a purpose has prevented you from accomplishing what you've wanted thus far in life, right? After all, you probably wouldn't be picking up a book like this if your life were perfect in every way and you were completely satisfied. Now, can you agree that if you were to claim a purpose for your life, then you would be much more able to begin creating the outcomes you desire? You would have defined the why behind your actions

> and decisions. You would be able to provide satisfactory answers to your inner five-year-old. You would be more focused. And, through your actions, decisions, and life's journey, you would create the experiences that you desire. Your sense of purpose will be the source of meaning in your daily life. Therefore, as you define and connect to it, your purpose will also become a source of energy and power.

If you can accept the previous two statements, then you are ready to begin seeking.

Dowsing Within for Purpose

The first step toward change is becoming aware of your purpose. You have to be aware of your purpose for it to impact your daily life. *Many* books and exercises out there are meant to help you identify your purpose, and most of them boil down to the two major roads of discovery that I describe below. Neither road is right or wrong, and both can get you to the end goal of greater awareness of your purpose. So, choose one and try it. If you come up dry, then change tacks and go the other way!

Road 1: Listening Within

Traveling the road within relies on your ability to listen to your internal knowing. Perhaps this is a part of you that sees more broadly or clearly—your higher self. This might also be your soul—your connection to the divine, or the channel of communication between God/the Universe and you. This is the seat of wisdom and intuition within you that has guided you throughout your life.

It is my belief that we all have this space and connection within us, but each of us has developed a different level of trust in its guidance. If you are at all aware of this connection within you, then this road of turning within yourself to engage your question of purpose can be a wonderful first step. When you build your relationship to that part of yourself, you deepen your trust of it and use its guidance more often in your daily life decisions.

I frequently equate the practice of listening within to that of dowsing for water. Dowsing is a practice of divinatory exploration in which the seeker attunes him or herself to the energy flowing within the earth and, using a special stick or rods, walks the ground to locate the best place to dig a new well. In other words, seekers who dowse tune in to what they want and then watch for the cue that they have found it.

How does dowsing for water apply to uncovering your purpose? Finding your purpose can be a simple two-step process:

1. Get quiet and ask your higher self/divine connection/inner knowing two questions: Why am I here? What is my purpose? Then listen for its answer.

2. Watch for a change in your internal state. You may experience this change as an internal welling of joy, a sense of rightness, a peaceful knowing, or an experience of awe. The inner shift is your dowsing rod telling you that you've uncovered something powerful and worth exploring deeply.

If this quiet, internal conversation feels too simple for you, then you could also try writing it as a discussion. Get quiet and write the questions—"Why am I here? What is my purpose?"—on a sheet of paper or in your journal. Then allow the answers to well up from within you or be downloaded to you, and write them down. Don't question or judge them; just write and observe. Then, again, watch for your internal state change.

I believe that dowsing within is the simplest and most direct route to uncovering the sense of purpose quietly dormant within you. However, this simple and straightforward method is not easy for everyone, particularly for those who lack a strong sense of connection to their intuition, to the divine, or to their higher self. If you are one of those people, the outer-world road might be the easier one to take.

Road 2: Identifying Impact

On this road to purpose, rather than looking primarily within yourself for the answers, the process is to reflect on your life and identify the times and places that have felt the most powerful, joyful, and impactful both for yourself and for others.

Often this brainstorming exercise is best done through reflection and writing. So, grab some paper, your journal or our worksheet listed in the resources below, and ask yourself the following questions:

- What activities in my life have been the most enjoyable? Fun? Exciting?
- When have I experienced a sense of fulfillment? The true pleasure of accomplishment? The feeling of having done good work?
- What am I particularly gifted at? What do I do better than many people I know? What can I do easily that others find to be a struggle?
- When have I done something that provided a tremendous value or benefit to someone else? At what moments have I had the greatest impact on others?
- What would I like to have people say about me after I have gone? What legacy of feeling, actions, or experiences would I like to leave behind me?

As you write your answers, remember that you are brainstorming. There are no wrong answers. Capture everything that pops into your head, even if it seems silly, and definitely if it has nothing to do with your current work or job in the world. Don't limit yourself. This is a big world, filled with endless needs and opportunities. If your greatest love is baking but you've never done it professionally, there is no reason why you shouldn't include baking on your list.

Once you've completed the brainstorming exercise, review your answers and watch for your internal state change. When do you feel that sense of joy rising up within you? Or during which of those events or activities have you felt it in the past? These are your clues. These emotions are your dowsing rod for identifying your purpose.

It's ok if your purpose feels a bit vague at this point. The next three chapters will help you bring it into focus. Maybe right now all you know is that it has something to do with creating beauty through jewelry, gardens, or art. Perhaps it has something to do with caring for kids or the elderly. Maybe it's about building airplanes or innovations in technology. Right now just become aware of the direction and your connection to that calling. Then, in the upcoming three chapters we'll help you create more clarity.

Embracing Your Purpose

For some people walking these roads, clarity of purpose will come like a bolt from the blue, a sudden sense of calling. Or it might feel like the gentle pull of gravity, as if a zip line were pulling you straight toward your purpose.

Others might need to take some time repeating the exercises and becoming attuned to your internal shift of emotion and energy. The primary goal of this chapter is to open your heart to seek your answer. Set your intention to become open to finding your purpose, to knowing your answer. This opening creates the conditions to make its discovery possible. After all, you will never find the answer to the question you don't ask. Live in the question.

It might be that you uncover a sense of purpose that feels powerful and true for you in this moment, but in a month, a year, or a decade it loses its juice. That's okay! That means it's time to explore and refine. Perhaps you just need greater clarity (see Chapter 2: Show Me the Energy), or perhaps you're in a moment of significant life transition and your focus is changing to manifest something new (See Chapter 6: When Purpose Changes). Each phase of your life is different, and how you manifest your purpose may shift with time. That doesn't make your sense of purpose here and now any less true, valuable, or powerful. This present moment, and the power of your connection to purpose, will fuel your growth and everyday actions. It will allow you to create both the life and the legacy that you want in this world. Live it, love it, embrace it with your full being, and bring it into your daily life and awareness.

Next Actions

✓ If you have used the methods described in this chapter and still have not found your purpose—that is, you have not felt that internal shift that indicates you're on the right path, even if it's a little bit fuzzy—then here are two suggestions:

1. Give it time. Repeat the reflective questioning above whenever you have a moment to pause—before you go to bed each night, as you wait for the train, while you drink your coffee in the morning. Simply give yourself some time to live in the question.
2. If you continue to feel confused and stuck, then you might want to pick up Tim Kelley's *True Purpose* (see **Resources,** below). It is one of the better guides to finding purpose because it provides 12 specific, actionable techniques, rather than just engaging the issue philosophically or theologically.

✓ If you have gotten a sense of your purpose, even if it feels kind of strange or fuzzy at the moment, then now is the time to keep it fresh and nurture it. Think of it like the first little flame of a fire that you're building. Take nurturing actions to keep the little flame alive: write about it, read about it, talk about it, meditate on it, draw it, breathe life into it. In this early stage, you might struggle with taking action on it, but we'll get there, no rush. The goal at the moment is to make sure that your little flame doesn't go out again and that you don't relapse into drifting and wandering aimlessly. Nurture your purpose flame every day, if only for one moment. For some more help with this task, take a look at Chapter 4: Your Purpose Statement.

Resources

Dowsing for Purpose Worksheet. www.InspiredActionBook.com/Resources.

Kelley, Tim. *True Purpose: 12 Strategies for Discovering the Difference You Are Meant to Make*. Berkeley, CA: Transcendent Solutions Press, 2009.

Leider, Richard J. T*he Power of Purpose: Find Meaning, Live Longer, Better*. San Francisco: Berrett-Koehler Publishers, 2010.

Niurka. *Supreme Influence: Change Your Life with the Power of the Language You Use*. New York: Harmony Books, 2013.

—2—

Show Me the Energy

Thinking about your purpose and putting it into action should enliven you. It should bring forward a sense of dedication, excitement, and joy. The energy that emerges from your being when you live and act *on purpose* is authentic and noticeable. If you are not feeling fired up and excited when you think about or take action on your purpose, then further reflection might be required.

Below are several questions designed to help you get that energy flowing.

Is My Purpose Big Enough?

Too frequently we set our sights too low out of fear, hesitation, or what our rational mind calls "being realistic." But allowing these obstacles to influence our definition of our purpose stifles our authentic sense of ambition and achievement. We unwittingly restrict or cap our energy flow because of our fears. For instance, we might fear the possibility of overreaching and failing. Or we might fear that achieving our goals will so completely change our lives that we will no longer recognize ourselves or remain connected to our roots. Whatever your particular fear, you can unleash the energy of purpose by making the goal big enough to magnetize your enthusiasm to achieve it. This energy will help you summon the courage to face your fears and to take risks. Ray Bradbury offered some words of wisdom on this topic: "Living at risk is jumping off a cliff and building your wings on the way down." Your purpose will be big enough to propel you off that cliff. It forces you to trust that you will learn how to build your wings as you fall.

Is My Purpose Focused Enough?

We human beings relate to our world through stories. When you think about your purpose, are you clear on who or what will benefit from your commitment to it? Imagine the stories. If you can't envision the interpersonal or tangible benefit that will result from living your purpose, then it's time to get more specific and focused. With whom are you working (if anyone), and toward what end? For instance, what type of suffering are you trying to ease? What accomplishment are you trying to make possible? The problem with a purpose that's too general is that it's hard to get passionate about something that doesn't speak specifically to *you* and shows you the lived benefit or outcome for the world around you.

Is My Purpose Action-Oriented Enough?

An authentic sense of purpose draws us forward. It defines our path through life and, like a beacon, guides us in how to act and where to go. While some purposes are focused on an overall way of being in the world, even those purposes correlate to certain actions that are congruent with that way of being and certain actions that are not. If your purpose doesn't clearly lead you to the actions you will take to live in alignment with it, then you might want to shift your understanding of it—or the language you use to express it—until those actions become clear. Living fully *on purpose* provides you with a clear guide or benchmark for your actions that will propel you into manifesting them.

Am I Experiencing Resistance?

Resistance is a fearsome beast that may raise its powerful head and try to demoralize you or distract you from your important work. If the energy around your purpose is feeling stifled, and you are comfortable with your answers to the previous three questions, resistance is likely the culprit. Steven Pressfield, in his book *The War of Art*, provides an excellent overview of the many ways that resistance can keep you from your purpose. We will explore how to dissolve and overcome resistance more thoroughly in Chapter 3: Dissolving Resistance, but for now you should know that, as Pressfield says, "Resistance will point to True North." In other words, "The more scared we are of the work or calling, the more sure we can be that we have to do it."

Next Actions

✓ Set aside some time (for instance, a half hour per day for the next week, or a half day on Friday or Sunday) to reflect on, research, and meditate about your purpose. Grab a notebook or your journal and just freewrite about the ideas, issues, and possibilities that arise when you think about your purpose.

✓ Find someone who shares your purpose or is at least playing on a similar field, and schedule time to talk with him or her about your ideas, visions, and understanding of what could be possible. Whether it's a phone call, coffee, or dinner, sharing with another person may help you to deepen or clarify your commitment to your purpose.

✓ Draw pictures or create a collage of your purpose in action or manifestation. What would the outcome look like?

✓ Write a eulogy for your life from the perspective of its end. Imagine who would be giving it and what he/she/they would say. What have been your accomplishments and achievements? How did your sense of purpose define your legacy?

Resources

Pressfield, Steven. *Turning Pro: Tap Your Inner Power and Create Your Life's Work.* New York: Black Irish Entertainment LLC, 2012.

Pressfield, Steven. *The War of Art: Break Through the Blocks and Win Your Inner Creative Battles.* New York: Black Irish Entertainment LLC, 2002.

—3—

Dissolving Resistance

Every road to every dream begins with your decision to walk it and the action of taking the first step. However, so many of us get daunted by the idea of the journey. We dwell on our fear of the obstacles and challenges that might appear miles down the road, and our imagined monsters become larger and scarier, locking us into what I call scared-bunny mode. We become frozen in inaction.

We are not rabbits, however, and most of our predators exist primarily in our own minds. But that doesn't mean the predators don't exist. Our greatest predator, writes Steven Pressfield, is resistance:

> *Resistance is the most toxic force on the planet....It prevents us from achieving the life God intended when he endowed each of us with our own unique genius.*

We each have work that we are here to do. We have gifts that we are uniquely able to give to others. When we allow resistance to defeat, discourage, or delay us, we are harming not only ourselves, but also the entire world, including friends, family members, and co-workers who might need what we have to give. Others may benefit directly from your life's work, or perhaps they will simply be inspired by seeing you live it. Either way, resistance is the monster to be conquered.

What can you do to conquer your fear and dissolve your resistance? As I stated earlier, the road to any purpose, goal, dream, or outcome starts with two things:

1. The decision to commit yourself to the path.
2. A plan of action that shows you the first step to take.

Task 1: The Decision to Commit

In my experience, such decisions are not made once and finished. Indeed, with resistance gnawing at your heels, it is easy to end up mired and frozen again. So, try turning your decision to commit into a daily practice. Each day, lock resistance back into its cage by recommitting to your purpose.

How this daily practice of recommitment manifests in your life will be unique to you, but here are some ideas to get you started:

- ✧ Evoke the energy of joy and commitment within yourself. Then repeat a series of affirmation statements during your morning routine— in the shower, in front of a mirror, or before your first sip of coffee. What could you say? I am connected and committed to my purpose. I am focused on living my purpose fully today. Best of all would be to create and use your purpose connection button, which we cover in Chapter 4.
- ✧ Engage in a brief daily reflection or journaling session on future possibilities. What will living your purpose make possible for you or others? How can and will you bring more value, beauty, and goodness to your life and to the lives of those around you?
- ✧ Meditate. Turn your purpose statement into a mantra, or draw warm energy from the earth and from Spirit to feed yourself and your purpose.
- ✧ Make a declaration upon getting up each morning: "I love my life, and I am here to ______."

Task 2: The Action Plan

The second part of dissolving resistance involves creating a plan of action and taking the first step that will help you shift your focus from the awe-inspiring end of your journey to its very simple beginning. As Antoine de Saint-Exupéry said, "A goal without a plan is a wish."

When climbing a mountain, if you continuously look at the top, you're likely to trip over a lot of rocks. Therefore, the fastest and surest way to actually get to the top is to start with the first few steps. Here are some questions to help you get started:

- **What is the exact next step?** Drill down and make it specific. Your next step should be a specific task that ideally takes 5 to 10 minutes, but definitely takes no longer than an hour. Examples: "Call John re: repairs"; "Email Stephanie to schedule meeting"; "Research hotels in Florence"; "Order copy of *Inspired Action* for Jessica."
- **Based on your calendar, could you take that next step today?** If not, pick a specific day this week when you can commit to that step.
- **Is there anyone who can help you on your journey?** Support and encouragement from others can help you get moving again when the resistance monster looms. Who could be on your team, either actively working with you toward your goal or serving as your cheering and coaching section, providing accountability and encouragement as needed?

As you tackle these questions, remember this key idea: It's best not to focus on possible problems with your journey right now. Address them when (or if) they arise.

Could your plan be much more elaborate and involved? Sure. But the essence of dissolving resistance is taking *simple and continuous action* by asking yourself, "What is the exact next step? When will I do it?" The best way to build momentum is to take one such step toward your intentional future each day. Once you get into a rhythm of action, then more big picture advanced planning might be appropriate, but for now conquer resistance through simple, continuous action.

According to Adam Markel, CEO of the personal development training company Peak Potentials, there are two kinds of habits: habits of doing and habits of not doing. If resistance has held you entrapped in the latter, then it's time to start developing the former. For more information and ideas on developing new habits, take a look at Chapter 14: Habits: The Power of Patterns.

I will conclude with an insight that my mother shared with me about getting her dissertation finished. The project felt so big and daunting that she avoided getting started. Her key to moving forward was deciding that the first step would be simply to sit at her desk for 15 minutes. She didn't have to *do* anything. She just needed to commit to getting her "butt in the chair." From that small step, the further actions of reviewing research, writing notes, and drafting small sections of the dissertation became much easier over time.

What is your "butt-in-the-chair" action? What can you do to just start showing up for your purpose and life's work in the world?

Next Actions

- ✓ During the next two weeks, practice identifying and scheduling the next actions for your purpose-driven plan. Afterward, reflect on your progress. Has taking action become easier? Is resistance still getting in the way? If so, break down the tasks into even smaller steps, or ask someone to be your partner in the process.
- ✓ When you find your mind mired in what-ifs or thoughts about possible obstacles or challenges, tell that little voice in your head, "Thank you for sharing" and refocus either on your purpose statement or on your exact next action. Even better, practice asking more empowering questions of yourself. You can learn more about the formula for empowering questions in Chapter 34: Leading by Example.
- ✓ Momentum is your best friend when countering resistance. Make taking action on your purpose a regular event in your life, either daily or weekly. Plan it ahead. On what day(s) could you take action? For how long? Imagine how adding that piece would feel in the flow of your day. The more predictable taking action becomes, the easier the momentum is to sustain.

- ✓ Make an audio recording of your affirmations to play as you brush your teeth or drink your coffee in the morning. Always begin by evoking a positive emotion before you listen to them; for instance, open yourself to feeling committed or unstoppable. Use this practice as your talisman of recommitment to keep your mind focused on your purpose and goals.

Resources

Canfield, Jack, and Janet Switzer. *The Success Principles: How to Get from Where You Are to Where You Want to Be*. New York: HarperCollins, 2005.

Markel, Adam. 2013. *Peak Potentials Training Programs.* http://bit.ly/NewPeaks.

Pressfield, Steven. *The War of Art: Break Through the Blocks and Win Your Inner Creative Battles*. New York: Black Irish Entertainment LLC, 2002.

—4—

Your Purpose Statement

Have you ever noticed that what you focus on expands? Focus on a problem, and everything becomes about the problem. Focus on a joyful experience, and everything feels joyful. Wouldn't it be great if you could just push a button and experience the beautiful feeling of being connected to your purpose? What if we helped you install that button?

Your Purpose Connection Button requires two ingredients:

1. A clear purpose statement (The experience being triggered.)
2. A charged emotional anchor (The button to be pushed.)

Your Purpose Statement

There's power in words. The more you focus the language of your purpose, the deeper your understanding and experience of it will become. Consider the mantras, or repetitive ritual words, that are used in most of the major spiritual traditions. Christians say the rosary or the Our Father. Buddhists and Hindus have rhythmic ritual mantras for meditation and prayer. In the Jewish tradition, I remember the beautiful intensity of the ritual words to commence the Seder dinner that my uncle, Calvin, would speak.

At first your purpose may emerge as a general sense of who, what, and where you want to impact, but a general *sense* will never carry you as far on a daily basis as a strong, clear purpose statement can. Choosing specific words to connect you clearly to your purpose can be an act of setting a spiritual intention. Regardless of your spiritual or religious background, with these words you will manifest your highest understanding of your life's purpose each time you speak them. The effort of clearly defining these words will pay off greatly over time.

Elements of a Purpose Statement

A strong purpose statement includes two parts:

1. A specific statement of whom or what you are working for or with
2. A defined outcome—the result or benefit of following your purpose

Based on these elements, the formula for an effective purpose statement is as follows:

I + [verb] + [group of people or focus of work] + so that + [outcome].

Here are some examples:

- I care for animals that have been abandoned so that they will be restored to health and joy.
- I craft our company's message so that we can serve and improve the lives of even more people.
- I teach children so that they will stay curious and develop their love of learning.
- I lead the people on my team brilliantly so that we can create the best products for our customers.
- I love and nurture the elderly so that they can live with care and dignity in their final years.
- I do improv comedy and teach acting so that I can bring joy and fun to people's lives.
- I create awareness of how we all can take better care of our planet so that we and our children can live more sustainably with the Earth.

Here is my own purpose statement:

I teach ambitious entrepreneurs how to connect with purpose and create the systems, habits, and mindsets to manifest that purpose in their everyday lives.

The Benefits of a Purpose Statement

A clear and congruent purpose statement will help you do the following things:

- **Focus your decisions and actions on a daily basis.** Your purpose statement helps you decide which actions are really essential on a daily or weekly basis. It gives you a clearer way to answer the question, "Does this task or project support or align with my purpose?"
- **Measure your progress and success.** Your purpose statement gives you a way to gauge your progress during quarterly and annual reflection times (see Chapters 47 and 48). During these reflections you will ask, "How much of my energy and time am I dedicating to my purpose? How can I make further progress? What will be my next measure of success? What project should be my next major focus?"
- **Communicate clearly and gain associates and allies.** A well-crafted purpose statement is easy to communicate to others. How many times in your life have you been asked, "What do you do?" What if you could surprise your conversation partner by saying, "I work with corporations so that they can be better stewards of our planet"? Isn't that a more compelling answer than "I'm an environmental consultant"? You never know when the person you're talking with might become an advantageous partner or ally on your path.
- **Ritually renew your commitment to your purpose.** I began this chapter by comparing a purpose statement to a mantra. One of the most powerful benefits of having a clear purpose statement is your ability to repeat it easily and frequently to yourself and to others. A daily reminder of the work that

comes from your core will both help you through the rough times and feed your energy for all sections of your journey.

Create and Charge Your Emotional Anchor

Your emotional anchor is the second ingredient for your Purpose Connection Button. It is a symbol of your purpose that triggers the feeling you get by connecting to that purpose. An emotional anchor can be anything—a physical object, such as a piece of jewelry; a part of your body that you touch or bring your hand to, like your heart; or a movement, such as a fist pump. One of my clients chose to squeeze the index finger of her right hand, which became her magic finger to evoke the powerful emotional state she needed to stay on course. I encourage you to make your anchor something accessible that you will either keep with you or be able to repeat whenever you need it.

Once you've chosen an anchor, it's time to charge it up. You can go to www.InspiredActionBook.com/Resources and listen to our Purpose Connection Button audio exercise for help with this process, or you can read the following instructions:

1. Take a couple deep breaths, relax, and close your eyes.
2. Notice how easily you can remember a time when you felt unstoppable—when you were certain that you would succeed. Bring that experience into your mind and body as if it were happening right now. Breathe how you were breathing at that time, feel what you were feeling, see what you were seeing, and hear what you were hearing. Drop back fully into that moment.
3. Make the moment bigger, brighter, crisper, and clearer. Bring the feeling of being unstoppable up to a peak. You are completely certain that you can succeed at whatever is in front of you. Now, pour that feeling into your anchor. Touch the object or part of your body, or make your anchor gesture. Feel the connection. Charge your anchor with that emotion. When you feel it connect or click in, take a deep breath and clear the

screen mentally and emotionally. Come back to the present moment.

4. Now, how easily can you remember a time when you felt completely clear and focused on your task. Do you remember that? You were in flow, and the world dropped away, leaving you clicking away easily on the project at hand. Drop into that moment fully, as if it were happening right now. Breathe how you were breathing, feel what you were feeling, see what you were seeing, and hear what you were hearing.
5. Again, make the moment bigger, brighter, crisper, and clearer. You are so clear, so focused, and everything is just moving along easily. Raise the feeling to a peak, and then pour that feeling into your anchor. Touch the object or part of your body, or make your anchor gesture. Feel the connection. Charge your anchor with that emotion. When you feel it connect or click in, take a deep breath and clear the screen mentally and emotionally. Come back to the present moment.
6. Finally, notice how easily you can remember a time when you felt like joy and excitement were just pouring out of you. Can you remember that? Bring yourself fully into that experience of complete joy and excitement. It's filling you up and radiating out of you. Drop fully into that moment as if it were happening right now. Breathe how you were breathing, feel what you were feeling, see what you were seeing, and hear what you were hearing.
7. One last time, make the moment bigger, brighter, crisper, and clearer. The joy and excitement are thrumming through your whole body and vibrating out of you. Raise the feeling to a peak, and then pour that feeling into your anchor. Touch the object or part of your body, or make your anchor gesture. Feel the connection. Charge your anchor with that emotion. When you feel it connect or click in, take a deep breath and clear the

screen mentally and emotionally. Come back to the present moment.

8. Now bring the two parts together. Touch your anchor object or make your anchor gesture and feel the focused, certain, unstoppable joy rise and wash over you and fill your being. When you feel those emotions flowing through you, say your purpose statement, either aloud or in your mind. Speak it with certainty, power, and joy. Surround it with those feelings, and perhaps even repeat it and your anchor gesture once or twice more. Feel them connect, and know that whenever you want to evoke these emotional states and connect to your purpose, all you need to do is to touch or repeat your anchor and open yourself to reconnecting with this moment right now: focused, certain, unstoppable joy for your purpose. It's waiting for you at your fingertips.

Next Actions

✓ Draft your purpose statement. Play with active and vibrant verbs. Define your target audience or focus even more specifically. Make your outcome compelling. Make your purpose statement easy to say and to remember.

✓ Make pressing your Purpose Connection Button a daily practice. Charge your anchor; feel the emotion of focused, certain, unstoppable joy flow into you; and speak your purpose statement. Start your day with it; do it as soon as your feet hit the floor, or before you walk out your door in the morning. Hit your purpose connection button before you walk into that important meeting or conversation. The more you use it, repeatedly and intentionally, the stronger it will become.

✓ If you find yourself naturally feeling an emotion that you'd like to connect to your purpose, then charge your anchor at that moment and stack the emotion into your Purpose Connection Button. Build the feeling up, bring it to a peak, and feel it connect to your anchor.

- ✓ When someone asks you what you do, experiment with telling him or her your purpose statement rather than stating your company, position, or title. You might discover fascinating people and have great conversations because you give people a sense of your core rather than just the outer-world titles and trappings.
- ✓ Look over your plans for the day or week and ask yourself, "How do these plans support my purpose?" You don't have to align *every* action you take to your purpose, but if you aren't taking purpose-aligned actions regularly, you may discover that you've lost momentum and focus.

Resource

Niurka. *Supreme Influence: Change Your Life with the Power of the Language You Use*. New York: Harmony Books, 2013.

—5—

Time for a Commitment Audit

If you have become clear on your purpose, then it's time to clean house on your commitments. No matter how much we may wish to be superheroes capable of being in many places at once, being brilliant at everything, and leaping tall buildings in a single bound…the reality is that we are human, and we have limits.

You only have so much time and energy, but remember: you have the ability to choose where your time and energy will go. As we discuss in Chapter 1, the goal is to live *at cause* in your life as the creator and captain of your journey. *You* are in charge of your life's commitments, and you have the ability to say "Yes" or "No," as well as "Not now" or "I'm done." And now your newfound clarity about your purpose gives you a benchmark or measuring stick against which to evaluate your current commitments.

I have done this process of reevaluating my commitments numerous times in my life. I will grant that every time has been slightly harder, since my life has continuously become more complex and has included more people who rely on me. But I will also affirm that the process has been worth it every single time.

If you cannot commit to each of your responsibilities—including your relationships—with a full and clear heart, then the time has arrived to reevaluate and possibly release them. This process of reevaluation is a commitment audit. It has the following steps:

1. Brainstorm a list of all the commitments on your plate, big and small. Think about commitments in your personal life, family life, work life, volunteer work, and other areas. In addition to time commitments, include relationship commitments—to your life partner, kids, friends, family members, and colleagues. Both people and activities require energy. On my list I

certainly included my cats, my houseplants, my car, and my home, all of which regularly require my effort, care, and attention. Ask your spouse or a close friend to help you make sure you've thought of all your commitments. It's amazing how many small responsibilities we accept without thinking or simply out of habit—and those tasks might be the first to go.

2. Consider your commitments in relationship to your purpose. Which commitments fit your needs and passions? Which ones are draining you? Take some time to simply reflect on each commitment. Address these questions:
   - How do you *feel* when you simply think about each commitment?
   - Which commitments excite you? Which ones feed your heart, mind, body, or soul? Which ones bring you peace?
   - Which commitments make you sigh with frustration or annoyance? Which ones make you internally (or audibly) grumble?
   - Which commitments give you a sense of fear, trepidation, or slightly overwhelming possibilities? Consider these items in light of Chapter 3: Dissolving Resistance. If you're slightly afraid of a particular commitment, then that might mean it's really important.
3. **Figure out what needs to go.** Anything that generates more frustration, annoyance, or grumbling than pleasure or peace is a strong candidate for removal from your life. These are activities, responsibilities, or people that are draining you. It's time to come up with a plan to phase these items out of your life and begin saying no to anything new that is likely to frustrate, anger, or drain you.
4. **Decide what can be trimmed down.** Some commitments and responsibilities can't be removed from your life immediately or easily, but you might be able to reshape them. For example,

what responsibilities could you delegate? Are there simple tasks that a colleague, volunteer, family member, or hired helper could accomplish for you? Can you begin succession planning—that is, planning to remove this responsibility from your plate and transfer it to someone else's over time? For more help with delegation strategies see Chapter 37: Delegation Plans.

5. **Decide what you can put on hold for later.** Perhaps now is simply not the time for a particular commitment to be in your life. Although you would find this commitment interesting, exciting, or valuable at some point—or perhaps it benefited you in the past—now you need to focus on other needs. I did this with dating during a period of time when I was single. After dating for two years with nothing substantial on the relationship front I made the decision to take a break from dating to focus on my business until I achieved a specific business goal. It took about 9 months to reach that goal. Three weeks later I went to my first event to start *putting my self out there* again, and that's where I met my husband Brian. Putting a commitment on hold doesn't mean you won't come back around and make a large investment in it in the future. It might just be time to push the pause button for now.
6. **Decide where you want to grow your investment.** Consider both the commitments that feed and excite you and those that scare or overwhelm you. What would it mean to deepen your investment of time and energy in those areas? Is there one that you could really focus on and engage more fully?

Ideally, you will emerge from the commitment audit process with some new clarity about where you want to deepen or narrow your focus and what commitments are not bringing value to your life. Now, it's time to take action.

Next Actions

- ✓ Brainstorm your next steps. Consider first the commitments to be removed or phased out. Whom do you need to talk to? What actions need to be taken to extract yourself from those responsibilities? What skills and information would need to be transferred, and can you document them to help the person who follows you? Start creating your removal or phase out plan and add appropriate tasks to your master list. See Chapter 24 for more info on tasks and your master list.
- ✓ Repeat the above process for the tasks you intend to delegate. Whom do you need to talk to? What do you need to communicate so that your successor can help and support you effectively? Create your delegation and communications plan. (See Chapter 37: Delegation Plans.)
- ✓ Finally, begin exploring how to deepen your involvement in commitments that will feed your purpose, excitement, and engagement with life. This step is the reward after you have done your audit and cleared the decks of all the responsibilities that drained you. What is the next step? Whose advice do you want to seek? What research do you need to do? What is one specific, tangible step that you could take this week to grow this area of your life? Capture these tasks on your master list too.

—6—

When Purpose Changes

Few things in today's life are guaranteed; nor can we expect them to remain the same for long stretches of time as previous generations could. The days of lifelong commitments to a company or a job have virtually disappeared. Your focus and your purpose may change several times throughout the course of your life. It may go through refinements, clarifications, or enormous course changes. So, what do you do when such a time comes for you?

My mother's life has been full of course changes. A truly accomplished woman, my mother has, thus far, led a life story with at least five chapters:

- Chapter 1: She grew up as one of eleven children in an Iowa farm family that, fortunately, encouraged and highly valued education.
- Chapter 2: She went to college and then graduate school to earn her PhD in clinical psychology and organizational development. Then she practiced as a psychologist for the next decade.
- Chapter 3: Following a family move and the closing of her private practice, my mother decided to go back to school and get an MBA, which resulted in her career during the early 1990s as an executive coach (back in the days before coaching was well known.)
- Chapter 4: After growing her successful coaching career, she wanted to expand and internationalize her work. So, she spent more time traveling and attending conferences as a strategic consultant and advisor for organizations and associations

across the world—in the United States, Costa Rica, India, Mexico, Russia, and Samoa.

- Chapter 5: After a decade of jet-setting, she retired from her fast-paced career and rediscovered the sweet renewal of being a homebody. She surprised everyone by falling in love with drawing and painting, which resulted in her getting a bachelor of fine arts in her early fifties and realizing that art was her new core passion.

My mother, blessedly, is still healthy and active, and who knows what Chapter 6 of her life might bring? But I think her journey so far provides an impressive example of the varied expressions that one's life purpose might take.

What have been the chapters in your life? Are you in a transition moment right now? What does that mean for you? How do you handle and navigate the experiences that come with such transitions?

Here are some suggestions for how to handle changes in purpose.

1. Keep things simple and focus on the basics. Remember to breathe. Take extra time to rest and renew yourself every day; focus on "extreme self-care," as expert coach Cheryl Richardson would say.
2. Expand your focus and start back at the beginning. If you jumped immediately to this chapter and have finished reading it, go back and walk carefully through Chapters 1 to 5. Doing the exercises in those chapters will probably give you a clearer picture of what the purpose of your next chapter might be.
3. Embrace the change. If your vision of your next chapter is beginning to become clear, then give yourself permission to let go of the previous chapter and embrace the next. Grieve its closing if you need to, but you must release the old to make space for the new.

Course changes are an inevitable and essential part of our lives. The better we learn how to manage ourselves and our energy through them, the better the outcome will be.

Next Actions

✓ If you are going through a purpose change (or even if you're not), it's time for extreme self-care. What actions could you take today to take better care of yourself? More sleep, better food, more time doing things you love? Brainstorm a list of possible actions. Then choose one, and make a commitment to do it every day for the next week. If possible, add another one the following week, or if necessary discontinue the first and start the second.

✓ Give yourself a renewal period. Choose a deadline in the future: three months, six months, one year, whatever feels right. During this time, give yourself permission to focus all your available time and bandwidth on renewal and exploration. Combine some of the extreme self-care activities you brainstormed above with expansion and exploratory activities that help you to widen or deepen your understanding and connection with your new purpose. Such activities might include taking classes related to your new focus, reading books on the topic, talking to people who are doing similar work, or taking a retreat to envision, imagine, and plan for this new phase.

✓ Give yourself permission to grieve and release. The previous chapter of your life had its own blessings and challenges. Take time to reflect on, appreciate, and understand those structures and patterns, and then release yourself from them. If necessary, have a party or go through a ritual that allows you to celebrate, honor, and acknowledge the end of one chapter and the beginning of the next. Include people you love if it feels appropriate, or make it a private celebration of your transition.

✓ Clean house! To start something new, you have to make space for it to grow. Now is the time to remove anything from previous chapters of your life that will not provide value to the next chapter. When I say "clean house," I certainly mean taking time for some physical reorganizing of your home or work environments. However, I also suggest reviewing your time commitments. Now might be the time to phase out any commitments that do not align with how and where you are moving forward. (For more on this, see Chapter 5: Time for a Commitment Audit.) Walk into your new life feeling lighter and ready for what may come.

Resource

Richardson, Cheryl. *The Art of Extreme Self-Care: Transform Your Life One Month at a Time*. Carlsbad, CA: Hay House, Inc., 2009.

Part 2

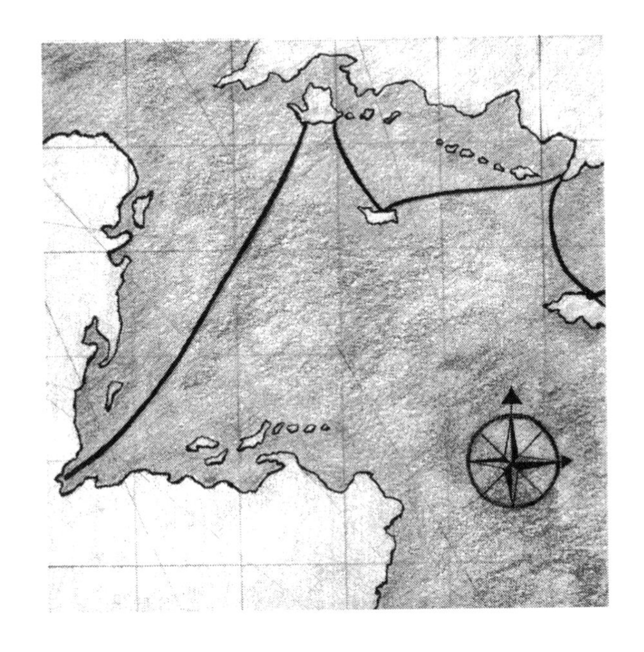

The Route: Passion, Dreams, and Lifestyle

—7—

Create Your Life List and Lifestyle List

While your purpose is meant to be the core focus and driving force for your life, that doesn't mean that every waking moment of every day needs to be directed there. Life is about exploration, learning, and growing. As Henry David Thoreau says, "I wanted to live deep and suck out all the marrow of life." It's time to let loose completely and imagine!

Have you seen the movie *The Bucket List*? Two older guys, both in the hospital in varying states of health, set out to accomplish their list of all the things they want to do before they "kick the bucket." The characters in the movie get motivated to undertake their adventures only after recognizing their mortality. But why wait? Life is here to be lived to the fullest, now! Each day you have a choice to make the day memorable—to work toward a once-in-a-lifetime dream experience, or to just get up, go to work, and go back to sleep, mechanically, one more time.

Personally, rather than focusing on the end—kicking the bucket—I choose to consider this project to be a *life* list. It is a summary of all the activities, outcomes, and dreams that I would love to check off during my life. As an innovation on the classic life list concept, I have decided to segment mine into two lists: a life list and a lifestyle list. On the life list go all those one-time achievements, adventures, and accomplishments that would bring passion and excitement to my journey. On my lifestyle list are the more habitual actions involving how I want to be in the world and who I am becoming: meditating each day, practicing yoga, doing cardio exercise regularly, engaging in a daily writing practice. In fact, that's a good way to think of this list: What are the practices that you would like to incorporate into your daily or weekly life? Perhaps you've wanted to start a gratitude journal. Perhaps you've wanted to have a regular game night with your family. Or maybe you want to spend some time reading each day.

Why create two lists? Because the methodology for working on your life list is very different from the way you'll make progress on your lifestyle list. The life list is a set of goals that can be broken into projects and tasks that can be checked off as *done*. On the other hand, on your lifestyle list are the elements that when embroidered together evoke the richness of the everyday life you want to create; they are habitual practices that don't have a precise beginning or end. These practices might wax and wane throughout your life as new ones arise and others fade away. For instance, once the kids go to college, that game night will probably no longer be a weekly event. But new practices may take their place. My mother took up painting after I left for college, and now she has a studio in her home where she can paint or draw every day.

Why are these lists so important? Because it is impossible to live your best life if you never take the time to define what your best life looks like! Both my life list and my lifestyle list are living documents. I have tools that I use to keep its items visible and vibrant to me every day. I also have established an annual ritual with my husband for my birthday. Every year on my birthday we go out to my favorite restaurant and bring with us the book that holds our lists. With a fruity cocktail in hand we look over his list, my list, and our shared list. We check some things off our life lists, and we talk about the memories of completing them. We add new items and occasionally remove ideas we've become less excited about (for instance, "Maybe I no longer care about performing with my harp at an Irish pub...."). Then we go through the same process with our lifestyle lists. What practices have we ingrained deeply this year, what do we want to develop further, and what new ideas have arisen? My life list and lifestyle list keep me passionate, curious, and engaged in my life as broadly and deeply as possible.

How to Start Your Life List

If items for your life list don't immediately start jumping into your head, there are many different ways to prime the pump.

Here are some questions that might help you get started:

- **Where have you always wanted to go?** France, Taiwan, Bali, the battlefields of the Civil War...?
- **What have you always wanted to see?** The Statue of Liberty, sunrise over the Rio Grande, a meteor shower, a breaching whale...?
- **What would you really love to learn?** How to speak fluent Italian, how to bake excellent croissants, how to deep-sea fish...?
- **What experiences would you love to have?** Skydiving, hiking the Appalachian Trail, sailing around the world...?

Hopefully, these questions will get your ideas flowing. The goal is to dig deep into your heart and mind for experiences that would thrill and enrich you. What could you do to turn blah into wow for you? Dream big! Every outcome starts with the idea. Capturing your ideas is the first step toward creating them.

How to Start Your Lifestyle List

To create this list, think about practices that you intend to weave into your daily or weekly life. Some of them you may already do; others you may have just heard about. What are the elements that would fill your daily life with beauty, intentionality, and joy?

Can you think of a few practices you want to include on your lifestyle list? Here are some examples: meditating, drinking morning smoothies, reading, playing golf, writing morning pages, practicing yoga, taking a weekly night out with your sweetheart, praying each evening, reading your Bible or inspirational books, paying a compliment to someone each day, taking a deep breath before starting your car, and reading to your children each night.

One of the great habits I have adopted is to ask people I admire to share their daily or weekly practices. This is one way to discover their recipe for success, whether it be success in their career, their relationships, or their parenting. What are the habits that make a difference?

You might come up with quite a number of items on this list as well. It may look like your personal recipe book for a richly lived life. Now, taking action on these items will involve building habits or routines, so if that's where you feel called to start, take a look at Chapter 14: Habits: The Power of Patterns and Chapter 15: Your Ideal Week Vision.

Bringing Focus to Your Lists

With both your life list and your lifestyle list, you'll make the most headway when you focus, so you might want to choose just one item from each list to start working toward. You can always choose a different one next season (see Chapter 48: Seasonal Planning). Sometimes fortuitous opportunities will allow you to check items off with very little effort from you, or you may be guided to see that now is the time to work toward an item that you did not choose initially. For instance, if your company wants to send you to Japan, then the answer is yes, and it's time to check that item off your list!

Next Actions

✓ Just start writing. Anything that pops into your head will do for the moment. Remember, you can always change your mind later. You have a whole lifetime to manifest these dreams.

✓ Think back to when you were a child. What were your biggest dreams when you were five years old? How about ten? Keep paging through your life in five-year segments, and see whether there are any old dreams that you'd like to dust off and add to your list.

✓ Talk to your partner, and create your lists together. You might learn a lot about each other—the dreams that you share, the lifestyle elements that matter to each of you, and the adventures that you never considered on your own but would be tons of fun to have together.

- ✓ Watch the movies *The Bucket List* or *Last Holiday* for some great laughs, poignant moments, and fun ideas for your list.
- ✓ Browse the bookstore or library aisles, and see what jumps out at you. Places to visit, things to do, and skills to learn might launch themselves at you from every direction.
- ✓ Ask people you admire about their daily and weekly habits. Many successful people consciously or unconsciously have developed a recipe for success that you can uncover and emulate.

Resources

The Bucket List. DVD. Directed by Rob Reiner. Starring Jack Nicholson and Morgan Freeman. Warner Bros., 2008.

Editors of Life. *LIFE Heaven on Earth: The World's Must-See Destinations.* New York: Life, 2011.

Ferriss, Timothy. *The 4-Hour Workweek: Escape 9-5, Live Anywhere, and Join the New Rich.* New York: Harmony, 2009.

Last Holiday. DVD. Directed by Wayne Wang. Starring Queen Latifah and LL Cool J. Paramount, 2006.

Man, John, et al. *The New Traveler's Atlas: A Global Guide to the Places You Must See in Your Lifetime.* New York: Barron's Educational Series, 2007.

Miller, Caroline Adams and Dr. Michael B. Frisch. *Creating Your Best Life: The Ultimate Life List Guide.* New York: Sterling, 2009.

—8—

Dream Check: Refine Your Life List

In the course of any good brainstorming process you may kick up an enormous number of ideas. If you were to weigh each one, you'd discover that some are true dreams, core passions, or must-haves. Others are lovely adventures, full of excitement and fun. And, most likely, a few just kind of sounded good at some point. The beauty of a life list is its status as a living document—something that can be continuously updated, altered, and revisited as your ideas and priorities change. I want to help you think about those changes from a few different angles.

Never Accept "You Can't..."

Do not let anyone tell you that you can't do something. No one should have the power to crush your dreams, and you are the only person who can give that power to them. We discuss this in Chapter 3: Dissolving Resistance. If there's a voice in your head (or a real voice coming from someone else) saying that you can't or shouldn't want something that you feel called to do, that probably means this dream is what you should focus on doing *first*. After all, look at Diana Nyad who at 64-years-old finally accomplished her 35-year goal to swim non-stop from Cuba to Florida. After five attempts and spending many hundreds of hours training for her 53-hour ocean swim, she finally accomplished her dream. Her mantra? "Find a way."

Live *Your* Dreams, Not Someone Else's

We unwittingly—and sometimes even begrudgingly—adopt a lot of life dreams from the people around us. The fact that your mother has always wanted you to become the chief of neurosurgery at a major hospital doesn't mean this goal needs to appear on your life list. And the fact that your father-in-law had a life-changing experience at an ashram in India doesn't mean you need to make this goal your own—no matter how much he wants to connect you to his guru. Make sure the items on your list spark a true feeling of passion in *you*, and pitch out anything that feels like an obligation. The one exception I'll offer is that it can be fun to share some dreams with your partner or a friend, but make sure that you both have space to say no without leaving anyone feeling crushed.

Create the Shape, but Hold It Loosely

Some dreams on your list will probably not be reached. As a wise man said, "I'll still have things on my to-do list when I die." The same can be true for your life list too. Ideally, you will never stop dreaming and engaging with the world around you, and thus your list will continue to grow, shift, and change. Some items will fade in importance or excitement at different phases of your life, while others will come to the foreground. Remember, your life list isn't a rigid catalog of tasks to be accomplished. Rather, it is a capturing of the breadth of your interests and passions. It is your personal map to "live deep and suck out all the marrow of life," as Henry David Thoreau said.

Pick One Place to Start

Dreams are like fireflies; if you try to go after every single one in the field at once, you likely won't catch any. You have to choose one light to follow and track it until it's within reach. But remember the previous idea: hold it loosely. If you have too many expectations about what reaching your goal will be like, then you might feel let down or miss out on the reality of the experience. Just follow it, hold it, and soak it in with joy and wonder.

Ask the Experts

Sometimes, with the really big dreams, we discover too late that we fell in love with the idea of something rather than the lived reality of it. For instance, many people might put "write and publish a novel" on their life lists. For some, this goal is the expression of a longtime dream that they have ignored. For others, writing a novel is something they would like to be able to *say* they did, but they have little understanding or excitement about the actual process of getting there.

This is your chance to make a dream check: do you want the *imagined* outcome, or do you want the lifestyle and lived reality of achieving that dream? If you're unsure, then ask someone who's done it and find out what you would really be in for. Traveling around some parts of Africa and Asia might sound lovely and exotic, but if the realities of poverty are going to rip your heart out, then you should at least be prepared for it before setting out.

The overall message here is to engage your list, question it, embrace it, and allow it to be a true expression of a vividly lived life of following your heart. While others may provide inspiration, they can neither direct nor limit your heart's desires. This is your life. Craft it intentionally.

Next Actions

- ✓ Review your life list and check in with yourself. Does each item spark a sincere sense of passion in you? Are you interested enough to commit to the good, the bad, and the ugly that might come with working toward and achieving it? Don't let anyone tell you it's too hard if you really want it. But similarly, don't fool yourself into ignoring the journey by focusing purely on the final goal.
- ✓ Find someone who has already accomplished your dream, and ask for two things: top three highlights from the experience and three "wish I'd known"s. Either you'll end up more prepared for the experi-

ence, or you'll be able to toss that dream in the trash before you find yourself standing knee-deep in a Florida swamp, swatting mosquitoes, and wondering why you thought gator wrestling sounded like fun.

✓ Look over your list and choose one item to start working toward. Make it big enough to motivate you to commit to getting it done. Then do whatever planning, brainstorming, or research is necessary as your very first step. What is one small task that you could do tomorrow to move you closer to that dream?

Resource

Miller, Caroline Adams and Dr. Michael B. Frisch. *Creating Your Best Life: The Ultimate Life List Guide.* New York: Sterling, 2009.

—9—

Freedom: The Real Wealth

The days of the static nine-to-five job are coming to an end in many companies and industries. This shift has happened partially because technology has opened up so many more possibilities in terms of providing the needed tools for remote work, accessing company information remotely, and staying in contact with teams and resources around the globe. However, I believe that the shift also stems from a growing recognition that flexibility of time and location is the true wealth in our world today.

Amid the growing buzz about work-life balance, *Inc.* magazine quoted a statistic that 30 percent of small-business owners would rather have more time than more money. More and more people are beginning to recognize that what matters most is the freedom to be where they want to be and to participate more deeply and fully in their lives, both professional and personal.

This has been a major focus of my life since 2008, when I began to design my work responsibilities as tasks that could be accomplished from anywhere with a computer and Internet access. Perhaps you are feeling a desire to do the same. This type of change might mean changing careers or negotiating greater flexibility within your current job.

To help you consider how to maximize your freedom of time and location, let me walk you through many of the logistics that you'll want to consider to implement your flexible work plan.

Crafting a Flexible Work Plan

To get started, answer the following questions:

✧ **Which of your current work responsibilities do not require specific times or locations?** Think about all the tasks you do at work on a weekly basis. How many of these tasks could be done from anywhere with a computer, an Internet connection, and the appropriate documents or digital resources?

- **What tools or resources would you need in order to accomplish these tasks in a location other than your workplace?** Think about files, contact information, technology setups, and office supplies.
- **What environments or situations will you investigate to test out your ability to be productive in alternative locations?** It might sound great to be able to work from anywhere, but you might discover that while working at home in your PJs it is really hard to not be interrupted by family members who want your attention, dishes that "need" to be washed, or laundry that "needs" to be cleaned. You might solve these problems by creating a dedicated space and time for work in the home, or you might want to consider working in cafés or libraries, at the beach, in your car, and so on. What environments actually work for you?
- **Who would have to be on board to test out your plan?** Whose support or blessing would be required in order to do a trial of your flexible work plan? Certainly your boss or supervisor has to agree to it, but potentially you'll want your co-workers and close family members also to be on board. Get the right heads together, and strategize about how to make this alternative work effectively.
- **What would a preliminary test look like?** Rather than trying to get everyone on board for a full-blown, permanent solution, conceptualize a test scenario. Perhaps you could work remotely one to two days per week for three weeks, reevaluate and strategize about how to improve the setup, and then repeat the test for three months. Eventually you will learn techniques and strategies to increase your productivity when working somewhere other than at your desk. (Keep reading this book, and

you'll be well underway!) Your success on a small scale will help ensure that your boss and co-workers will support your desire to increase your time away from the office.

Challenges and Benefits of a Flexible Work Plan

One of the major challenges of shifting away from a standard nine-to-five office environment is losing the structure it imposed on your life. I know an amazing number of failed entrepreneurs who fell apart at least partially because they couldn't create enough structure in their lives without an office and co-workers who were expecting them to show up each day. When the structure isn't provided to you, it becomes your responsibility to create it. You still have to commit to showing up for work at particular days and times. The difference might be showing up with your computer at your dining table, home-office desk, library study space, or beach chair each day.

Similarly, don't expect that the work you struggled to get done in eight hours at your office is miraculously going to take only three hours just because your location has changed. There is no guaranteed "geographic cure" for hard work. Yes, you can take a break in the afternoon to go grocery shopping if needed, but that means you might be working a bit further into your evening than you would have otherwise. The biggest time gain is the reduction in commuting time, which is a definite win.

For a flexible work plan to succeed, you will likely have to choose functional work locations, create systems that ensure you have the tools you need to work effectively (see Chapter 22: Checklists for Everything and Chapter 17: Activity Kits), and create a schedule that reserves the time you need to get things done (see Chapter 15: Your Ideal Week Vision).

The biggest change that accompanies your flexible work plan will likely be an experience of increased integration of your work and personal lives. Success is no longer about trying to balance either work *or* home; it's about how you can blend them and get both types of tasks done adequately. At first this may be challenging as you and your family or friends adjust, but over time you may find that this blended life has many rewards.

And what exactly *are* those rewards? For starters, you can save time by shopping at off-peak hours. You can find new creative inspiration by changing work locations regularly. You can pause your work to see your daughter's baseball game and then make up for that time after she's gone to bed. Or you can bang out that major project from 6 to 9 AM, when your mind is fresh, rather than spending two hours getting ready for work and commuting in rush-hour traffic, by which point your freshness and clarity have faded.

While a flexible work plan might not be possible for every person in every career, it is a feasible choice for many knowledge workers. Now is the time to explore how it could benefit you.

Next Actions

✓ Create your flexible work plan. Answer the questions above to brainstorm the best way to make such a plan work for you.

✓ Read the other chapters that will be essential for making this kind of lifestyle productive—for starters, Chapters 15, 17, and 22.

✓ Talk to your boss and get permission for a trial consisting of remote work for one day each week for three weeks. Even that limited experience will teach you a lot about what works and what doesn't. Then you can make any needed changes and repeat the experience with even greater success.

✓ Install Skype or a similar video conferencing platform on your computer. You might be surprised how great it can feel to have face-to-face meetings with colleagues, clients, or business partners but not need to travel to make it possible. I meet with most of my clients via Skype these days, and it's *so* much better than a phone call.

Resources

Ferriss, Timothy. *The 4-Hour Workweek: Escape 9-5, Live Anywhere, and Join the New Rich.* New York: Harmony, 2009.

Morgenstern, Julie. *Time Management from the Inside Out: The Foolproof System for Taking Control of Your Schedule—and Your Life.* New York: Henry Holt/Owl Books, 2004.

—10—

Envision the Possibilities, Then Make Them Manifest

Have you ever attended a conference or a workshop intended to help you move forward in life and motivate your next steps? Perhaps you left invigorated, enthusiastic, and raring to go to make some big changes in your life. Then, if you're like many people who attend such conferences, a few days or weeks passed, and your life hadn't changed at all. You were right back in the same grind with the same problems and patterns that you'd been struggling with for months or years. Given how hopeful and powerful you'd felt just a few days or weeks earlier, perhaps you were confused and baffled at your lack of progress.

People have two common responses to this outcome:

1. "The conference speaker must not have been that good, since I didn't actually learn how to apply the information to create change in my life."
2. "I must be a real slacker since I had this great insight about how to move forward in my world, but somehow I'm still right where I've always been."

My guess is that the truth is somewhere in the middle. Yes, a really great teacher helps you see how you can apply new insights to your life. But once you've left the conference or workshop, the responsibility shifts to you to carry out the next steps and to manifest the actions.

The same is true about reading a book like this one. You can read it and feel inspired and excited, but if you don't actually reflect on the material, do the work, and take action on the ideas, then it just becomes another book collecting dust on your shelf. The real-life challenge inherent in self-help situations is that it can be difficult to make our life's dreams and desires *tangible* enough to motivate our continued action and attention.

Often we have a vision once, and then we allow it to fade into the semiconscious or forgotten sections of our minds. The striking moment of insight and the shimmering vision of a possible future fade like last night's dream and then appear only briefly as half-remembered flashes. Why is this? Because we have not learned the techniques to give our dreams, our possibilities, a tangible or visual expression here in our physical daily world where we can interact with them not just once, but again and again. We need a vision manifestation tool.

What might such a tool look like? Many of us wish that a genie would pop out of our coffeemaker and make the new reality appear instantaneously. However, most likely we need to do the work of creation ourselves. We need a stake in the ground to focus us and to hold us to our goals and intentions.

Here are some great examples of the kind of manifestation tool I'm talking about:

- ✧ **A vision board.** Gather images from magazines and catalogs, print out pictures from the Internet, or take your own photographs to represent your goals or dreams. Use the images to create a collage on a piece of large poster board. Then hang it in a place where you will see it each day. Feeling bashful about sharing your dreams with the people around you? Then paste the images into a Dreams Book—a scrapbook that you can flip through regularly on your own.
- ✧ **A digital vision board.** Essentially this is the same idea as above, but in this version you collect digital images, create a collage in a graphics program like Adobe Photoshop, and set the final image as your desktop background or the lock screen on your tablet. There are even some great ready-made apps for this if you're an iPhone/iPad user. Another idea is to use the collected pictures as your computer's screen saver.

- **A goals video.** Some great and really easy programs out there can help you create a short goals video with images and music that call forth your vision. A few I've tried are iMovie (for Mac, iPad, or iPhone), Animoto (PC and Mac), Windows Movie Maker (PC), and Bloom* (iPhone).
- **A vision story.** Write about your visions. As you create your dreams and goals with words, give them as many specifics and contexts as possible. Describe them to your mind and heart in the present tense, as if they exist in the current moment. Give your story emotion. How do you feel now that you are living your vision? Scientific studies have shown that the brain can't tell the difference between reality and something vividly imagined, so create plenty of juicy details in your story. Then reread your vision story every day. I recommend reading it first thing in the morning or last thing at night so that you program your subconscious to spend each day making that vision become true.
- **A series of mantras or affirmations.** Take one or more of your dreams and write a series of short sentences stating what is true about yourself or your life now that you have achieved your goal. Examples: I love living actively in my healthy and fit body. I travel the world and inspire people with my message and work. I meditate each day for 20 minutes and feel focused and refreshed. Phrase all sentences in the positive and in the present tense. Read or speak them and vividly imagine their truth as already completed and present. Write these mantras or affirmations on index cards that you can flip through regularly, or record them on your smartphone's voice recorder so that you can always hear your voice speaking your dreams with confidence and certainty that they are true.
- **A sculpture representing your dreams.** Pick any 3-D medium that feels appropriate to you. For instance, you might use clay or paper-maché. Or perhaps you could collect physical objects

representing your goals and dreams and build them into a sculpture.

- **An altar to your future.** Gather objects that represent your goals and dreams and choose a space in your home that you look at regularly—perhaps a side table in the living room or bedroom, perhaps a mantelpiece or a bookshelf. Arrange the items there intentionally and with care. Then spend a few minutes each day just sitting or standing near your altar and reflecting on the dreams or goals represented there and the actions you can immediately take to make them happen.

The visions and dreams you have for your life are possible futures awaiting you. While others might help inspire your awareness of them, you are the only person who can actually manifest them. Give yourself the tools to begin making them tangible and to maintain your focus on creating them in your life.

Next Actions

- ✓ Review your life list and your lifestyle list and decide which items you want to incorporate into your vision manifestation tool. Pick one of the methods described above, and make it happen! Collect the necessary resources. For instance, go to the bookstore and buy some colorful magazines with evocative photography. Browse online and clip pictures (PC: right-click/"save image as"; Mac: two-finger click or Control & Click/ "save image as"). Pinterest can also be a *great* resource for such photos.
- ✓ Create a habit or ritual of interacting with your vision manifestation tool. Choose a time of day. Then attach this new action of reviewing or reflecting on your tool to something you already do easily and regularly. Give yourself a few minutes to just pause, breathe, meditate, or reflect on the images, items, or words that you see, and allow them to settle in to your conscious and unconscious mind. Feel these items rekindle your heart's excitement about that possible future. Picture them vividly as already complete and present in the here and now.

✓ At first, you can allow your subconscious mind to do a fair share of the work of aligning you with the dreams you've incorporated into your tool. Eventually, however, when you take your daily reflection time, it will be helpful to finish by defining the very specific next step that you are going to take today or tomorrow to help make that dream come true. Make it something small and doable, something that will take only a few minutes or at most an hour of your time and attention (unless you happen to have more time to dedicate that day). Make it specific enough that when you return to reflecting on your tool, you'll be able to say, "Okay, one more step done. What's next?"

Resources

Assaraf, John, and Murray Smith. *The Answer: Grow Any Business, Achieve Financial Freedom, and Live an Extraordinary Life.* New York: Atria Books, 2008.

Pinterest. http://bit.ly/PinInfo.

Collage apps for smartphone/tablet. Search the App Store and you'll find plenty of options.

Bloom*– Mindbloom. http://bit.ly/bloomApp

Part 3

Mending Your Sails: Energy Management

—11—

Action or Reaction Mode?

Imagine this scenario: You have carefully planned what you want to do first thing tomorrow morning. You're going to start that important project you've been thinking about for months. When morning comes, and you're just about to take that first step, you check your email and get detoured into a lengthy response to your boss about what she perceives is a major issue in an upcoming presentation. After that, the phone rings with a call from your child's school principal, who requests a meeting to discuss some concerns…and this turns into a lengthy conversation in which you cover most of the information that you will likely cover again in the meeting. Finally, just to add salt to the wound, you open the fridge to find there is no milk for your coffee, so you decide to run down the street to the café for a latte. Upon returning from the café you look at the clock and discover that it's already 1 PM. Frazzled, you moan, "Where did my great morning work time go?"

Have you ever had mornings like this one? Does it feel like you often get derailed before you even get started? In today's life, it has become absurdly easy to live in constant reaction mode. We run, hop, and jump when the phone rings, when the email dings, and when the laundry buzzer zings, and whatever important or purposeful action we were doing—or, worse, intending to do—gets left by the wayside.

It's so easy to forget that we don't need to be automatons responding to the stimuli of every sound or request around us. We have one supreme power that is entirely in our control: the power to *choose* what gets our attention in this moment. Granted, when your child is crying or your boss is yelling at you about something, it's hard not to give that your full attention, but in so many other, smaller circumstances we allow ourselves to become derailed by much less important and even irrelevant items.

Stephen Covey writes about this power to choose in his book *The 8th Habit: From Effectiveness to Greatness*. While on sabbatical in Hawaii prior to working on his first major bestseller, *The 7 Habits of Highly Effective People,* he went to a library and wandered the stacks. He pulled a book off the shelf at random, (Victor Frankl's *Man's Search for Meaning,* as it happens) and in it he read three sentences that inspired much of his impressive thought-leadership:

> *Between stimulus and response there is a space.*
>
> *In that space lies our freedom and power to choose our response.*
>
> *In those choices lie our growth and our happiness.*

The greatest skill we can learn is to expand the space between stimulus and response and exercise our freedom to choose our response—to choose what gets our attention in this moment and to choose what happens next. This means living in action mode rather than reaction mode. This skill is essential to develop if we want to live more "on purpose" because so many aspects of our lives are designed to interrupt and distract us, and it's so easy to simply allow ourselves to go with the flow. The inevitable question becomes: how do we start to acquire this skill? It's as simple as A, B, C, and D.

Step 1: Awareness

To start developing the ability to choose your responses, simply become aware of that space between stimulus and response. The next time something dings, rings, flashes, or knocks on your door, before you jump to your standard reactive response, just pause. Feel the space. Take a breath. Just notice how strong your urge to react is. Then, if necessary, continue with the automatic action you were inclined to take. Try this several times today and just notice how "big" your space is. How strong are your automatic responses? Their strength might differ depending on the stimulus. You might want to continue this awareness practice for a few days to explore and discover more.

Step 2: Brainstorm

After spending some time feeling and becoming aware of your space, choose one experience to reflect on. For example, let's start with the "new message" notification sound on your computer's email program. Now, completely outside of that moment when it dings, consider your options. What choices do you have when you hear that sound next time? Here are a few:

1. Stop what you're doing and see what has come in
2. Ignore the sound and keep doing what you were doing
3. Go into your email program's sound settings and turn off the notification
4. Chuck your computer out the window

Can you think of others? Even extreme options might be worth considering. Brainstorming has no limits after all!

Step 3: Choose

Consider all of the possible responses you brainstormed. Think about the possible consequences of each choice. Are the consequences life-threatening or job-threatening? Could you handle the consequences mentally and emotionally if they became problematic? What is the likelihood that your new response will lead to a dramatically bad outcome? What would you gain by making this choice?

Now, to continue with our example, choose a response to try the next time your new email notification dings. Commit to the choice, and get ready for the opportunity to make it.

Step 4: Do

The next opportunity has arisen: your email program dings its cheerful "new mail" noise. So, take that breath, feel that space, and make your new choice. What happens? Is there an immediate difference? Perhaps in how you feel or in what happens next? What are the actual consequences over the next couple hours or days? Are they catastrophic? If not, then try the same response again. Or, go back to the **Choose** step, choose a different possible response, and try that one next time. Wash, rinse, and repeat until you have changed your automatic programming and expanded your ability to choose in that moment.

Following Up

If you have success with small changes, such as responding to your email notifications in a new way, then apply the same process to other circumstances—the phone ringing, the doorbell, your phone's text notifications, your child's insistent requests, your partner's less appealing personal habits...anything. As Frankl reminds us, between every stimulus and response there is a space, and in that space lies your power to choose.

It can also be helpful to reflect on what the ABCD process reveals about you. Does it help you realize that you have been acting out of fear or out of habit? If you can identify where your standard response is coming from, then you'll be able to bring the right resources to bear to change it. If it's a fear, then challenge your belief about the possible frightening consequences, and, if appropriate, seek the help of a counselor or coach. If it's a habit, then it's time to change the pattern in your brain by repeating the ABCD process consistently. For more help, you can take a look at Chapter 14: Habits: The Power of Patterns. With enough practice you'll shift the balance in your life and increase your ability to act with purpose.

Next Actions

✓ Learn more about what the space between stimulus and response looks like for you. Stephen Covey believed that the "size" of your space comes largely from your family and your environmental conditions. Some people go through life with very large spaces between stimulus and response. Others, because of their personality, upbringing, or environmental circumstances, have been conditioned to have very small spaces and thus tend toward knee-jerk, automatic reactions. The size of your space might also vary in different areas of your life. Perhaps at home your space is larger, while at work it tends to be rapid-fire reactive—or vice versa. Is your space different around certain people or members of your family? Give yourself time just to learn about your own space without judging or trying to make any changes.

✓ Grab a piece of paper and write "Chances to Choose" at the top. Then brainstorm a list of all the events or moments during a typical day or week when you are in reaction mode or are functioning on autopilot as you respond to stimuli. If necessary, carry the list with you for the next day, and at each break in the day reflect on whether any additional reaction moments could be added to your list. Each of these items is an opportunity for you to exercise your own power of choice. Pick one item, and experiment with the ABCD process for the next couple days.

✓ Set a goal for yourself. If you have experimented with making a more proactive choice in one type of circumstance, then set a goal to repeat your new response for an entire day, a week, or a month—whatever feels appropriate. It's best to start small and then build on your previous successes. If you relapse into your automatic response, don't beat yourself up; just recommit to your new response for next time. New habits take some attention to build, and the best way to succeed is through commitment, clear actions and goals, and a resilient attitude.

Resources

Covey, Stephen R. *The 8th Habit: From Effectiveness to Greatness.* New York: Free Press, 2005.

Duhigg, Charles. *The Power of Habit: Why We Do What We Do in Life and Business.* New York: Random House, 2014.

Frankl, Victor E. *Man's Search for Meaning.* Boston: Beacon Press, 2006.

—12—

Leveraging Your Body's Rhythms

We've all heard about early birds and night owls. Some people get up in the morning ready and fresh, eager to meet the day. Others drag their way out of bed each morning, but at around 7 or 8 PM they are picking up energy and ready to tackle creative, exciting projects. You probably know which side of this equation you fall on, and you might even recognize that it has shifted once or twice in the course of your life, depending on your circumstances.

While these bodily energy rhythms are not set in stone, they have a dramatic impact on our abilities to focus and to be productive at different times of day. The official term for this energy cycle is *circadian rhythm*. We flow through one full circadian cycle each day. What is less well known is the role of our ultradian rhythms. These mini-cycles, which happen throughout our day, allow us to easily focus on a given task for a while (generally 30 to 120 minutes) before needing a break.

We humans are not machines to be switched on or off. Our circadian and ultradian rhythms are parts of our body's natural cyclical existence, and the best way to increase our productivity overall is to learn about our body's cycles and plan our tasks accordingly. To explore this possibility we can apply the ABCD formula to this challenge, just as we did in previous chapters.

Step 1: Awareness

Begin by taking stock of your usual energy levels. Do you tend to have more fresh, creative energy first thing in the morning, late at night, or somewhere in between? Reflect on recent days or weeks. Don't include those random all-nighters when adrenalin keeps you going but normally you would be fast asleep. Look at your body's natural tendencies. You will begin to see your own circadian rhythm.

Now, track yourself for the next few days. When you are digging in to a project or sitting down to work, how long do you tend to focus before wanting to stop and stretch, get up and go to the bathroom, or grab a cup of coffee? This period of focus might vary a bit throughout the day, but in general there will be a point at which your brain or energy hits the wall and you need to stop for a break before you can continue. For some people this period might be only 30 minutes. For others it might be almost 2 hours. Paying attention to your energy and mind will help you to notice and determine the length of your natural ultradian cycles.

Step 2: Brainstorm

After increasing your awareness of your body's natural tendencies, you can address the next question: how do you use this information to increase your productivity? First, when planning your tasks or appointments for each day, reserve your most creative and high-energy time for the tasks that most require it. In other words, don't use that time to check email, to wash dishes, or to do your laundry. Those minor, relatively mindless tasks can be accomplished just as easily at a different time of day, thus preserving your high-power time for the crucial projects. Right now, try brainstorming the kinds of projects you could most effectively work on during your high-energy time. What would give you the greatest bang for your buck?

Second, segment your projects into tasks that are small enough to fit easily into your natural ultradian rhythm. Try to fit the task to your flow rather than forcing your flow to expand for the task. This might mean setting timers to give yourself permission to stop working on a big project by the end of your natural cycle, or at least to take a break at that time. I can frequently link two ultradian cycles together with a five- or ten-minute break between them, but rarely can I work constructively on any single project for longer than that. Now, try brainstorming ways to leverage your natural ultradian cycle so that you'll work more effectively on your major tasks and activities.

Step 3: Choose

Look at your schedule and task list for tomorrow, and segment the day into blocks that match the size of your ultradian cycle (for me that's 90 minutes). After reserving time for getting ready in the morning, traveling to and from daily destinations like the kids' school or work, and eating meals, you probably have space for three to six ultradian cycles each day. I have roughly two in the morning, two in the afternoon, and two in the evening. On most days, my two morning cycles are dedicated to writing, planning presentations, and any additional creative heavy lifting. That's because my mind is freshest in the morning, so those blocks are very important to get such creative activities done. My two afternoon cycles are for outside meetings, phone calls, and administrative work like checking email that doesn't require a ton of creative brainpower. Finally, my two evening cycles are for self-care (such as exercise), social time with my family or friends, and standard housework such as laundry and cleaning.

Try arranging your day tomorrow in blocks like these (or if necessary pick a more open day next week). What activities or projects will you slot in to your morning, afternoon, and evening cycles? Create a rough plan for the day, either right on your calendar or on a separate sheet of paper (or electronic file). Giving appropriate consideration to your daily circadian power time, assign one (yes, *one*!) major activity or project to each ultradian cycle box.

Step 4: Do

Implement your plan. Test out your theories. What worked, and what didn't? Did you feel more focused? Did you get more done? When the plan had to change, what was the cause? What interrupted you, or what factors in your day did you not consider? Based on what you learned from your first attempt, try creating a plan for the next day. Continue to consider your circadian and ultradian rhythms.

In time, you will become an expert at planning your activities, meetings, and tasks to fit your rhythms, and you will discover that doing so both increases your overall productivity and brings you a greater sense of peace and natural flow in your daily life.

Next Actions

✓ Talk to your partner, family members, close friends, or housemates about your discoveries about your circadian and ultradian rhythms. Enlist their support to help you protect your power focus time from interruptions. This will help enable you to be more present for them at other times.

✓ Make a list of all the current projects and activities that require your highly focused attention. Then make another list of projects and activities that are largely mindless. Use these lists to help you plan your tasks for each upcoming day or week.

✓ Pay attention to your bedtime. As my friend and colleague Lisa says, the battle is won the night before. No matter how much of an early bird you are, failing to go to bed at a reasonable hour and get your full night's sleep diminishes your effectiveness during the following day's cycles. Lack of sleep might simply delay or shift your peak time, but it might eliminate your power focus time completely. Protect your energy whenever possible by making wise decisions at night.

✓ Connect the insights from this exercise to your Life Rhythm Map from Chapter 15. Perhaps you'll want to change your ideal week in order to leverage your cycles and power times more effectively.

Resources

Loehr, Jim, and Tony Schwartz. *The Power of Full Engagement: Managing Energy, Not Time, Is the Key to High Performance and Personal Renewal.* New York: Free Press, 2003.

Schwartz, Tony. *Be Excellent at Anything: The Four Keys to Transforming the Way We Work and Live.* New York: Free Press, 2010.

—13—

Your Energy-Management Plan

Multitasking, duo-tasking, uptime, downtime...we have been led to think about ourselves as computers with on/off switches. The time-management and technology gurus of the past few decades have largely focused on how to get more out of the day by doing our activities more quickly and efficiently. These experts seem to suggest that if we're awake, then we must be "on"—that is, consistently and incessantly productive, making the most from every single minute. The only "off" time is when we sleep.

This human-machine approach is wreaking havoc on every part of human life today. Increased stress, poor health and self-care, damaged relationships with family and friends, and other fundamental problems are traceable to this "Go, go, go!" approach to living. I believe that it has to stop.

Humans are not machines. We do not have an endless supply of consistent energy pouring into us from a cord. We are beings of nature with inherent cycles to our attention and functionality. If all we do is pour energy out, then we will suffer the whirlwind of illness, exhaustion, and depression that ensues. It's time to shift the paradigm and instill a new approach to our daily lives.

Fortunately, energy-management experts Jim Loehr and Tony Schwartz have defined the differences in this new paradigm. They suggest we shift our thinking to view life as a series of sprints rather than a marathon. This requires embracing the cyclic nature of our personal energy and focusing on how to build our energy capacity on all levels: physical, emotional, mental, and spiritual.

The Holistic Approach to Energy

In Chapter 12: Leveraging Your Body's Rhythms, we discussed specifically how to take advantage of your natural circadian and ultradian rhythms. That method helps you take the energy that you already have and use it to greatest effect at appropriate times of the day. Now, I want to challenge to you get curious and recognize what you could do differently not just to use your existing energy cycles better but actually to increase your capacity to perform.

Your personal energy can be either increased or drained through a variety of avenues. Think about your physical state. When was the last time you got a bad night's sleep and felt significantly less energized the following day? What happens to your energy after you eat an overly large and less-than-healthy lunch? On the flip side, do you ever get a buzz right after working out, going hiking, or attending a yoga class?

What emotional states have you been spending time in frequently? Have you experienced mostly excitement, joy, and peace? Or have you more often felt frustration, anger, and a sense of being overwhelmed? Do some people in your life consistently bring you down? Do others often lift you up and leave you feeling great? We've all felt how contagious emotional energy can be. There are even times when I'm in a good mood space, and I'll choose not to talk to certain people because I want to maintain that energy.

On a mental level, many of us spend a huge amount of energy on decision-making from the moment we get up until we go to sleep. Do you pride yourself on your ability to multitask? Be honest: when was the last time you caught yourself texting (or emailing) and driving? Have you woken up in the middle of the night with your brain in an incessant whirr of thoughts? Conversely, have you felt that great experience of flow in which you're so focused and clear that time seems to fly by?

On a spiritual level, we've already discussed the power of acting "on purpose." That sense of commitment and rightness can feed you and keep you on course. Have you occasionally felt as if your stated values aren't in alignment with your actions? Have you felt the joy of putting your core skills into service for a great cause or for someone you care about? Have you experienced the passion of getting up in the morning and knowing that you are going to do something meaningful and energizing that day?

All these questions are aimed to give you a sense of how each of the four levels of your human experience might build or drain your energy. This is the basic premise behind energy management as an approach to productivity. You are at your most effective if you have created adequate energy *capacity* for the task at hand on all four levels: physical, emotional, mental, and spiritual.

Awareness: Energy-Management Self-Assessment

To help you get clear on how well you manage your energy, and to provide concrete ways to improve your energy capacity, I encourage you to pause reading for just a few minutes, go online to www.InspiredActionBook.com/Resources, and take our Excellence Assessment. This productivity self-assessment will look at all the key areas of productivity including the four facets of energy management and give you some immediate insights on areas you can improve. It will take less than ten minutes for most people.

Now that you've taken the assessment, what are your areas of strength? What areas could use some attention? Once you know where the growth opportunities are, you can begin planning how to shift your habits and create rituals to address those areas. If you come away with a laundry list of areas of improvement, that's okay. When you decide to start making improvements, the best method is to focus on one at a time.

Just get curious about your results. Awareness is always the first step before creating something new and different.

Brainstorm & Choose Your Road to Change

Now that you have achieved greater awareness about your current energy-management patterns, as well as some other key areas of productivity, it's time to get curious and get creative. It's time to change your life and create your new actionable energy-management plan.

In our work at Chosen Course, we like to use the metaphor of building a bridge from where you are to where you want to be. You might want to print out one of our Change Bridge worksheets at www.InspiredActionBook.com/Resources. Then, to get started, choose one of the areas from your self-assessment that you would most like to improve, and start considering these categories of questions:

- ✧ **Where I am now.** What have been my patterns in this area? What's been showing up for me in this context?
- ✧ **Desired outcome.** What would my preferred outcome look like? What would I rather do instead? Who is a model of possibility, someone who has mastered this area? What specifically are they doing differently?
- ✧ **Bridge-building paths.** What are several possible ways that I could create better results in this area?
- ✧ **Why pillars.** Why is it important for me to improve this area? How would my life be better if I achieved this?
- ✧ **Preparing for potential problems.** In the past, what has gotten in the way? What obstacles might distract me or hinder my results in the future? How might I address these problems if they arise?
- ✧ **Enlisting support.** Who might be able to help me make these changes? Should my supporters be my cheering section, partners on my journey, models of desired behavior, or expert guides to help me take action?
- ✧ **Next step.** With my plan in hand, what would be the next step I could take today to begin creating my success?

Do It: Take Action

- ✧ Right before you take that next step, take a moment to envision your successful outcome. Close your eyes. See yourself, feel yourself, and hear yourself masterfully doing this new behavior you're creating. If you find that you're having trouble seeing this vision, then you might be interested in trying our New Behavior Generator Visualization to help you create and integrate this new behavior even more fully and clearly and to begin creating your success immediately. For more information, visit www.InspiredActionBook.com/Resources.
- ✧ Once you have the vision of your success locked in, remember the last time you felt unstoppable. Bring that memory and feeling right into this moment, and charge up your vision with that emotional state of being certain, being unstoppable. With that energy propelling you, take your next step. Take action as quickly as possible to lock into your consciousness the change that you've chosen to make.

Next Actions

- ✓ If you're having trouble brainstorming possible strategies, then ask your friends for help. Post it on Facebook or Twitter. Try YouTube and Google. Get some crowd-sourced solutions for how other people solve this problem.
- ✓ Consider making your plan with your partner or a friend. Habit changes can be easier when you have social support and a positive-minded person to hold you accountable—to make sure that you are staying with your commitment.
- ✓ Keep an energy log that tracks both the habit you're focused on and your energy level on that day on a scale of 1 to 5. Consider checking in with yourself two or three times during the day. Give yourself some solid data to determine how effective your changes are.
- ✓ Once you've locked in your first energy-management change, go back to your assessment and repeat this process with the next one.

Focusing on one per quarter or season tends to works best; more than one per month is generally too much.

Resources

Change Bridge Worksheets. www.InspiredActionBook.com/Resources.

New Behavior Generator Visualization. www.InspiredActionBook.com/Resources.

Chosen Course Excellence Assessment. www.InspiredActionBook.com/Resources.

Loehr, Jim, and Tony Schwartz. *The Power of Full Engagement: Managing Energy, Not Time, Is the Key to High Performance and Personal Renewal.* New York: Free Press, 2003.

Schwartz, Tony. *Be Excellent at Anything: The Four Keys to Transforming the Way We Work and Live.* New York: Free Press, 2010.

—14—

Habits: The Power of Patterns

Have you noticed that when you get up in the morning, you take certain actions without thinking about them? You move from your bed to the bathroom to the kitchen and take care of the needful things almost without any conscious thought. Now, while I am an advocate of being present in daily life, I do believe that these small automatic routines are an essential part of our existence. They allow our conscious minds to rest.

In fact, we are biologically programmed to create habits. Our minds are constantly looking for cues that tell us which routine to start next, because when we find a cue and start our known routine, our brains can rev down and rest until the routine is done. Stated simply, habits reduce mental strain and stress, and most of us certainly appreciate having less stress in our lives.

The challenge is that we develop many of our habits by default rather than with clear intention, so they might not serve us as much as they could. How much more powerful could our habits be if we intentionally crafted and created them?

Fortunately, science has been advancing and helping us better understand how to make the most of our natural habit-forming patterns. In his book *The Power of Habit,* Charles Duhigg summarizes his studies on the role of habits in our lives, how habits get created, and how we can change them. The key is this pattern: cue, routine, reward. Every habit you have consists of a cue that tells your brain to begin a specific, established routine that results in a specific, consistent reward. That reward may be something physical or tangible like the coffee you drink during your afternoon break, or it might simply be a feeling or state, such as the connection and relaxation you get from checking Facebook or watching YouTube videos. A cue might be an action that precedes the habit, a specific time on the clock, an interaction with a certain person, or an emotion. Whenever you experience that cue, you automatically execute a prewritten script of behavior that to leads to your reward.

It's likely that you already have many habit patterns as constants in your life. Here are some of the more common routines for many people:

- Morning wake-up and getting ready
- Arriving at work
- Getting home from work and settling in at home
- Going to bed at night

However, there are plenty of other times when establishing patterns might help you "get the job done" in normal activities of life:

- Exercise routines or circuits
- Preparation rituals for doing creative work
- Helping your kids with their homework
- Transitioning between activities
- Wrapping up at the end of your workday
- Planning your meals for the week

Can you think of other times when habit patterns would be appropriate for your life? There are virtually limitless possible examples. For instance, I have been learning to sail, and I discovered that the process of rigging a sailboat is another perfect time to establish a powerful, reliable pattern. Think about your activities and life, and you'll begin to identify some examples that are relevant for you.

If our aim is to craft our habits more intentionally, then we must focus on two possible outcomes: a shift in an existing habit or the creation of a new one.

Creating or Changing a Habit

If you want to shift an existing habit so that it will serve you better, then you already have an established cue, routine, and reward. If you're creating a new habit, then you need to identify the new cue, routine, and reward for this pattern. This might be easy in some cases and a bit confusing in others.

I continually study my own habit patterns and change them to meet my current needs. One pattern that I've been developing recently is my morning writing habit, which has allowed me to finish this book. The morning writing habit itself is an example of creating a new pattern. However, this new habit also relied on my first changing some of my existing patterns.

For instance, to be successful at my new morning writing habit, I needed my laptop to be available in my bedroom first thing in the morning. Since my laptop generally gets used in my office throughout the day, I needed to shift my evening getting-ready-for-bed pattern to include taking my laptop upstairs with me. I simply needed to incorporate this additional step into my existing routine.

The cue for this modified going-to-bed pattern is my thought about heading upstairs. If I miss that cue, however, then the physical act of putting my hand on the banister reminds me that two objects should be in that hand: my laptop and my water bottle. Now, I had already been in the habit of making sure that I had my iPhone with me before I walked upstairs, since my phone is both my alarm clock and my audiobook that helps me go to sleep. So, in this case, all I needed to do was shift my routine to include grabbing all three items: the iPhone, the laptop, and the water bottle.

A minor adjustment, right? In this case, the reward was the sense of satisfaction I would get from knowing that I was prepped and ready for a productive morning writing session.

After I made this adjustment to my bedtime routine, the process of creating my morning writing habit became so much easier. Writing has become the first thing I do in the morning. The cue is waking up. Then I've crafted the routine to include the following steps: go to the bathroom (since a full bladder is a definite distraction), light my candles, turn on my writing playlist, grab my laptop and draft, and curl up back in bed to write. This routine is especially powerful because I've built in several rewards. First, I get to stay in my warm bed longer in the morning. Second, I get that internal win of having gotten my writing done and out of the way before the rest of my day begins. Finally, I give myself 15 minutes of Facebook time immediately after I finish my session, which allows me to rest, to connect with folks I love, and to celebrate my morning win with a status update.

Now, let's break this process into steps that you can apply for yourself:

1. **Identify the change you want to make.** The easiest aspect of a habit to change is the routine itself, since your established cue will naturally propel you into the process of execution that results in a given reward. Changing the cue or the reward can be more challenging, but it is also possible. And creating a full cue-routine-reward pattern may take a little more thought and effort.

2. **Identify your cue.** What specific sight, sound, thought, or feeling will tell you that it's time to begin the pattern? What will happen *immediately before* your new routine? Identify something specific, such as my examples of waking up, putting your hand on the bannister, or the even earlier cue of the thought that it's time to go to bed.

3. **Identify your reward.** What's the *why* of making this change? What's the benefit that you'll get from this new effort? The reward must be compelling enough to make the new routine worth committing to.

4. **Visualize your success.** Take a couple minutes and walk through the exact new sequence in your mind. Imagine all the details of completing it successfully. See your cue, imagine yourself immediately taking the new action of completing the routine, and feel yourself receiving the reward. If you're shift-

ing an existing pattern, the changes you're making may not be huge, so this simple visualization process will just help you lock it in. If you're creating a new habit pattern, particularly something that involves behaviors that are new to you, you might try our New Behavior Generator Visualization exercise that you can find at www.InspiredActionBook.com/Resources.

5. **Practice your pattern.** Put your new pattern into action. You may find that your new or revised routine happens easily and immediately. You might catch yourself blowing past your cue and missing the new steps a couple times. If possible, go back and take the steps immediately when you notice that you've missed them. If you miss the pattern completely, try repeating the visualization step above and locking in your awareness of your cue even more clearly.

It can be beneficial to track your progress in creating your new habit. This can be as simple as a blank calendar that you mark with an X for each day when you successfully execute your new pattern. Smartphone apps can also help. I use one for iOS called Streaks, which is essentially a digital version of putting X's on a calendar.

Following Through

Remember to think of this process as practice. You are practicing a pattern of success in life. Each day is simply another chance to practice. Don't make it stressful, and if it doesn't come immediately, then here's the key question: What could I do to make it even easier for me to complete this habit each day? Following my own example, could I have done my writing habit each morning without having my laptop already in my bedroom? Yes, but having it there already made success so much more likely. Shawn Achor, author of *The Happiness Advantage*, calls this the "20-sec rule." How can you reduce the resistance to starting a habit by making it take 20 seconds or less? For him, the new habit was morning exercise, and the key to making it easy was to sleep in his workout clothes and put his gym shoes next to his bed.

Shift, adapt, get curious, and get creative. Establishing one new habit pattern might require you to change two or three other small routines, but everything is possible. Craft your life like a sculptor, and you will be delighted with the masterpiece you can create.

Next Actions

✓ Start by choosing just one habit that you want to shift or create. Focus is the key here. Practice it until it becomes easy. It might take three weeks or three months; give it whatever time it needs. If you find you're struggling, don't give up. Just get curious. Remember the key question: How could you make the routine even easier? Would it work better at a different time of day? Would a different cue be more powerful?

✓ Do you want to encourage someone else to create new powerful patterns or to participate in yours? Think about the other person's cue, pattern, and reward. How will he or she know that it's time to act or to get involved? What are the specific steps that he or she would need to take? What could the reward be? Train yourself and others just as you might train your beloved puppy—with curiosity and positive reinforcement—and you'll be surprised at the results.

✓ Make habit crafting a part of your regular self-development. As part of your seasonal review ritual, you can pause to check in on the habit you've been developing. (For more information, see Chapter 48: Seasonal Planning.) If you feel like it's becoming solid and automatic, then choose a new powerful habit pattern to begin crafting into your life.

Resources

Achor, Shawn. *The Happiness Advantage: The Seven Principles of Positive Psychology That Fuel Success and Performance at Work*. New York: Broadway Books, 2010.

Duhigg, Charles. *The Power of Habit: Why We Do What We Do in Life and Business*. New York: Random House, 2014.

Kolberg, Judith, and Kathleen Nadeau. *ADD-Friendly Ways to Organize Your Life*. New York: Brunner-Routledge, 2002. This book has great sections on patterns and establishing habits, both for those coping with ADD and for the rest of us just trying to simplify our routines in life.

—15—

Your Ideal Week Vision

It's happened again. You have gotten to the end of the week and are confused about why so many things didn't get done or why you didn't make the progress that you were hoping and planning for. Where did the week go? And why did you feel like you were constantly zooming from one place to another and shifting back and forth between activities at a whirlwind pace?

Ending the Epidemic

I have seen this experience with so many clients and colleagues, and I have definitely had that feeling myself from time to time. We pack our schedules with commitments to various people (and rarely to ourselves). We say yes to anything that could even potentially fit in to the calendar space in front of us, but at the end of the week we feel wiped out, run-down, and haggard. We look back and begin to feel that familiar frustration: some of the things that we had intended to accomplish simply didn't happen.

This experience is epidemic in our lives today. But I have seen an exercise that consistently brings light to this challenge and can put you on a path to resolving it. You have to step outside your daily activities for a couple hours and create your vision for an ideal week. This form of planning has many names, including time mapping and unscheduling. I prefer the term *life rhythm map* because it raises your awareness about the current rhythms of your life and encourages you to reflect on how you want to change them. This exercise captures the cadence and flow of the days in *your* ideal week. Completing the exercise also offers insight about why that end-of-week exhaustion and confusion have hit you again, and what you need to do to change them.

The Weekly Life Rhythm Map

Here's the process:

1. Think of all the major areas of your life: work, family, friends, personal care, community activities, home care, and so on. Grab several sheets of paper, and write each area of your life at the top of one sheet. Draw a line down each paper, making a wide column on the left and a slightly narrower column on the right. For more help, download our Life Rhythm worksheets at www.InspiredActionBook.com/Resources.
2. In the left column of each sheet of paper, brainstorm all your current commitments, goals, or projects for that area. Give yourself plenty of time to do this, and make sure you get them *all*. Everything you've said yes to, or dedicated even 30 minutes a week to accomplishing, deserves a place. Don't forget the minor daily-living items: getting ready in the morning, eating meals, relaxing and taking care of yourself, doing dishes, doing laundry, running errands, and so on.
3. When you've captured all of your commitments, then go down the list, and in the right-hand column, write your truest, best, most accurate guess of how much time you spend on each activity each week. Make sure to include any travel or prep time for the activity too! If it has to happen on a certain day, at a certain time, or with a certain rate of frequency (including monthly or biweekly), then note that too. Now it's time to chart out your ideal weekly rhythm. Personally, I tend to do this as a digital spreadsheet in Microsoft Excel or iWork Numbers, or you can create a new calendar using Google or another calendar program. However, any grid-based chart for a week will do. For templates both digital and printable, visit www.InspiredActionBook.com/Resources. The example below will give you a good idea of the result you're aiming for. The most important thing is to equate length of time to space using the size of the blocks. So, download, print, or draw a chart for

yourself. I recommend making 1 block equal to either 15 or 30 minutes of your day to give you the appropriate level of detail. I am also a fan of color-coding the different life areas.

4. Start by entering all the fixed elements (if you're writing on paper, I recommend using a pencil):

   - **AM get-ready time.** When you wake up, how long does it take you to get ready in the morning?
   - **Commute.** How long is your commute to work?
   - **Lunch break.** How long is your lunch break, and when do you usually take it on weekdays?
   - **End of work.** When is your commute home from work, and how long does it take?
   - **Bedtime.** What time do you go to bed (or *want* to go to bed, since this is an ideal week)? How much time do you need to get ready or to wind down before bed?
   - **Weekly appointments.** What standard meetings, classes, or weekly commitments structure your week? Think of staff meetings, kids' sports, church, yoga class, and so on.

   Is your week starting to fill up? Are you beginning to see what little time is left for all the *less*-structured projects or activities? You will likely see that instead of having wide-open days brimming with possibilities, you have roughly three large blocks each day: morning, afternoon, and evening.

5. Go through each of your brainstormed sheets and begin entering the remaining projects, activities, and commitments in the available white space. You might group together certain kinds of work. For instance, follow-up phone calls and emails might just be grouped as "admin time," and you might give it two small blocks (one before lunch and one after lunch). Or, a group called "house maintenance" might include laundry,

cleaning, and repairs, and you might slot it in on Sunday afternoons.

6. Notice if you are having trouble fitting certain commitments into your chart. Are your days seeming crammed, with no white flex space left? If so, you are probably beginning to see why you get that frustrated feeling at the end of the week. Now you have reached the decision point in this exercise. What needs to give? What can you eliminate, reduce, delegate, or postpone either to make everything fit or to actually bring a bit of breathing space into your days?

7. Do a few final accuracy checks:

   - Imagine your way through yesterday (or any other day in the past week). Visualize it step by step, and think about any activity (or group of actions) you did that adds up to at least 15 minutes of your time and attention on a regular basis. Have you accounted for those activities in your ideal week? If not, find a place for them—or decide to change your commitments.

   - Did you leave enough space for travel or prep time to/from or before/after activities?

   - Is there adequate rest and relaxation time in your ideal week? Remember, humans are not machines; we need more downtime than just sleep. Is that time incorporated into your days? (For more information, see Chapter 13: Your Energy-Management Plan.)

Now that you have created your weekly life rhythm map, you can begin shifting your reality to fit the ideal. Be prepared; this may take time. You might want to keep a copy of your map near your regular calendar, so that you remember how precious your time is before you say yes to that additional project or volunteer commitment.

If your most creative time is in the morning, then try to schedule meetings and appointments with other people for the afternoon, so that you can leverage your creative energy at its peak time. This won't always work, but my experience is that whoever makes the clearest request tends to control scheduling conversations, and this person's needs get respected.

Also, remember that you might need to reevaluate your map regularly—perhaps every three to four months—because seasons change and new commitments and projects need to be worked in to the plan. Updating the map tends to take less time than when you first create it, unless a major life change requires a full rethink. However, having a clearer understanding of how your time is being spent and how much space your current commitments take up is the key to never having that "what-happened-to-my-week" feeling again.

Next Actions

✓ Complete your weekly life rhythm map, and begin adjusting your scheduling and plans to match your *ideal* week over the next two to four weeks. In those weeks, revisit your map at least weekly and make any tweaks that become obvious or necessary with lived experience.

✓ Encourage your partner to create his or her own map, and then compare them together. Talk about your mutual time and how you want or need to spend that time to take care of your relationship and your joint responsibilities. Use this as a conversation to illuminate pressures that you've been feeling, and ask for the time and support you need for each other's personal health and the health and happiness of your relationship.

✓ Print a copy of your weekly life rhythm map, and keep it posted by your desk or folded into your calendar or capture book as a reference and reminder for planning and decision-making.

✓ Write or enter an appointment on your calendar for three months from now to revisit and update your weekly life rhythm map for the next season.

Resources

Morgenstern, Julie. *Time Management from the Inside Out: The Foolproof System for Taking Control of Your Schedule—and Your Life*. New York: Henry Holt/Owl Books, 2004.

Life Rhythm Map Templates. www.InspiredActionBook.com/Resources.

Fiore, Neil A. *The Now Habit: A Strategic Program for Overcoming Procrastination and Enjoying Guilt-Free Play*. New York: Tarcher/Penguin, 2007.

Part 4

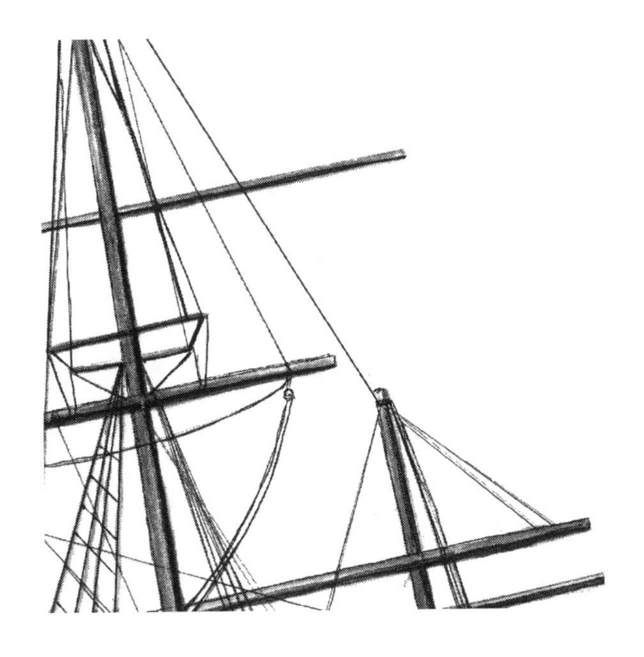

Rigging and Spars: Tools and Systems to Get Organized

—16—

8 Steps to Organizing Success

Why Does Being Organized Matter?

Organization means less wasted time in hunting for things. You would spend less money buying duplicate items and on late fees for missing bills. Most of all, living an organized lifestyle gives you more energy to focus on what matters because your environment is designed to support you.

Imagine if you could find anything in your world in less than two minutes. Imagine if you could come home daily and not feel exhausted and overwhelmed by all the stuff. These are just a few of the gifts of organization.

> *"I really want to get more organized, but I have no idea where to start."*

This sentiment is shared by most of the organizing clients that my company has ever worked with, and part of our job is to teach them a basic method that will guide them through any organizing process. After over a decade of working in this industry, I became very familiar with the classic methods, such as Julie Morgenstern's SPACE method and Kathy Waddill's Nine Strategies for Simplifying Your Life. However, there was still room for improvement in giving people a specific and complete process to become more organized in any area of space or life. That's how I developed what we at Living Peace call the 8 Steps to Organizing Success.

There are three phases to any organizing project: Planning, System Setup, and Maintenance. The challenge is that many people ignore the importance of phases 1 and 3 and focus only on the system setup phase, but the beginning and the end are where many solutions go wrong.

As you get started, here is the most important thing to remember: these steps must be done in order for maximum success. The most frequent error people make is jumping to step 5 and buying containers before they have gone through the first four steps. That's a great way to spend a lot of money on things that you may not need or that may not be the best solutions. Trust me, the outcome is worth the work.

Planning Phase

1. Create the vision. If you know where you're going, it's much easier to get there. Many clients struggle with articulating their vision before we begin. An organizing vision springs from the answer to one question: how do you want this space to look, feel, and function when you're all done? We can dig in to more specifics by considering these further questions:

- What's happening in this space now, and what activities will happen here when we're done organizing?
- What words describe the feeling you'll have when you walk into the space?
- What will you see that's different when you walk into the space after we're done?

Answering these questions at the beginning of the organizing process gives you a beacon to guide your work—a clear understanding of what you are creating and moving toward. Without it, you may find yourself knee-deep in stuff and wondering why you started this project in the first place.

Similarly, if you're working with anyone else, whether it be family, friends, or a professional organizer, having a clear vision of the outcome you want helps you clarify actions and communications, and it can illuminate decisions that you did not consider previously. For instance, you really want to move the bill-paying activity from the living-room couch to the kitchen desk. What would need to be different in order for that to work?

As a final reminder, focus on making your environment fit your life right now, not a previous chapter of your life or a fantasy future version that might happen someday. Make sure you create a system that lives in your present reality with you.

For all these reasons, starting with a vision and undergoing this planning phase is crucial to bringing about the best possible outcome. Then you can dig in to the system setup.

System Setup Phase: SWABS

As you set up your organizing system, remember the acronym SWABS: sort, weed, assign, buy, set up.

2. Sort everything into categories. The first—and crucial—step in setting up an organizational system is to define the categories of items currently in the space and then physically sort everything in the space into those groups. As an example, I'll tell you about my recent reorganization of my office storage closet. Some of the major categories of objects in the closet were filing supplies, archive paperwork, paper and notepads, envelopes (various kinds), labels (various kinds), pens/markers/highlighters, electronics/computer-related items, and fasteners.

Now, since my closet was reasonably well organized in the first place (that is, most of the objects in it really were office related), I immediately began making more refined categories. If your office has become a dumping ground for many things in your home, then your categories might include gift wrap, gifts to give, kids' toys, books, paperwork (all kinds), and office supplies (more generally).

When sorting, it's best to find a "Goldilocks" level of category: not too big and not too small, but just right. Otherwise, you can get trapped in either having just three categories for everything in the room (which is probably unhelpful) or having 50 micro-categories and spending all your time sorting sizes of binder clips rather than making a real impact on the space. I would say aim for 6 to 12 categories, and you're probably in the right zone.

3. Weed/relocate each category. After going through everything in your space and grouping things into categories, now is the time to make the "hard" decisions about what stays and what goes. Remember, there might be several options for things that will go:

- Relocate it to a different room/space
- Give it to a friend or family member
- Donate it to charity
- Give it away on Freecycle or a similar reuse community
- Sell it on eBay, craigslist, consignment, or through an auction
- Recycle it
- Trash it

Why is it important to sort first and to weed second? Because you will make stronger weeding decisions when you see all of what you have in a particular category. Does this mean that you never pitch something immediately rather than placing it in its category? No. If you know it's trash or you'll never want or need it again, put it immediately in the trash or in a donation pile. However, by sorting first, you may be surprised to discover that you have 17 staplers but only 8 rooms in your house. Even if you put one in every room, there would be a lot left over. That is why seeing all of a particular type of object together will allow you to make clear and solid decisions to keep the best and release the rest.

The end of this step is when you clear from your house all of the trash, recycling, donations, or sale items. Watch out: those bags of stuff for charity can become a new kind of clutter in a random corner if you don't follow through and take action to get them out of your life.

4. Assign homes. At this point you should have gotten down to *clear categories* of just the objects you want to keep. Now is when you take a look at these items and start thinking about how, when, and who will use them. Here are some questions and guidelines to help you.

- *How frequently do you use these items?* Do they belong in accessible "prime real estate" locations, or could they be stored in less convenient places for the one or two times a year that you look for them.
- *Who needs access to them?* Consider the usage of others in your home. If your kids will be using these items unsupervised, then you'll want to make sure they are stored within easy kid reach. If your spouse is significantly shorter or taller than you are, then that would be a similar consideration regarding the long-term storage of items that are shared.
- *Under what circumstances do you need or use these items?* Perhaps they are used in conjunction with another set of items and thus should be stored together. Or perhaps this is paperwork that you would need if you got audited, but you are unlikely to access it otherwise. In other words, it's really just archive rather than active at this point and could be put into storage somewhere more remote than your desk file drawer.

Think about the questions above, and then consider where each group of items might go in your space. Choose the drawers, shelves, or closet space that makes the most sense based on your answers, and consider what additional kinds of storage solutions would either add necessary storage space (a new filing cabinet, shelving unit, or armoire) or make the storage space you have more functional (baskets, bins, plastic drawer units, or drawer organizers).

Now make your shopping list. Take detailed measurements of both the spaces you will be placing things (like dimensions of the closet shelves) and the general volume of any category to be stored.

5. Buy/locate appropriate containers. This is the step that everyone loves because it means going to the store and picking out all the new boxes, bins, and baskets that you will look at and enjoy. Before immediately trooping off to buy new things, however, I encourage you to look around your house for any unused containers or tools that could be repurposed for your newly organized space. We frequently forget to shop in our own home before heading out to the stores, and we might save ourselves both time and money by simply relocating a current under-utilized resource.

During step 4, you should have created a very specific shopping list of items to locate or to buy. So...go to it! Here are a few things to keep in mind:

- *Size.* Keep your measurements with you during your search. If a container won't fit the space you want to put it in, or if it won't hold the full volume of a collection of objects, then it is *not* the right tool for this purpose. Also, consider the size of the items to be stored inside the container. Use smaller containers for smaller items and larger containers for larger items. Think of all the LEGOs that get lost at the bottom of a large toy chest, and you'll recognize why this is important.
- *Aesthetics.* If you don't like the look or feel of a container, then you'll be disinclined to use it. Find tools that feel good to your hands or please your eyes. Then you'll be happier with the result and more likely to maintain the system moving forward.
- *Visibility.* Clear or open containers can be helpful because they give you immediate visual cues about what is inside. This is particularly important if you are a visual person. Similarly, if the goal is to hide the clutter, then you might prefer containers that are opaque.
- *Manageability.* If you are going to be lifting a container, putting it down, or moving it around, then consider how heavy it will be when fully loaded.
- *Sturdiness.* Will the tool be able to handle heavy use? Will it stand up over time to regular wear and tear?

6. Set up and label the final system. Now you take all your new containers and your sorted and weeded categories and bring the two together. This step is the final implementation of your new organizing system.

Don't skimp on the labels for your new system. I'm a fan of using a label machine to mark bins, shelves, or drawers for several reasons:

- Labels remind you of where things go and what you decided long after the fact, which makes the system easier to maintain. It's easy to forget which shelf or drawer is supposed to hold an object you're putting back, particularly if it's one of a kind—without a label, there's no cue about where the object should go after you remove it.
- Labels communicate shared systems to multiple people using them. If a container is labeled FILING SUPPLIES, your co-worker will probably pause before sticking the printer cartridge in that container and might pause to look for the appropriate location.
- Labels keep categories clear and together. If each place is clearly labeled for a specific type of item, then every item's home becomes more obvious, and items without homes can be identified easily and dealt with thoughtfully rather than just getting shoved on any shelf that has room.

These five SWABS steps will result in a beautifully organized and functional space in any office or home. Whether your space stays that way likely depends on *also* completing the final two steps in the maintenance phase, below.

Maintenance Phase

7. Identify and develop habits. Maintenance is about habits. If you don't work to develop good habits for putting things into their new homes, then your system will dissolve and you'll end up starting over.

- What will you need to do on a regular basis to ensure that your space stays as beautifully organized as it was by the end of system setup? Return items to their assigned homes, certainly. Anything else?

✧ How frequently will you put things away? At the end of each day? Once a week? Only when the clutter "ick" factor starts bugging you again?

Your long-term results will vary based on the answers to these questions. And if you're used to living in cluttered spaces, then you might need to work actively on developing the habit of putting things away more frequently. (For more help with habit development, see Chapter 14: Habits: The Power of Patterns.)

8. Evaluate and update. Your needs will change in time. The best system in the world for right now will need to be updated, tweaked, or overhauled as new projects and needs arise. In reality, organizing is never actually *done* because our lives are constantly changing, and thus our systems need to change as well. If you pay attention, you might be able to just slightly tweak systems to shift with you, but at some point you will likely need to start fresh back at step 1 and establish a new system to fit your new normal.

When you walk through all eight of these steps in order, any organizing project you take on—from your desk drawers to your garage—will fall in line and become maintainable and sustainable for the future.

Next Actions

✓ Pick one space in your home or office and get started with the 8 Steps. You might start with a small space, like a closet, if you want to see rapid results in a few hours. If you tackle a whole room in your house, be prepared to dedicate several multi-hour sessions over the next few weeks to see it through to the end. We prefer to work in three-hour sessions to keep the progress and energy manageable.

✓ Find an organizing buddy. Talk to friends or family members, and find someone who also has an organizing project in mind. Schedule sessions together (about three hours is good) once per week and alternate weeks in each other's spaces. Working together will get the job done faster and be a lot more fun!

- ✓ If you are overwhelmed by this process or are aware that organizing has been a lifelong challenge for you, then hire a professional organizer! You can either hire a local organizer to work with you in your space hands-on, or you can work virtually by phone or Skype with an experienced organizer to coach you through the process. My former organizing company Living Peace has team members trained in virtual organizing who can work with you anywhere in the world. You can find out more at bit.ly/LivingPeaceOrg. To find an organizer in your local area take a look at the National Association of Professional Organizers (bit.ly/NAPOInfo).

If you can't remember any time in your life when you've been organized, then you might want to work with a specialist in chronic disorganization. You can find a specialist through the Institute for Challenging Disorganization at bit.ly/ChallengingDisorg. The right support and guidance can make a project that feels utterly overwhelming both easy and fun.

Resources

Institute for Challenging Disorganization (ICD). http://bit.ly/ChallengingDisorg.

Living Peace Professional Organizing. http://bit.ly/LivingPeaceOrg.

Morgenstern, Julie. *Organizing from the Inside Out: The Foolproof System for Organizing Your Home, Your Office and Your Life.* New York: Holt Paperbacks, 2nd Edition, 2004.

National Association of Professional Organizers (NAPO). http://bit.ly/NAPOInfo.

Waddill, Kathy. *The Organizing Sourcebook: Nine Strategies for Simplifying Your Life.* Chicago: Contemporary Books, 2001.

—17—

Activity Kits

The activity kit is one of the greatest and simplest organizing solutions available. These kits can help you accomplish many different tasks more easily. One of the key principles of organizing is to keep like items together, but sometimes we don't recognize that what makes certain things alike is not necessarily what they *are* but rather how we *use* them.

How often have you gone running all over the office or the house to collect the various items you need for a certain project or activity? Wouldn't it be great if you could permanently minimize all that running around—particularly for activities that you do daily or weekly?

Activity kits can take many different forms. To help you start thinking about kits that you might choose to create, here are a few examples of successful kit solutions my team has developed for ourselves and for our organizing clients:

- ✧ All the members of my staff have a **toolbox of organizing supplies** that they take with them to every client's space. It's a simple plastic toolbox with a lift-out tray, and inside are the most frequently used items for organizing: Post-it notes, Sharpies, scissors, a stapler, Scotch tape, a label maker with extra cassettes, highlighters, and so on.
- ✧ In my trunk I keep my **gym bag**, which always has my gym shoes, one to two changes of gym clothes (after I use them I bring them in the house for washing and set out a new set to take to the car the next morning), my armband for my iPhone and headphones, a combination lock, hair ties and clips, a towel, a water bottle, a swimsuit, and so on. Because of this activity kit, I rarely need to plan ahead to go to the gym. If I have an

opening in my afternoon, I can just drive over and get in a workout.

- ✧ A client of mine is in sales and spends most of his time driving to meet with clients, so he put together a **traveling office**. In his work satchel he placed standard forms and reference sheets that he used with clients, several of his favorite pens, his laptop, an extra power cord that lives permanently in the kit, a small stapler, a calculator, and some other relevant items.
- ✧ Another former client is an avid quilter who frequently has several major projects in the works at once. In her craft room we set up a group of **project baskets** where she now stores all the items she needs for an individual work-in-progress: the appropriate color thread; the pattern or notes; stacks of cut quilt pieces (frequently in ziplock bags); and other tools, stencils, or design elements that are unique to that project. Whenever she is in the mood to work on a specific project, she can just pull down that basket and get to work.
- ✧ Several of our clients successfully use **bill-paying kits** that include all the necessary items to take care of the weekly bills: checkbook, calculator, envelopes, stamps, pens and pencils, folder for bills to pay, and so on. Paying bills is just a matter of opening up that kit.
- ✧ More recently, my husband and I created two sailing kits. One with everything we need to take with us on the boat in a waterproof bag: hats, sailing gloves, sunglasses, sunscreen, water bottle, etc. and another kit to live in the car with a change of clothes for both of us and a towel in case we flip the boat!

To help you get started, here are the steps for making activity kits:

1. Brainstorm the various activities in your life that would benefit from a kit, and choose one to start with.
2. Ask yourself the following questions:

- ✧ What supplies do I use for this activity?
- ✧ Do I have (or might I buy) extra supplies that I can dedicate to live in my kit without needing to fish them out continuously for other reasons?
- ✧ What kind of container will be most appropriate to hold my kit? A bag, basket, or bin, perhaps?
- ✧ Where should my kit live, so that it will be convenient for engaging in the activity?
- ✧ What habits will I need to form in order for my kit to work optimally? (Think about my gym clothes example: I had to get in the habit of bringing in my gym clothes for washing and putting new sets in the car.)

3. Collect all the necessary items. If necessary, buy or order additional supplies to live inside your kit. This is one time when duplicate items can be a blessing—one for your kit and one for more general use.
4. Pay attention when you use your kit. Did you miss any items that should be added? If you can't keep everything in the kit itself, then include a checklist of additional items to grab—for instance, you might also need to pack your medicine, laptop, or a ziplock bag of fresh dog food. (See Chapter 22: Checklists for Everything.)

There must be some activity in your life that would benefit from having a kit. Give it a try!

Next Actions

✓ If your first kit is successful, then go back to your brainstormed list and try another. How much easier might life be if what you needed were ready to go at a moment's notice?

- ✓ Use kits with your kids. This is a great approach for organizing and teaching organizing skills to kids. If you keep all the items for one type of activity together, then your children can learn to pull out that kit when they want to do that activity and put all the items back together and away when they're done.
- ✓ Give kits as gifts. For example, a moving kit can be great for your friend who's facing relocation. A small toolkit might be a wonderful present for a person who has just graduated from college and is starting life on her own. What about a diaper-bag kit with a packing checklist to help a new mom stay organized? There are so many types of kits that people could use. Get creative! One of my favorite presents for a bride is a Wedding Day Emergency Kit with all the last-minute solutions that might become essential on her important day.

—18—

BARFT:
Managing Your Incoming Paperwork

Paper, paper, there's always more paper! With the introduction of tablet computers, the amount of paper in people's lives is finally lessening a bit. However, during my years as a professional organizer, the number-one issue that our clients have repeatedly identified is managing the mountain of paperwork that is part of their daily lives. I remember futurists of the 1990s predicting that with the increasing popularity of the personal computer, paper would soon be history. Instead, computers made it easier to print everything! As a result, most of us have more paper in our lives than any previous generation did.

What's so tricky about paperwork is that for a given stack of it on the corner of your desk, you might need to make anywhere from 10 to 200 decisions to make that paper end up elsewhere. We frequently tell clients to be prepared for the fact that organizing paperwork tends to be both challenging and slow. If you think about it, four inches of height on a shelf in a closet might hold two to four sweaters and thus require only two to four decisions. The same space of paperwork on your desk, however, is a couple reams of paper that need individual attention. So, begin with patience...and a deep breath.

BARFT: Five Categories for All Paperwork

At this point, I'm pleased to tell you that essentially every sheet of paper in your world falls into one of five categories, which I have unattractively coined as BARFT. While it's not the prettiest acronym in the world, many of us feel rather like our paperwork has barfed all over our lives, so at least it's accurate.

Bills to Pay

I always like to start here because of all the papers in your life, bills are items for which your failure to find and act on them can negatively impact your bank account, your credit score, or both. Bills deserve their own special place and category.

Action Items

This type of paperwork includes forms you have to complete and return, services or products that you want to research, and notes from your child's teacher that require a response. Basically, action items are papers that require you to take a follow-up action before you can pitch it or file it. If you're using a task management system, then you might also want to build a habit of recording the necessary action on your master list before putting the papers into your Action Items file or bin. That will ensure that you have a reminder of the task in a useful location rather than relying on the paper itself to be your reminder. For more information about setting up your master list see Chapters 23 and 24.

Read

This is where all those catalogs, magazines, newsletters, and reports belong—those lovely, bulky items that you want to curl up and flip through at some time in the near future. I encourage you to get very clear about what's realistic to keep in this category. I have seen "To Read" piles that are several feet high—or occasionally, with some of our hoarding clients, entire houses or rooms full of paperwork that the client wanted to read someday. Set a limit. It could be a spatial limit (no bigger than a designated basket) or a time limit (if I haven't gotten to it in X weeks or months, then it can't be that important to my life.) Either way, don't let the "shoulda-coulda-woulda" of the "To Read" mountain take over your environment or your energy.

File

If a piece of paper's only value is as a reference or in case of future emergency (perhaps your taxes get audited—*shudder*), then it probably just needs to be filed appropriately. Think very carefully before you immediately toss everything in here, though. When would you need this item again, and under what circumstances? Could you find the information easily online or on your computer if necessary? What's the worst thing that would happen if you didn't have it? The 80/20 rule often applies to paperwork: people access only 20 percent of their files on 80 percent of the occasions when they search for files. That means 80 percent of our paperwork hangs around our workstations for absolutely no good reason. Don't accumulate thoughtlessly. Remember: the more you keep, the harder it may be to find what you really do end up needing.

Trash (or Recycling, if You Prefer)

Here's the truth: *all* of that paper will eventually end up in the recycling bin. You just get to decide how long a sojourn in your world it will take in the meantime. Perhaps it goes to Action or Read first, or it travels through your filing system until it gets purged. But a significant amount of paperwork can and should go directly into the trash (do not pass go, do not collect $200). Some examples:

- **All mailed envelopes.** The envelopes that paper arrives in just create bulk. They also mean you have to take time folding and unfolding things before you know what they are. Pitch the envelopes and save time and space.
- **Unsolicited junk mail.** Unless your response upon looking at it was, "Wow, I've been looking for one of those!" it's trash. When you need it, you will be able to find it again. Behold the power of the Internet!
- **Inserts that come with your bank statements and utility bills.** They are essentially the same as the example above: unsolicited junk.

I'm sure I could think of more examples of papers to trash, but perhaps a good suggestion is to set some rules that allow you to make quick decisions about what stays and what goes.

Next Actions

- ✓ If you have a pile of random paperwork on your desk, grab four sticky notes and give them the following four titles: *Bills*, *Action*, *Read*, and *File*. Pull over your recycling bin and start sorting. Every one of the pages in that pile will fit in to one of these categories. It's time to decide which one.
- ✓ Set up a permanent paperwork-processing system. Choose a specific place (basket, bin, folder, or other container—anything other than an unlabeled, drifting pile will suffice) where you will always put each of the four main categories—Bills, Action, Read, and File. Keep a recycling bin or trash can, and a paper shredder (if necessary), near your processing system location.
- ✓ Practice, practice. At the end of each day, or when your mail arrives, collect all loose paperwork in your world and practice sorting into the BARFT categories. Once you get used to the system, staying on top of it rarely requires more than five minutes a day. With this processing done, you'll have your paper information teed up and ready when you are for that bill-paying session, reading, or to knock out a few of your actions items.

Resource

"Overcoming Paper Clutter: BARFT Your Papers."
www.InspiredActionBook.com/Resources.

—19—

Carrying a Capture Tool

Have you ever had a moment when a great idea comes to you, but you don't have any way to write it down? Or perhaps what comes to you isn't a great idea but an item you need to pick up at the grocery store or a book recommendation that you want to be able to remember later. One of the most essential tools for a productive lifestyle is a capture tool.

While my mother says that a slow or spacey memory is one of the pains of growing older, I would argue that trusting your mind to be able to bring up important information when requested is a massive challenge at any age. Inevitably, that recommended book's title will skip right out of your head 30 minutes later, and you won't remember that important grocery-store item until you're driving home from the store after picking up everything else that's less important.

The concept of writing things down to help ourselves remember them has been around, literally, for centuries. In his book *Hamlet's BlackBerry: Building a Good Life in the Digital Age,* William Powers describes the wax-tablet gadgets in use during Shakespeare's time as on-the-go capture tools. If capture tools helped Shakespeare capture his brilliance, then we can at least learn how to rely on them to remember to pick up some eggs.

Now, you might be saying, "Okay, I've been writing grocery lists and to-do lists for years. How is this different? A capture tool puts all of that information at your fingertips at any moment rather than scattered around your world on a plethora of different scraps of paper or Post-it notes.

What Makes a Capture Tool Work?

A capture tool is only effective if it meets the following criteria:

- **It's with you, or within easy reach, at all times.** David Allen talks about the necessity of "ubiquitous capture." You must always be able to capture information immediately and easily as soon as your mind churns it up. Thus, your capture tool *must* be portable and convenient to carry.
- **It allows you to subcategorize and reorganize information easily.** Putting that grocery item in the middle of your notes about this afternoon's meeting will probably mean that you forget to pick up the eggs yet again. So, you have to be able to subdivide your information or easily move it where it will be most useful.
- **It fits your preferred working style.** For some people, a smartphone with a few well-designed apps accomplishes this goal. For others, there will never be a substitute for a good notebook and a pencil. For many years, I used a hybrid of both: I would capture some types of information electronically in my smartphone and other types of information in writing on the fly. The key is having clear logic and knowing which information belongs where. There is no one right answer, but you do have to find the system that feels easy and natural for you. Don't let marketing sway you into believing that you'll transform from a confirmed Luddite into a gadget wiz overnight.
- **It's trustworthy.** If you frequently have to go hunting for your notes in your book or gadget and fail to find them, then you will begin to resist using the tool—a certain death knell. Make the sections of your capture tool clear and easy to find. Have *one* place for each category: *Books to Read, Movies to Watch, Tasks, Meeting Notes, Computer/Internet Passwords (properly encoded), Grocery List,* and so on.

✧ **It always has space to write more.** If you use a paper system, then make sure you always have adequate paper available to add or the next capture notebook is ready to go when your current one gets full. My favorite paper system is the Levenger Circa System which I have used and recommended for years. It looks like a spiral notebook but functions more like a flexible binder because the paper in this system is punched like an old-school Rolodex, thus making it simple to move pages around, remove them, or add more paper wherever you want. See **Resources**, below, for more information.

Using a Capture Tool

The most important idea with a capture tool is to pick ONE system, keep it simple, and stick to it. Multiple notebooks and tools generally mean more places to look and more potential confusion. Create a relationship with your capture tool. It needs to be your one go-to resource for capturing information. Occasionally I've had clients express the concern, "What happens when everything's in one notebook, and you lose the notebook?" My hope is that by following the practices in this book you are becoming both more organized and present enough not to have that happen. However, if you're really afraid of losing information, go digital with a cloud-based system. Then, even if you lose the device, you still won't lose the information.

Your capture tool is your absolute best friend for navigating life today. Invest appropriately with your time, energy, and money to keep that friendship strong.

Next Actions

✓ Choose your preferred capture tool, and begin carrying it with you everywhere.

✓ Practice capturing everything as it pops into your head. Think of a task? Reach for your capture tool. Someone mention a book for you to read? Reach for your capture tool. Don't trust your mind to remember that detail 15 minutes later. If it's important, or if it requires future attention or action, then grab your capture tool and make a note in an appropriate place.

✓ Seed your environment for effective capture. If you're using a paper system, such as the Levenger Circa System or a loose-leaf binder, then keep the appropriate type of paper and pens in all the places where you spend time: your desk, your bedside table, your kitchen, the bathroom—whenever you might need to capture the idea that just popped into your head. Then you can add that page to your notebook or binder.

✓ If you're using a digital system, get comfortable with having that smartphone always within arm's reach... even in the bathroom. Additionally, you might want to look for cloud-computing solutions that will allow you to access your information from any computer with Internet access, so that with or without your smartphone in hand, you'll be able to get to your lists to add or access information. Evernote is a great option for digital note capture and Asana.com is my favorite digital task management tool.

Resources

Allen, David. *Getting Things Done: The Art of Stress-Free Productivity.* New York: Viking, 2001. For the origination of the concept of ubiquitous capture, this is the place to go.

Asana. http://bit.ly/AsanaTasks. This web-based task-management tool has become my favorite for my own team. With a great web interface and apps for smartphones, now I've found it just as easy to capture tasks directly into my task-management system. It makes life so much easier.

Evernote. http://bit.ly/EvernoteDigitalNotes. This program is the current king of ubiquitous and convenient digital-information capture and storage.

Levenger. http://bit.ly/LevengerCirca. These products are "Tools for Serious Readers"—and writers, and anyone with an appreciation of a high-quality paper productivity system. Junior-size Levenger Circa Notebooks have been my right hand for years. Staples also has a knockoff brand (Arc) that can do the job. I find Arc's paper quality to be lower, which means that pages fall out more often. I make the higher investment for a trustworthy tool, but you will make the best choice for you!

Powers, William. *Hamlet's BlackBerry: A Practical Philosophy for Building a Good Life in the Digital Age.* New York: Harper, 2010.

—20—

Making Calendars Work for You

How many appointments do you have today? Meetings, classes, picking up the kids at school, drinks with friends...so many plans and commitments fill our lives. I don't know anyone between the ages of 5 and 105 who doesn't benefit from having a calendar to help keep track of activities and commitments.

In previous decades there was essentially only one option for managing such information: a paper calendar, either hanging on your wall or in a book to carry around. Now the options seem almost limitless, and it has become confusing to determine the best system for *your* life.

I want to help by giving you some guidance about the calendar options available and the best ways to make the most of the option you choose.

What You Need in a Calendar Tool

Let's start at the beginning. What do you *need* and *want* your calendar to do?

Generally, a calendar *must* be able to do two things:

1. Provide space to record appointments and commitments on specific days.
2. Be available when you need it to consult current commitments and make new ones. In other words, if you're at the doctor's office and need to make your next appointment, then your calendar information must be at hand in order to make sure that you don't double-book yourself.

Depending on your preferences, you might *want* your calendar tool to do the following:

- ✧ Share your availability information with others to help them schedule something with or for you, or to help them plan their own schedules.
- ✧ Segment your appointment information into work and personal categories, or among members of a family or team, so that you can see what commitments you have made in all sections of your life or with various people in your world.
- ✧ Display time in the way you prefer to think about it. If you plan by the week, then a weekly view will be extremely valuable. If you prefer the long view—the month at a glance, with only a couple commitments per day—then you'll want to see that displayed. If your days are packed with meetings, calls, and commitments, then looking at more than one day at a time will be overwhelming.

These characteristics are pretty basic, but depending on your needs or wants, they can dramatically influence which system will work best for you.

One last important question: do you prefer paper or digital? Both are right! There are definitely pros to the flexibility of a digital solution, but if you are uncomfortable interacting with or entering information digitally, then it simply will not work for you. It's better to create a system that you trust and are comfortable with rather than forcing yourself to use technology simply because others think it's cool. (Now, if you work for a company that requires digital calendars, you might have to spend some time creating an appropriate hybrid solution, but don't give up hope.)

Two Key Concepts for Using Calendar Tools

The following two tips will help you get the best use from your calendar tool:

1. **Choose ONE main calendar.** For *Lord of the Rings* fans, think "One ring to rule them all." It is essential to keep *only one tool*

as the daily, standard, and reliable spot for your information. For this tool you have essentially two options: 1) a paper planner that you carry around with you everywhere, or 2) a digital calendar that syncs to your smartphone or other handheld device. Either is fine, but identify your "one ring"—your master calendar—on which anything relevant to your commitments and activities will exist.

2. **Make a habit of writing in and checking your calendar.** If your calendar is going to be a system you can trust, then you have to get in the habit of interacting with it consistently. If you fail to write things on your calendar, then it will constantly be giving you incomplete information and you won't trust it; thus, it won't work. If you fail to consult it regularly, then you won't get the information you need when you need it, and you've just defeated the whole purpose of writing things down: getting information out of your head to make running your life easier.

Calendar Systems That Work

For paper lovers. Any portable paper planner book *can* work. I'm a fan of the roughly five-by-eight-inch size because it provides enough space for writing but isn't too bulky and still feels portable. My personal favorites are the Levenger Circa System calendars because you can easily blend your calendar and capture tool into one flexible tool. However, this department is filled with many different products, so play with them. Find the one that makes sense for your life and the kinds of information you want to keep with you. Know what each of the available sections provides, and make sure it feels good in your hands—after all, that tactile experience is one of the best benefits of paper over a digital device.

Paper/digital hybrids. If you really prefer paper, but your company requires a digital calendar, or if you prefer digital but don't want (or have the budget for) a smartphone, then a hybrid paper/digital system is likely your way to go. The secret to making a hybrid system work is acknowledging that the digital calendar is the master calendar. Everything needs to be added there consistently. However, printing out your upcoming weeks will both satisfy your desire to interact with paper on the fly and provide increased portability (without a smartphone) for your digital calendar.

Depending on how fast things move or change in your world, or how many other people might schedule appointments for you, either weekly or daily you'll need to print a new copy of the upcoming two to four weeks of your digital calendar to carry with you. Then, when you are having scheduling conversations, you can take out those pages, consult them, and write in new appointments. Finally, at the end of each day or week, you will need to enter any new appointments or changes into the digital version and print new copies.

This system has two main drawbacks:

1. You have only as much information as you print, so if you tend to schedule a lot of appointments or events many months into the future, the system will be less functional.

2. There is increased potential for information loss since you have added the step of transferring the information from the paper version to the digital format. Your commitment to this habit is key, and so you may want to make sure this additional element of complexity is outweighed by the benefits.

For digital lovers. There are tons of solutions out there. I have seen Google Calendar, Microsoft Outlook, and iCal used with great success. With any digital solution, the goal is to have your calendar information available on both your computer and your smartphone, as well as synced to a cloud/server system. Why is this important? Having a local copy on your device means that you have your information even when there is no Internet available. Meanwhile, having a cloud copy means your information is accessible even if your computer or phone is stolen or broken.

In the past, my main calendar was in Outlook, and I used a shared exchange hosting service to sync the information across all my devices, including my iPhone and iPad. If you are a Mac person, then iCloud will do roughly the same job: syncing your iCal information to multiple devices.

Since then, my company has shifted to Google Calendar, which is significantly less expensive for small businesses or home use and offers all the same benefits of syncing your information to your devices while maintaining it on the cloud.

Getting Fancy with Calendars

Once you start adding *wants* to the *needs* of your calendar—for instance, sharing information with others—your systems start becoming more complex. In this case, you aren't the only person who needs access to the information and the ability to schedule activities and commitments. This is where digital solutions excel. Sharing information with others becomes significantly easier using any of the three digital systems mentioned above.

However, here are some other options for calendar sharing:

Combination of a paper planner and a wall calendar (or chalk/whiteboard calendar). The key to this combination is that your portable paper planner always wins, and no additions get made to the home calendar without discussion or notification. You also have to build committed, consistent habits around adding necessary information to the wall calendar on a daily or weekly basis. Be warned: this is where most people get messed up with calendars. Something doesn't get added, the information becomes incorrect, and then you and your family/team make commitments without all the appropriate information.

Combination of a paper planner and a shared digital calendar. I've seen teams and families make a blended paper/Google Calendar system work. However, the burden falls on you, as manager of the family, to transfer information to the digital calendar whenever there are changes. This is a solution that several of my staff members have used successfully for scheduling their client appointments.

Shared digital calendars between platforms. There are reasonably easy ways to share calendar information between digital platforms.

Syncing solutions are available to transfer Outlook or iCal data to a Google Calendar account that can be shared with staff or family. Otherwise, you can set up a shared Outlook Exchange hosting service or use Google Calendar and create accounts for all of your team or family members. My company has used both systems successfully.

Identify and implement the calendar system that works best for you, and then stick to it.

Next Actions

✓ Evaluate your current system to make sure it is working adequately for you. Can you access your information when you need it? Can the appropriate people in your life easily access and share this information? Are you interacting with your calendar consistently and thus creating a trustworthy system?

✓ If you are considering moving to a digital system, play with the tutorial videos for whichever systems you might consider: Microsoft Outlook, Google Calendar, or iCal. The respective companies have all made some tutorials, but also try checking YouTube for third-party reviews that will give you a sense of what the user experience is like and what other people have found useful and valuable about a particular tool.

✓ For you paper lovers, play around on Levenger.com with their Circa options, or look for another solution that will give you a calendar/capture tool combination. You'll need to carry both, so you might as well make it two for one.

✓ Poll your friends. Find out who uses what systems and what they like and dislike about them. Weigh their answers against your known needs and wants.

✓ Try color-coding your calendars, either by person (if you're frequently responsible for family commitments) or by areas of your life (e.g., work, social events, and athletic events). You will be able to see at a glance who is up to what activities or how much time each area of your life is getting from you.

Resources

Google Calendar. http://bit.ly/GcalInfo.

iCal. http://bit.ly/iCalInfo.

Levenger Circa System. http://bit.ly/LevengerInfo.

Microsoft Outlook. http://bit.ly/OutlookTime.

—21—

Task-Management Tools (a.k.a. To-Do Lists)

As with calendar-management tools, a seemingly infinite number of task-management tools is available today. As a productivity expert, I have seen and used many of them, either for my own purposes and research or in my work with clients.

What so often gets lost in the feature fervor, or in the excitement of playing with or setting up a new task-management tool, is the simplicity of what these tools really need to do for us. They store actionable information in a way that allows us to retrieve it, to be reminded of it, or to act on it easily. That's it.

A simple list written on a piece of paper will do the same, as long as you don't lose the paper. But that's one of our challenges. Many of us have such chaotic lives that we frequently *do* lose the important piece of paper, or our list is so long that it requires many pieces of paper. At that point, we begin to feel so overwhelmed by our list that we start another one that's simpler. Does this sound familiar?

The next several chapters provide some basic strategies that will help you to avoid such frustrations in the future. All the strategies rely on first choosing a functional task-list system (an information storage and retrieval tool) that fits your needs. So, let's start there.

What Do You *Need* from Your Task Management System?

In order to be effective, a task management system must do all of the following:

- Capture and store all of your current commitments, projects, or, as productivity guru David Allen calls them, open loops
- Display your information in a way that makes sense to your mind and enables you to take action
- Include some level of portability in order to allow you to reference it in your decision-making throughout the day

What Might You *Want* from Your Task Management System?

In addition to the necessary functions, you might want your system to do the following:

- Prioritize actions according to what needs to be done today, soon, or later
- Track deadlines for particular projects or milestones
- Remind you of tasks when you still have adequate time to do them (rather than the night before the deadline)
- Re-sort information into different groups to enable both vertical planning (within project) and horizontal planning (across projects)
- Allow you to share tasks with others in order to ask for help or to facilitate delegation of certain project steps

Do these needs and wants sound familiar? You may have others, but I have found these to comprise the most common wish list of functions for a task management system.

The Big Question: Paper or Digital?

Now the important and immediate question is the same one we faced in the previous chapter on calendar tools: paper or digital? If you are a paper person, embrace it! Love your paper, invest in your paper, and make it a pleasure to work with. You will find that you are not alone in your love of paper, and you can let all those gadget folks live in their virus-ridden world of rebooting.

However, if you are a gadget geek who loves bells and whistles that pop up to remind you to brush your teeth in the morning, embrace it! The powerhouse functions available in some digital task management systems make paper lists seem positively Stone Age. The feature of a pop-up that reminds you of the day's tasks each morning is both lovely in its simplicity and convenient in a way that a paper list never could be.

You may, however, find yourself stuck in the middle. That's okay too! Whether you are living the hybrid lifestyle by choice or because the needs of others have made it necessary, have faith. There are ways to make this middle ground happy as well.

Task Management at Its Simplest

Any good task management system is made up of two parts:

1. A master list (or, more accurately, set of lists). This includes *all* of your current commitments or open loops. (See Chapter 24: Your Master List.)
2. A daily list. This is a very short list of tasks for today. Ideally it includes no more than four items. (See Chapter 50: Daily Planning).

That's it. Everything else is complexity, nuance, or gravy. Sometimes adding a *little* bit of gravy makes it taste better, but essentially these two pieces are all you need to keep things rolling.

Two Key Concepts

As with a calendar system (see Chapter 20), two key concepts will help you get the best use from your task management system:

1. You must create one seamless system in which ALL information has a clear place to live – professional and personal... everything.
2. You must build your habits to maintain the system. If you don't keep it up-to-date, you won't trust it.

These two elements are essential to building a system that will really work for you.

Common Disaster Situations

Now that we've glimpsed the ideal situation, let's take a tour through some scenarios showing what happens when a task management system falls apart.

- ✧ You write everything on the back of a napkin or a random Post-it note...and then promptly lose it.
- ✧ You try to keep all of your task information on your calendar. Most of our lives are far too busy and overcommitted for this system to be functional. You will end up constantly bumping activities from day to day until the situation becomes untenable.
- ✧ You set up a task management system but don't commit to maintaining it. Thus, the information on your lists rapidly becomes outdated. The system feels untrustworthy and thus unusable, and you end up starting over again. You blame the "bad" system, but it was really your unintended lack of commitment and maintenance habits that led you here.
- ✧ Your task management system becomes too complex to be functional. If you try to parse your information into 50 different versions or subcategories or assign seven different elements to every new item, you will end up in a mental boggle rather than in action mode every time you try to add something or act on something. You will spend your time inputting, reorganizing, or massaging your system rather than getting things done. I've

heard this referred to as "productivity porn." Be warned of the sirens of sophisticated systems; they rarely provide you with functional, real-world results.

Are any of these scenarios familiar? Has something like this happened to you? Okay, then you've felt the pain. Now, let's get down to discussing what kinds of task management tools might work for *you*.

Task Management Tools for Paper Lovers

Two systems work best for my paper-loving clients and friends:

1. Index cards. Create a stack of index cards with all your project/task information tracked and easily available to you. There are two primary ways to structure this system:

   ✧ You could have one card per project, and you write the necessary tasks (i.e., next actions—see Chapter 25 for more details) on the back. Then, each day, you review all the cards and create a new daily card with your Inspired Action and 3 Bonuses. (For more about this planning method, see Chapter 50: Daily Planning.)

   ✧ You could have one card per type of task or context (e.g., calls, email, errands, computer-related, @home, @office). This structure, recommended by productivity guru David Allen, can be very functional for some people, and allows you to only review tasks that you are capable of taking action on in any given moment. If you're not at home, then those tasks aren't possible right now so you can focus on reviewing the cards that are possible given your current location, time, energy, or resources.

2. Notebook or Binder. You could use either my perennial favorite, the Levenger Circa System, or a small binder with looseleaf pages. In my opinion, being able to add pages where you want them or to move things around is invaluable to a functional task management system, which is why I steer away

from standard bound notebooks. With either of these options, you can create lists just as outlined above: either one per project or one per context/type. It's best not to do both types of lists. While displaying task information in multiple formats can be good in different contexts, with a paper system this strategy would double the amount of work required to maintain it. Choose one method or the other, and run with it. (The one exception to this rule is your list of delegated tasks. Everyone benefits from this context-based list because it ensures that balls don't get dropped. For more information about good delegation methods, see Chapter 37: Delegation Plans.)

Paper/Digital Hybrid Task Management Tools

Whether you are using a blended system because it's required of you or by choice, the biggest challenge with a dual system is to minimize dual work. As I said earlier in this chapter, at its simplest, any task management system includes a master list and a daily list. The most successful hybrid systems I have seen keep the master list digitally and the daily list on paper, or vice versa.

What appears to be most important with a hybrid system is that when you are trying to decide what to do in the moment, there should be only one place to look. Similarly, when you are either adding new items or planning for your upcoming week or quarter, there should also be only one place to go to get the full-story overview.

So, for the hybrid folks, read the sections above and below this one and choose one system for your daily list and another for your master list, and you'll be well on your way to success.

Task Management Tools for Digital Lovers

The number of available task management software solutions is immense. While I will tell you some of the most popular solutions, as well as my personal favorites, all of them fall into three basic types that are important for you to understand in order to choose the best tool for you:

1. A Word or text document that is synced across your machines (desktop, laptop, and smartphone/handheld) via Dropbox.com, Google Drive, or a similar service.
2. Evernote or similar cloud note-taking solution. Create a note for your master list that will automatically sync to all of your devices. Then either create separate notes for your daily list or cut and paste today's tasks to the top of the list each day.
3. Cloud/local-based software or app. This allows you to keep all your data both on the software company's servers (accessible anywhere with Internet access) and on your local machines (including your smartphone) for access when you're not connected to the Internet. Some examples are Asana, Wunderlist, iCloud Reminders, Remember The Milk, Outlook Tasks with ToDoist Plugin.

Are there others? Sure—an immense amount of tools that you could spend weeks researching, testing, and implementing. However, you'll notice two important factors in all these types of systems:

1. The emphasis on having both a local and a cloud copy of your information
2. The capability for your lists to be portable and accessible from anywhere via a handheld device

These factors are not optional, and if your current system is missing either of these elements, then it's time to reevaluate and either tweak it or find a new system.

What I have outlined here should be enough to get you started and to help you narrow down your possible task management options to two or three that you will want to investigate further in order to identify and commit to the one that will be best for you.

Next Actions

✓ Spend an hour or so researching and exploring the most promising systems for you according to your preferences above. An informed decision will help you commit to your system for the foreseeable future.

✓ Consider the importance of some of your "want" items. Are they really essential for your life, or would you be fine without them? I generally prefer to find the simplest solution that will accomplish my goal—but it can't be simpler (this is another David Allen concept). Remember the sirens of productivity porn, and don't allow yourself to be enticed by feature fervor.

✓ Ask your friends and family—particularly those who are well organized—what they use to manage their tasks. Then weigh their methods against the guidelines above to help you decide which of their solutions could work for you.

✓ Are you ready to give your system a test? Before you begin, I recommend that you read Chapters 22 to 25 to help you succeed in implementing the best possible system for you.

Resources

Allen, David. *Getting Things Done: The Art of Stress-Free Productivity.* New York: Viking, 2001.

Asana. http://bit.ly/AsanaTasks.

Babauta, Leo. *Zen to Done: The Ultimate Simple Productivity System.* CreateSpace Independent Publishing Platform: 2008.

Dropbox. http://bit.ly/DropboxDigitalStorage.

Evernote. http://bit.ly/EvernoteDigitalNotes.

iCloud Reminders. Built-in with the Apple iOS operating system.

ToDoist Plugin for Microsoft Outlook. http://bit.ly/TodoistOutlook.

Remember The Milk. http://bit.ly/RTMTasks.

—22—

Checklists for Everything

Imagine getting on a plane, sitting in your seat, buckling your seat belt, beginning to get comfortable…and then it hits you: the thing you forgot to pack has bubbled up to your awareness, and you are mentally (or actually) smacking yourself in the head and muttering curse words under your breath. Perhaps the same feeling has happened to you in the car on the way to your kid's sleepover party or on the way into your workplace for an important client meeting.

Whenever these moments have hit you—and we've all had them—they are the moments when you recognize that trying to remember everything by relying solely on your own brain generally leads to disaster. And, as my mother tells me, it only gets worse as we age. The simplest things become increasingly hard to recall at the appropriate moment.

This chapter is dedicated to helping you minimize those "D'oh!" moments in your life. What's the secret? Checklists! The hardest part about many of our routine tasks is, well, remembering the routine! So, don't make your brain work any harder than it needs to. How much time do you think you will save every day, week, month, or year if, rather than redoing the intensive thinking process for what needs to happen (or to be packed) each time a certain activity occurs, you just scanned down a checklist and grabbed what you needed?

Do you want to make it even easier? For many standard activities, such as packing for vacations, starter checklists are available online. Just do a web search for "vacation packing checklist," and you'll be delighted to see that many people have done the hard work for you. Use an online list to give you a head start on creating your own.

When to Use Checklists

Here is a selected list—by no means an exhaustive one—of occasions when checklists are helpful:

- **When you pack for trips.** Whether it's a vacation, a business trip, or a camping trip, most people have a specific set of items that they want to bring—some of which are likely essential to the trip's success. Create a separate checklist for each type of trip you go on. I have a list for attending conferences, business trips, taking vacations, and family weekend getaways.
- **When you prepare for business meetings.** Do you have a weekly staff meeting, or do you meet with prospects or clients frequently? I bet certain items are essential to bring, and certain activities are necessary to do before, during, or after those meetings. Why not create a checklist to help you prepare and stay on track at those times?
- **When you help your kids (or partner) prep for activities.** Create separate packing/prep checklists for each of your children's activities—one for standard school activities, another for soccer, another for music lessons, and so on. Then everyone can be confident that important pieces aren't being left behind when you walk out the door. Imagine the time you'll save by reducing those "Mom, I forgot my…" calls.
- **When you replenish your diaper bag.** A member of my staff swears by the value of her diaper-bag-packing checklist for ensuring that all baby-related contingencies are covered.
- **Seasonal Projects or Cycles.** There is a certain list of projects that you do at the beginning of each school year or prior to the holiday season? Perfect time for a checklist: Home decorations, gifts, holiday party planning, holiday cards, thank you cards, holiday meal preparations, etc. Since you only do these projects once per year a checklist can make it *so much* easier to remember all the essential projects or tasks relevant to each of them.

- **When you learn a new activity or process.** Have you ever been assigned new responsibilities at work or been taught a new computer system? These are great times to create checklists to help you reinforce and remember the needed steps to produce the intended result. If you're lucky, someone has already documented the process for you, but if not, create a simple checklist for yourself and then share it with your boss or co-workers. You are likely not alone in needing a cheat sheet, and you might help your entire team implement the process better.

What Checklists Look Like

There are tons of systems that you could use to create your checklists. The important thing to remember is that it must be reusable. The whole point is to do the thinking once and then make the task easier for every time it happens in the future. Thus, scribbling your checklist on the back of an envelope will not be a long-term improvement. Here are some good options:

- **Create a Word document or Evernote Note.** You can print the list and check off items each time the activity arises. We use this type of list with client packets and mailings so that our administrative staff ensures that all necessary items get included.

- **Create forms.** While this is similar to the Word doc suggestion above, forms walk you through a process—for example, prep for an upcoming meeting—and bring all the necessary information together so that you feel confident and ready to go. We use forms for our staff-meeting prep. These forms contain several questions that prompt staff members to think ahead about issues, tasks, or questions that they want to discuss during the meeting. Using the forms helps staff members thoroughly prepare for the meeting and keeps the meeting itself running more smoothly.

- **There's an app for that.** There are a lot of great checklist apps for your mobile device; just do a search. Apps that are specific to packing lists come preloaded with possible items and activities for pre- and post-trip, while more generic programs allow you to create custom lists, check things off, and then reset the list when you're done.
- **Create wipe-off lists.** Print or write a list, and then get it laminated. (Most print/copy centers have laminating machines.) Then you can use dry-erase markers to check items off and just wipe it fresh when you're done. I've seen this work very well for kids' checklists. You could even create a little flip book of index card–size checklists for each of your kids' activities. By including stickers or images on the cards, you can add visual interest and help even very young kids use the checklist effectively.
- **Use a whiteboard.** If you want a semipermanent list at home or in your office, grab an appropriately sized whiteboard, write the items or prompting questions with a Sharpie (permanent marker) or adhesive letters, and then keep a dry-erase marker nearby to check items off regularly. The permanent marker will stay in place when you wipe with a dry paper towel, but if you want to remove it, you can use nail-polish remover (acetone). Use the adhesive letters for a more permanent version, or a chalkboard with paint.
- **Have notepads printed.** It's a lot easier to have short-run notepads or other products created these days. Once you're pretty sure you've got a particular process or list nailed, create some standard notepads and have them printed up by a company like Vistaprint. This inexpensive solution might be appropriate if you want to make a list easily available to your entire company (or family) or to keep a stack of short checklists immediately on hand for yourself.

Really, any system that provides a permanent list and allows you to refer to that list easily can be a checklist. Can you think of other methods for creating checklists in your life?

It's time to save your brainpower for where it matters most. Give your brain a break from trying to remember the easy stuff, and delegate that responsibility to a checklist.

Next Actions

✓ Brainstorm all the times in your life (or in your family's or team's lives) when a checklist might be valuable. Ask others to help you brainstorm, if appropriate. When was the last time you had one of those "D'oh!" moments?

✓ Choose one of these times and create a checklist of items or questions that will help the activity run smoothly. Search online for starter lists that will get you going. Ask for input from family, friends, or teammates here too. Many minds make light work.

✓ Identify and implement the best checklist methodology for that situation. Different methods may be appropriate for different situations, depending on who needs access to the information.

Resources

Gawande, Atul. *The Checklist Manifesto: How to Get Things Right.* New York: Metropolitan Books, 2010.

Real Simple: Life Made Easier. http://bit.ly/RealSimpleInfo.

Vistaprint. http://bit.ly/VistaprintInfo.

Part 5

Your Helm and Rudder: Task Management Essentials

—23—

The Brain Dump

Zoom, zoom, zoom...Our brains are spinning constantly at a breakneck rate, and most of us have barely gotten up in the morning when we begin to feel overwhelmed by all the actions that we "need" to take or the commitments and appointments that we've made. Sometimes those are actions for today, but just as often they are for tomorrow, next week, or three months from now.

The fact is that when your mind is whirring about so many different topics, you *cannot* rely on it to consistently churn up the information you need in order to focus effectively for today without guidance and assistance.

Have you ever gone to the grocery store, wandered the aisles, and racked your brain to remember all the things you were supposed to be picking up? Then, as you are driving home—or, even worse, entering your kitchen—you remember the essential item that you had told yourself to pick up but had forgotten completely while in the store? Our memories are amazing; we can retain vast quantities of both useful information and complete flotsam. However, that doesn't mean that your brain can reliably offer up the details you need at the most convenient time for you to be able to take action. Relying on your memory whirlpool is a trap that will rapidly sink you.

In any effort to get a spinning brain to calm down, a worthy first goal is a thorough brain dump. It's time to get everything out of your head and down on paper (or the digital equivalent) immediately. Specifically, I'm talking about your commitments and action items; everything that needs your attention and action to move forward. Grab a notepad, and don't worry about structure, grouping, or format. This exercise is purely about *getting it down*. Logical lists aren't needed at this moment—and don't worry, because in other chapters we'll talk about how to make your lists optimally effective. Right now, you just want to capture everything that you're thinking about, wondering about, stressing about, or planning to do.

What *is* essential for this exercise is to get *everything actionable.* Leave no area of life untouched: work, personal, family, home, community, everything. If you have a responsibility to act on something in some way whether for yourself or a promise to someone else, then it should appear on your list. Recognize that you are not truly creating a to-do list. While everything that appears here will require your action or attention, this brain dump will consist of haphazard scribblings of projects, tasks, dreams, and goals—and that's exactly what we want. Just get it *all* down, and I'll help you sort it into a more functional system later.

There are several ways to make sure you get everything out in a brain dump. Here are some suggestions:

- **Review your calendar appointments.** Look at both the past few months and the upcoming 6 to 12 months. That will likely jar both current and future commitments into your mind including upcoming trips, birthdays, and major projects.
- **Glance through your active paperwork.** If you have piles of paper on your desk or workspace, they probably represent something that wants your attention and might be full of actions or commitments to be captured.
- **Wander around your home and/or office.** Write down all the repair projects, things to be returned, collections of stuff to be reorganized, or items to be cleaned or maintained. This includes the outdoor areas of your home too—the shed, the garage, the car, the yard, and so on.
- **Review your strategic life plan for this year.** What projects or activities in your life plan haven't yet started manifesting in your everyday life? Take note of them on your brain dump. (See Chapter 46: Your Strategic Life Plan.)

- **Wander your mind over all the people in your life.** Have you made commitments to anyone? What about upcoming birthdays, anniversaries, or other special events? Have you and a friend been talking about planning a fishing trip? What about a girls' night out? Are your parents (or in-laws) coming for a visit sometime soon? What about your pets: do they need to go to the vet soon?
- **Reflect on yourself.** Does self-care appear somewhere in your brain dump? Are there activities to help you accomplish your personal goals, such as eating healthfully, working out, having more fun activities, or getting some quiet personal time? Some of these goals likely involve habit building, but there might also be projects and tasks that will get you moving (for example, joining a gym might be the first project before you can start a habit of working out four times a week).

It is possible, even likely, that this brain-dumping exercise will take a few days to complete. That's okay. It's better to take your time and ensure that everything gets included. It's critical that the system you'll create from this information be trustworthy, and if only some information is there, you will have to continue relying on your unreliable brain. Uh, no…not the goal!

Get started! And trust me, your brain will eventually thank you for not making it work so hard every day.

Next Actions

- ✓ Carry your capture tool with you every day this week, and write down any projects, tasks, goals, or commitments that you come across. This week of jotting notes will be great practice for developing a consistent habit of using your capture tool to get information out of your head and down in writing. (For more information, see Chapter 19: Carrying a Capture Tool.)

✓ Ask close family members or co-workers to help you remember upcoming activities or projects. You never know when they might jar loose something that you didn't find on your own or tell you about a future project that you'll need to act on.

Resource

Allen, David. *Getting Things Done: The Art of Stress-Free Productivity.* New York: Viking, 2001. Allen is the originator of the idea of "mind like water" and the concept of moving your mind from whirlpool to zen stillness.

—24—

Your Master List

Elizabeth was a bright, savvy, enthusiastic entrepreneur who was starting her own counseling firm working with troubled teenagers and their families. With a vivacious personality and grand ambitions, Elizabeth's mind was a constant whirr of ideas, images, and language that she wanted to incorporate into her growing business's structure and operations.

When Elizabeth and I began working together on task management, her methods for tracking tasks and ideas reflected the state of her mind: little Post-its all over her home, a half dozen notebooks with no rhyme or reason as to their contents, and a lot of items that had yet to make it from her head to a piece of paper. Because her plans, projects, and actions were literally strewn across her world, she found it difficult to make decisions about what needed her attention today, this week, or sometime later.

The key for Elizabeth—and this will be true for you too—was to have all that information in one place, in one trustworthy system that will give all of your actions an easy and obvious place to live. We discussed systems like this in Chapter 21: Task-Management Tools (a.k.a. To-Do Lists). In this chapter, however, I want to cover the key elements you'll need to use your chosen tool effectively.

As we know with our physical stuff, if it doesn't have a clearly defined home, then it tends to float around our world and clutter up our space. The same is true with our projects and tasks. We write down random ideas, reminders, and notes from meetings or leave them floating around to clutter up our minds as well as our spaces. But how different might our results in life be if we pulled all of this information together into one place and gave it a logical order that allowed us to act strategically and effectively? That is the purpose of a master list: to give all that actionable information a home.

Goals, Projects, Tasks, and Habits

Before we dive in to the structure of an effective master list, it's essential to make sure we're on the same page about a few basic terms that people often get confused: goals, projects, tasks, and habits.

Goals. A goal is a statement of intention or ambition that is measurable, well defined, and usually tied to a deadline. A goal likely involves a series or combination of projects, tasks, and habits that allow you to achieve it. Your goal is the big picture of what you are aiming to accomplish. Example: "I will lose 20 pounds by June of next year." (Personally, I have been known to recommend that you throw out your SMART goals because sometimes it's more important to focus simply on achieving the outcome rather than pressuring yourself to either succeed or fail by a specific deadline. (SMART is an acronym for Specific, Measurable, Attainable, Relevant, and Time-Based.) You can find a video about my preferred alternative, Vivid Future Accomplishments (VFAs), at InspiredActionBook.com/Resources.)

Projects. A project is a series of tasks with a specific, measurable outcome and a clear beginning and end. It is generally made up of a group of tasks that are necessary to accomplish the defined outcome. Example: "Start a weight-loss program."

Tasks. A task is a small, bite-size action that can be done in one brief period (usually 5 to 30 minutes). Similarly, a next action (see Chapter 25) is always a task—specifically, the exact next task on your path toward a goal or within a project. Here are some examples of tasks: "Research Weight Watchers online"; "Request *The South Beach Diet, Atkins Diet,* and *Dr. Siegal's Cookie Diet Book* from the library"; "Read one chapter of *Cookie Diet.*" Before you can read a chapter, however, you would need to request the books; therefore, requesting the books at the library might be your next action, while reading the first chapter would not—even though both are tasks.

Habits. A habit is a task that you will repeat consistently in order to achieve your goal. Example: "Weigh myself each morning and log my weight." Habits are generally tasks that must be repeated either daily or multiple times a week in order for them to be effective. I often make a distinction between habits and repetitive tasks that occur weekly, monthly, quarterly, or seasonally because the strategies for tracking habits versus less-frequent repetitive tasks are different. (See Chapter 14: Habits: The Power of Patterns.)

The reason I wanted to start with these definitions is that most people's to-do lists are a giant jumble of all four of these categories. Although your projects should be aligned with your goals, a list that's an ill-defined mixture of the two is a recipe for confusion and inaction. Similarly, jumbling up tasks and habits can become counterproductive and inefficient, since tasks are single actions while habits must be done repeatedly to be effective. In fact, I will boldly say that habits should be removed from your master list entirely. Habits are routine patterns, and I believe that there are better systems than your master list for tracking and developing habits. (See Chapter 14: Habits: The Power of Patterns.)

With these definitions established, let's talk about how to set up a spectacular master list using your chosen task-management tool. (Chapter 21: Task-Management Tools (a.k.a. To-Do Lists) can help you choose the tool that will work best for you before beginning this implementation process.)

Turning "Stuff" into Actions

It all begins with your brain dump, so if you have not yet created that, then jump back to Chapter 23 and follow the instructions there. Get everything actionable out of your head and onto paper, where we can explore and play with it.

Once your brain has been dumped out thoroughly, you'll probably have a mush of projects, goals, tasks, and habits. That's okay! To make sense of that mush, grab a fresh sheet of paper and create three columns. (Or you can find our Outcomes & Next Actions worksheet at

InspiredActionBook.com/Resources.) At the top of the left column write "Outcome," in the middle write "Projects," and at the top of the right column write "Tasks." Then, starting with the first item on your list, take the following two steps:

1. *Identify the intended outcome.* Sometimes you will need to break up an item that you wrote initially in order to identify the goal or outcome that's relevant for this item. For instance, "Write a will" is a project, but a level up from that is "Complete estate planning," which would include writing the will, creating your living will, assigning a health-care proxy, and identifying beneficiaries for your accounts. By determining the outcome of "Complete estate planning," we can gather under it *all* the projects and tasks that are necessary to achieve it effectively.
2. *Identify the specific next action.* For each project or goal you will also need to identify the specific task that is your next action to move it forward. Using the example of writing a will, ask yourself, "What specifically would I need to do next?" Several possible answers might occur to you: call my lawyer, research estate attorneys, make a list of assets and accounts, make a list of beneficiaries to name in my will. You are the only person who knows which of these would be the best next action for you. So, you can capture all relevant tasks on your list, but you'll want to make sure that you've identified or starred at least one as your specific next action to start moving this project forward. Remember, a task or next action should take only 5 to 30 minutes to complete, so if you found a step that would take longer than 30 minutes, drill it down to something even shorter. "Find phone number for my lawyer" might be an example.

Start with your first item and clarify: is this a goal, project, task, or habit? Next, explore upward and drill downward with it to identify the appropriate outcome and next action that will move it forward and write each of these elements on your sheet in the appropriate columns.

Repeat with your next item, and continue down the list until you have clear outcomes and next actions for each entry from your brain dump.

You will likely discover that in some cases what was on your brain dump list was either a next action with an undefined outcome or an outcome in need of a next action. So, some items will just be transferred from your brain dump to the appropriate column, and then you can find the missing pieces to clarify the action.

If any habits have made their way onto your brain dump list, then I recommend setting them aside and handling them as discussed in Chapter 14: Habits: The Power of Patterns. However, you can pause for a moment to see if there is a larger outcome connected to that habit, and that outcome might inspire you to remember other tasks to be captured. For instance, "clean the cats' litter box" is definitely a habit (unfortunately, doing it just once doesn't keep it perpetually clean). However, if I explore up from that habit I might recognize that the outcome is taking excellent care of my cats, which might remind me that I need to call the vet to schedule their next annual physical. The task "Call the vet to schedule appointment" *does* belong on my master list, even if the habit of cleaning the litter box doesn't.

This type of thinking gets much easier with practice, and that's part of the purpose of taking this intermediate step between your brain dump and adding items to your master list. This helps you begin training your brain to recognize the differences among outcomes, projects, tasks, and next actions in a way that will make your task management so much easier and more effective in the future.

Organizing Your Master List

Having processed your brain dump and identified the outcomes and next actions, now it's time to develop the structure for your final master list and move your items into the right places in your new task-management tool.

First, it's important to understand that your master list is actually a group of sublists or buckets where your actionable information will find its home. Therefore, to create your master list, the next step is to clarify the appropriate buckets for *you* and how *you* think or operate best.

Active vs. On Hold

To help improve your focus (and reduce your sense of overwhelm), you may want to begin by reviewing your whole list and identifying which outcomes are active and which are on hold. Sometimes items that are important or relevant will appear on your mental radar screen, but now is simply not the best time. That's okay. Let's make sure that they still get captured so that you can come back to them later. They can live "on hold" until you're ready to devote some energy to them.

Take a moment to review your list and see if there's anything that you would put on hold. Perhaps it's either 1) not relevant right now, and thus not actively in progress, or 2) one of those "great ideas" that occurred to you at some point but that you have not committed to accomplishing yet. Creating a separate On-Hold Projects list gives these items a place to live while not confusing or cluttering up your world of active projects.

Active Project Buckets

Your active projects and tasks are the core of your master list, and creating some structure to these items will help you interact more easily with your system. Therefore, the first step is to choose one main system of categorizing.

Here are the categories that I have used most frequently with clients:

- **By project or area of your life.** Create a separate bucket for each project. Or you can create a list for each major area of your life, such as work, home, community, and personal.
- **By horizon.** Today, soon, and later are great horizons of focus that allow you to prioritize your actions.

- **By context of the next action.** Create a list for all your phone calls; errands to run; or tasks to complete on your computer, at home, or at work. In other words, where would you have to be, or what would you need to have with you, in order to be able to complete that specific task? This type of context grouping, popularized by David Allen, is still used widely many GTDers (devotees of David Allen's Getting Things Done system). Personally, the one list I do like to keep separate is my errands list, because then I can batch all the items that require me to be out and about in my car.

If you are choosing to use a paper master list, then I encourage you to keep these categories as simple as possible. It's very easy to create a lot of extra work for yourself by trying to get fancy here. In fact, this is one of the areas in which digital solutions excel because they make it easier to slice and dice the information by project and by horizon with just a couple clicks. The goal is to create clarity by having one place where each task belongs.

However, let me offer one way that a paper-based system can integrate both vertical project planning and horizontal priority planning. Create the core buckets of your master list by project/life area, and by default ALL these items become your Later list. Then, on a weekly basis, create a new Soon list by pulling a handful of items together from these buckets onto a fresh sheet. Then, on a daily basis, you would refer only to the Soon list to decide what to do, and you would capture new tasks in the appropriate project bucket for later. At the end of each week, you remove all completed items, bring your core project lists up-to-date, and create a new Soon list for the upcoming week. (For more on weekly and daily planning, see Chapter 49: Weekly Planning and Chapter 50: Daily Planning.)

Outcomes List

It can be valuable to keep a running list of only the active outcomes/major projects that you are working on. Occasionally, we might check off a task as done but forget to capture a new next action to continue moving that project forward. Your outcomes list can help trigger you to ensure that you always have a next action identified and captured in the appropriate bucket to keep the project moving forward.

Connecting Your Life List & Lifestyle List

One element that often gets missed is to create a relationship between your master list and your life list. For many people these lists feel very different, as if one is their "have to" list and the other is their "want to" list. Allow me to suggest that you loosen these boundaries and make sure that your master list has a *lot* of fun stuff on it too!

In Chapter 7 we discussed creating your life list and lifestyle list. If you've done that piece of exploration and play, then I highly encourage you to find a few projects and tasks from those lists, do the same type of outcome and next action thinking for those items, and incorporate them directly into your Active Projects list.

The only way life and lifestyle items will get done is if you have the option to *do* them, and we want your master list to provide you with a complete picture of your choices.

Remember, your Active Projects list is for discreet projects and tasks, *not for habits,* so make sure you take a look a Chapter 14: Habits: The Power of Patterns to help with those repetitive elements from your lifestyle list.

Bonus Lists

You may want to consider incorporating a few cool alternative lists into your system of core buckets on your master list:

- ✧ **Waiting Response.** Not to be confused with the On-Hold Projects list, the Waiting Response list helps you track tasks for which you are waiting for input or action from someone else. In other words, *you* cannot act further until you hear back from someone. Perhaps you've sent your client or colleague an email about a shared project, but you're waiting for a response. Or you've asked your partner to research flights for your upcoming trip to Hawaii, but you want to make sure that you remember to follow up. These would be great items to add to your Waiting Response list. This list allows you to keep track of and remain aware of tasks that have been delegated to someone else but are ultimately your responsibility.

- **Agendas.** Similar to meeting agendas, these lists help you track topics that need to be discussed with specific people in your life when you next see or meet with them. They are particularly useful for tracking questions or discussions to have with your spouse, assistant, co-worker, or boss. You might also keep such a list for each of your clients, children, or staff members. These lists have saved my brain many times. They help prepare me for both infrequent meetings (such as those with my financial planner or my doctor) and regular ones, such as my weekly meeting with my assistant.
- **Groceries to Buy**. We all go grocery shopping, but let's not clutter up our master list with a whole bunch of individual entries about buying milk and diapers. Rather, create a separate bucket just for these items. Personally, I prefer to use a dedicated app called Grocery IQ. It's great because if either my husband or I adds something to our list on the app, then it automatically syncs to the other person's phone. No more reminding each other to pick up something specific. Just update the list when you run out of milk, and everyone will know to pick it up on the next grocery run.
- **Errands to Run**. As I mentioned earlier, this is the one context-specific list that I find very helpful for batching any tasks that require running around town to the library, post office, mall, or elsewhere. It becomes easier to plan one trip and hit everything on the list if all these tasks are together.
- **Other lists as appropriate/necessary.** Certain sets of information lend themselves nicely to being separate buckets. Some

examples are Books to Read, Movies to Watch, and Restaurants to Try. All of these lists could clutter up your master list since often there's no sense of urgency or commitment to these items, but it's still helpful to record them in a predictable place. Personally, I consider most of these to be more reference lists than action lists. Unless I'm committed to picking up a particular new book that a friend recommended, I generally handle these items separately in my Evernote reference system. I had an executive client who traveled a lot and would keep a separate sheet for each of the cities that she visited frequently. On that sheet she would include info about restaurants to try, places to visit, favorite hotels, and more. But, obviously that information wasn't actionable unless she was in that town. That's why it remained in its own separate home and not on her core master list.

Essential Mindset Shifts

When you've completed this process, every goal, project, and task should have one home that makes sense in your system.

Allow me to pause and acknowledge that, for many people, after they create their master list they tend to feel even more stressed and overwhelmed than normal for a little while. Never before have they seen all their responsibilities in one place! This reaction is common. Take a deep breath, and realize that nothing's changed. These items were always there; they just weren't as visible and organized before. Now you're in a much better position to review and act on these items intentionally rather than reactively. With a master list you can decide strategically where to direct your attention, rather than just working on whatever floats across your mind or email inbox.

Additionally, I want to encourage you to shift your expectations. The point of having a master list is *not* to get it all done. When used properly, your master list *will never be done*, and it will never go away, unlike some of those to-do lists you used to create, complete, and pitch. It is a flowing, responsive tool that organizes all your actionable information, and as long as you're alive, you will likely have actions to do. Your master list is here to give those actions a home. Your part is to keep the information up-to-date and let your system do its job. That's the only way you'll learn to trust your system.

Now that you have this master collection of actions, if you're feeling confused about how to make sense of it all and stay focused *today*, then I suggest jumping to Chapters 49 and 50 on weekly and daily planning. They will give you the strategy for turning this collection of possibilities into a solid plan of action.

Next Actions

✓ Test out your system for the next two to three weeks. Make sure you capture new tasks consistently and keep the system up-to-date. Notice any minor adjustments or alterations that might improve your system or that will help you interact with and maintain it more easily.

✓ Improve your task-capturing skills by reading Chapter 25: What Is a Next Action? This chapter provides ways to identify and write down doable tasks—rather than just "stuff"—more consistently.

✓ Develop a habit of reviewing your full active master list at least once per week, so that you can add new projects and tasks and identify priorities for the upcoming week. For more information about using your master list in your planning and decision-making, see Chapter 49: Weekly Planning and Chapter 50: Daily Planning.

✓ If you're looking for a huge upgrade, consider maintaining your master list in a digital task-management system designed for *team* collaboration. Asana is my current favorite, although Wunderlist is a close second. It has revolutionized how both my business team and my husband and I handle our tasks, since it creates a high level of visibility on task progress and simplifies communications.

Resources

Allen, David. *Getting Things Done: The Art of Stress-Free Productivity.* New York: Viking, 2001.

Asana. http://bit.ly/AsanaTasks.

Babauta, Leo. *Zen to Done: The Ultimate Simple Productivity System.* CreateSpace Independent Publishing Platform: 2008.

Grocery IQ. http://bit.ly/GroceryIQapp.

Wunderlist. http://bit.ly/WunderListTasks.

—25—

What Is a Next Action?

The biggest challenge that most people face when looking over their to-do lists is that most of the items on it fall into one of two categories:

1. Horribly vague entries (e.g., Joyce Jones, cat litter, birthday party)
2. Enormous multiday projects rather than immediately actionable tasks (reorganize the house, create company website, plan vacation)

Do these categories sound familiar? As David Allen says, most people's task lists are full of *stuff* rather than clear and actionable tasks. As we discussed in the last chapter, a task is a simple, discrete action that takes 5-30 minutes to complete. A "Next Action" is simply the specific *next* task that will move a particular project forward. In other words, it's the task that comes first.

It's time to learn how to change the *stuff* on your lists into effective next actions by exploring the three essential elements of a good, next action task.

Element 1: Next Action Tasks Are Specific, Actionable, and Brief

The first and most important lesson is that every project on your master list needs to be broken down into clear, specific, and actionable tasks. What is the best way to get to the actionable tasks? Choose any Active Project on your master list and ask yourself, "What is the very first concrete action I would have to do to move forward on this?"

Then test the answer: would the next action you just identified take between 5 and 30 minutes? If not, then dig deeper. Look at the next action you just identified and ask the same question again: "What is the very first concrete action I would have to do to move forward on this?" Next actions often start with the following words: *call, email, research online, draft, order,* or *brainstorm*. Projects, on the other hand, are more likely to start with words like *plan, explore, create,* and *organize*.

Element 2: Next Action Tasks Always Start with a *Verb*

Since next actions require us to *do* something, they start with a verb. Ask yourself, "What do I need to *do*? Look at the "Horribly vague entries" list at the beginning of the chapter. Do you need to *call* Joyce Jones, or *email* her, or *meet* with her? These are very different actions that require different tools and amounts of time. And what about the cat litter? *Clean* it, *buy* more, *research* alternatives...? Again, each action requires different tools and amounts of time. And what about that birthday party? *Plan* it, *take* Cindy to it, *call* to RSVP for it? Planning a party is definitely a project, whereas taking Cindy to it would be an appointment, and calling to RSVP is a task. Do you see what a difference the verb can make?

When you glance at a vague list, does your brain fill in the details? Yes, maybe, but why ask your brain to redo the same thinking every time you look at the list? Figure it out once, record it, and then you can just review the list and act rather than churning over the same recall process every time you are trying to decide what you need to do *now*.

Element 3: Next Action Tasks Define and Simplify the Task

If you need to call Joyce Jones, then you might also want to define the purpose of the call: "Call Joyce Jones re: preparing research for next week's meeting." Including this detail in the task itself allows your brain to relax yet further. No more moments like this: "...

[pause]...Why did I need to call Joyce? Oh, right, the research." Let's consider another example: "Call plumber." How much easier would it be for you to take action if you saw "Call plumber re: repairing toilet (617) 555-1234"?

With these three guidelines, you will transform your task lists from jumbles of mush to clear and concrete tasks that make taking action easier and eliminate time wasted on rethinking the same ideas.

Alternative Next Action Strategies

Here are a couple additional tips for refining your next actions:

Set a length of time. If you find yourself at a loss for words when trying to break a project down to yield a clear, small next action, then try using a time limit: "Spend 30 minutes working on Abco presentation." Then, after you've completed your 30 minutes, either identify the specific next action that occurs to you and add that to your master list, or renew your original task to spend 30 more minutes.

Account for thinking time. Occasionally, the first step of a project is thinking time, so feel free to include tasks that are more mental than physical, as long as they are specific. Examples: "Brainstorm options for product launch marketing," "Define vision to set up baby nursery and identify needed elements." With next actions like these, you will usually end up with something in writing to guide next steps in addition to getting some good thinking done.

Next Actions

- ✓ Review your master list (see Chapter 24) and make sure that you have identified one clear next action task for every project and goal.
- ✓ Practice identifying next actions whenever you get into project-planning mode. Look for the verbs, and dig down until you have at least one clear action that will take you 5 to 30 minutes to accomplish.
- ✓ If something on your task list just never seems to get done, then ask yourself if you can make the task even smaller. Perhaps rather than

"Call plumber," the action could be "Look up plumber's phone number." When you find the number, you might feel ready to make the call too, but at least by looking it up and recording it on your list, you have gotten one step closer to the final outcome.

Resource

Allen, David. *Getting Things Done: The Art of Stress-Free Productivity.* New York: Viking, 2001.

—26—

Becoming a Better Time Estimator

During a visit to the Boston Museum of Science, some friends and I came across an interactive exercise and decided to give it a shot. The goal was to see how accurate your internal timekeeper was. You pressed a button and then, after guessing when exactly a minute had passed, you hit the button again. It was fascinating to see the varying results of the different members of our group. For some, a minute was only 37 seconds long; for others, a minute was actually 1 minute and 20 seconds.

The skill of time estimation is essential for a productive and effective lifestyle. Does that task take you 5 minutes or 15? There's a big difference. If you're ten minutes off on all the activities you do in a given morning, then it's no wonder that you tend to be late to your meetings and accomplish only half of what you had planned.

Your time-estimation skills might vary by context or by task. It's amazing how if we're asked to do something distasteful or something we simply don't like, our minds swell the task such that we think it will take forever. However, when you are in the middle of your favorite activities, time passes like lightning and you barely notice hours go by (a state that psychologist Mihaly Csikszentmihalyi describes as flow).

How Do You Store Time?

A particularly interesting approach to shifting your perception of time is to become aware of how you mentally store your time line. If you think of this moment as somewhere between the moment of your birth and the moment of your death, then you could say that this moment appears somewhere along your time line between those two points. Just for fun, and going with whatever is your first instinct, physically or mentally point to your past. Is it behind you? In front of you? Off to your left or right? Or perhaps it's above you? There is no right answer. It's just a matter of awareness. Now, point to your future. Do future events create a line stretched out in front of you? Is your time line running through your body, or are you walking on it as you would on a path? Is it doing any fancy turns, twists, or corkscrews? Again there is no right answer; this is just how you tend to view and store time.

Now, let's play with it a little. It's *your* time line; you have all the power over how you perceive and store it, and you can move it wherever you want. So, grab your time line (mentally or physically), and let's put it up like a yardstick on the wall in front of you, with your past to your left, your future to your right, and the moment of now roughly in front of you. Does that feel different? I call this method of viewing time Planning Mode because when you're trying to feel where you are compared to where you will be, it's much easier to judge the distance from here.

Think about the last time you tried to figure out what time to set your alarm to in order to arrive at a morning event on time. It's likely that you backtracked your way from the event's start time to your alarm clock's wake-up call. If you could see that plan for your future up on a wall, might you be able to judge the time differently and with a bit more detachment and accuracy?

Similarly, you can play with moving your time line to run straight through your body either back-to-front or side-to-side. Perhaps it passes through your heart or your belly, with your past behind you and your future ahead. Does that feel different? This mode is often called "in time." I call it Presence Mode because this way of storing time can allow you to be more fully present to what's happening right now. It's a great way to store your time line when you want to be present to your kids, to pay attention in a meeting, or to be fully present in bed with your lover.

Finally, if you move your time line down at your feet like a path you are walking, you are in what I call Action Mode. Walking on your path toward the future, you are aware of where you are now, what's coming ahead, and how to be responsive to it.

The objective of all this time-line playing is to demonstrate to you that you have control. You may have tended to store time and interact with it in a particularly way, but you can move it around based on the moment and what you most need. In fact, you might explore shifting it around intentionally depending on the needs of the moment. If you're planning out your day or a long-term project, move your time line into Planning Mode. If you're at an important lunch with a client or co-worker, then Presence Mode might be appropriate. If you're moving through a sequence of tasks, then Action Mode might be required.

Here's the kicker: I can almost guarantee that if you are frequently late to things, you're spending more time in Presence Mode than in Planning Mode. You aren't seeing clearly how this moment relates to the path ahead, and you're making decisions based on what's drawing your attention in the present rather than projecting how long the next sequence of steps will take.

Strategies to Avoid Lateness

Here are some specific strategies that might help you address this common problem.

- **Avoid "one more thing-itis."** This is the tendency to do just "one more thing" before heading out the door—checking your email, putting in that next load of laundry, and so on. This tendency made me late for years. I know that most of you "chronically late folks" recognize what I'm talking about, and I also know that you *can* become aware of when you are tacking on "one more thing." Just stop. It's time to go—this time with some grace and dignity, rather than in a giant rush.
- **Learn to love being early.** You can get a wonderful, peaceful feeling by knowing that you'll arrive with plenty of time. No rush, no urgency, and no panic are required. As I shifted from being frequently late to often early, I discovered this sensation

and almost began to crave it. The biggest hurdle for most people is the conviction that if they arrive early to an appointment, they will end up wasting time waiting around. Before the age of smartphones, avoiding this type of wasted time required more planning—people had to bring along something to read or do. You can still operate that way: for example, pack the birthday or thank-you cards you've wanted to write or that professional journal that you never get around to reading. A smartphone, provides a whole range of possible activities while you wait: respond to an email, check the stock market, watch a YouTube video, scroll through Facebook, schedule a doctor's appointment. It can be perfectly productive or appropriately recuperative time!

- ✧ **Expect the unexpected.** Assume that something unexpected is going to happen. Traffic is the most common event in this category. Plan in buffer time for the unexpected, and then get a reward of downtime at your destination if it doesn't happen. Living in the greater Boston area, it's not uncommon to find traffic on the local roads as well as on the highways. I started simplifying my travel planning: my destinations take 30 minutes, 60 minutes, or 90 minutes. Most places I go frequently fit into one of these three categories, and I spend less time fussing: "Well…it only took me 20 minutes last time, so maybe I can speed there in 15? By simply blocking time conservatively in 30-, 60-, or 90-minute chunks, I often get to enjoy a pocket of downtime because I've arrived early, or I get to avoid stressing when traffic turns out to be heavier than usual.

Test Your Time Estimation Skills

To become better at planning your time, the key still is to learn to judge more accurately how long particular tasks will take you. The only way to accomplish this is to gather some data about your current sense of time. Here is an exercise to try:

1. Grab a sheet of paper and create three columns. From left to right, label the columns Action, Estimate, and Actual (or grab our Time Estimator worksheet at InspiredActionBook.com /Resources.)

2. Think through your morning routine, from waking up to arriving at work or whatever your natural end point is. In the first column, preferably in sequential order, write down each of the steps of your routine—for example, waking up, brushing your teeth, getting dressed, making and eating breakfast, and so on.

3. Go down the list and take your best guess at how long each activity takes you, and write those figures in the second column. (Remember, we're aiming for accuracy, not speed.)

4. Tomorrow morning, grab your cell phone (most of them have a stopwatch function), a stopwatch, or any clock with a second hand, and actually time yourself as you do each activity listed in the first column.

This exercise will give you a sense of how accurate your internal timekeeper is. It is also interesting to see what activities and steps you forgot to write down as you go through your morning routine. Any activities that you forgot are steps that take up your time every day, but you didn't remember to include them originally. How often does that most likely happen in your life, and how much time is therefore unaccounted for in your daily planning?

So, how far off were you on your total morning-routine time? Five minutes? Fifteen minutes? More? Were you guessing too much time or too little?

Usually, we are slightly better at estimating the duration of tasks that we do frequently, as opposed to occasional tasks such as writing a report for work or doing a particular piece of research for a new project. However, being off on our project guesses can be even more detrimental to our daily planning and, indeed, to entire company-wide projects. This is exactly why good project managers always round up the departments' estimations of how long delivery of their segment will take. This practice is intended partially to allow for the unexpected, but largely to counteract most people's difficulty with estimating time.

This brings up the similarly challenging element of planning for the unexpected, which we mentioned before. If you live alone, then your morning routine likely has few X factors. However, add in a spouse, roommate, or kids, and who knows what might interfere with your estimations? Whether it's interruptions, delays, or just unforeseen steps to accomplish your goal, the universe has funny ways of making sure that you can't be too rigid about your planning. Remember the old adage, "Wanna make God laugh? Make a plan." While occasionally frustratingly true, adages don't excuse you from developing good time-estimation skills. As I suggested above, learn to expect the unexpected, and plan for it in advance. Perhaps you need to add 15 to 30 minutes of buffer time to every activity.

Two of the keys to peace of mind are knowing how much you can realistically accomplish in a day and being prepared for the unexpected. A significant part of our daily stress is self-initiated: we are victims of our own impossible expectations for how much we can get done. Accurate time estimation for both frequent and infrequent tasks will guard you from this unnecessary stressor and help you end each day feeling content with what you accomplished rather than frustrated by what didn't get done.

Next Actions

- ✓ Toy with your time line. Try moving it around into different modes before you start new activities, and just get curious. Does the activity feel different than usual? What do you notice about where your mind is focused? What mode might allow you to be maximally productive in each of your frequent activities?
- ✓ Try repeating the estimated/actual exercise for other sections of your day: getting settled in at work in the morning, wrapping up at the end of the day, getting home and making dinner, and so on. The more information you have about how long these routine activities take, the better you will understand how much actual work and rest

time you really have to plan during your day. Alternatively, repeat the exercise for your morning routine for an entire workweek to see if the results vary on different days.

- ✓ When planning your task list for tomorrow, jot down next to each item an estimate of how long you think it will take. Then, while doing each task, set a timer to measure the actual duration. How good are you at estimating unusual tasks versus routine tasks?
- ✓ Try this chapter's exercises with your partner or a friend, and discuss what you each discover about your time-estimation skills. This might reveal why one of you is frequently late and the other tends to arrive fifteen minutes early.
- ✓ Some tasks expand to fit whatever time they are allowed. Try reversing this exercise by giving yourself only the amount of time that you estimated to complete the task. Set an alarm for that time, and when it goes off, just stop. Occasionally, we allow ourselves to get off track by what I call falling down rabbit holes, and something that should have been finished an hour earlier has nudged us into a completely random other world. Watch out for rabbit holes, and find strategies to help stay more focused and get you out of them when you fall down one.

Resources

Csikszentmihalyi, Mihaly. *Flow: The Psychology of Optimal Experience.* New York: Harper & Row, 1990.

Niurka. *Supreme Influence: Change Your Life with the Power of the Language You Use.* New York: Harmony Books, 2013.

—27—

Batching Your Tasks

Do you want to create more time in your day or week? One of the simplest ways to accomplish this is batching your tasks. A significant amount of our time and energy is spent on simply getting started on any particular action, so the more we can group similar actions together, the less "getting-started" energy we'll need to use overall.

If you need more reasons why task batching is a great time and energy saver, however, read on!

The Wonders of Task Batching

Batching tasks is helpful in so many ways. Below are just a few of its advantages.

It helps reduce the mental energy of transitions. When you switch from one type of task to another, it takes time for your mind to adjust to the new activity. A client of mine once said that the feeling of switching tasks is like going around and around on a Ferris wheel, and when you need to get off to go on a different ride the momentum continues and the Ferris wheel won't stop. If you minimize the number of times that your mind has to switch between one activity and another by grouping similar activities, then you gain time for other pursuits.

Setup and cleanup time are done once rather than multiple times. For years, I have suggested to my mother that choosing a time once per week to pay bills would save her time. Every time a bill comes in the mail, she opens it, pulls out her computer and financial spreadsheets and checkbook, logs in to her online bill-pay system, pays the bill, records the transaction in the appropriate places on her spreadsheets and checkbook, puts everything away, and files the paid bill. While she does have the routine down to a science, she spends a good five-plus minutes pulling everything out, doing the task, and then putting it away *each time a bill arrives*. Due to her retired lifestyle, she doesn't mind the extra time and prefers the feeling of always having her bills paid immediately. However, many of us don't have—or *want* to have—the additional 5 to 20 minutes a week to do a particular process repeatedly.

Task batching can minimize unnecessary interruptions. When you suddenly think about something you want or need to do, a task-batching plan prevents you from having to stop the presses and take care of the action immediately. Instead, you *sort* that action into a group of its friends to be accomplished at a more convenient, planned time. For instance, let's say you remember that you wanted to call John about next quarter's financial projections. Rather than immediately picking up the phone and stopping the flow of your current work, you simply add the call to the time in your day that you've designated for phone calls.

Task batching can drastically reduce travel time. One of my favorite types of tasks to batch is errands. Rather than running out for something every day when the idea or need pops into my head, I choose one afternoon a week to drive around and accomplish *all* of those activities. This habit has several upsides:

- It minimizes repeat trips in a single week. Throughout the week, I make a single list for grocery items, visits to the mall, and so on.
- I can plan to run my errands on a day and time when the stores won't be busy.
- It turns errand running from something that needs to be squeezed in between important activities or appointments into a lovely and fun adventure out for the afternoon. Toss in lunch or tea at a local café, and it becomes a relaxing yet productive day.

The Best Tasks for Batching

Some types of tasks lend themselves especially well to batching:

- Calls
- Emails
- Meetings
- Errands
- Cooking! I know some folks who cook four to five meals on Sunday and keep them in the fridge or freezer for easy heating on weeknights.
- Bill paying
- Cleaning tasks
- Filing
- Weekly planning (see Chapter 49)

Tasks that can't be batched include dog walking, paying attention to your loved ones, sleeping, eating, exercise, and relaxation time. It's better to spend a little time every day accomplishing these activities because waiting for once a week or delaying for many hours may lead to disaster!

Task-Batching Tips

Here are a few final pointers for effective task batching.

- **Create a weekly structure for batched tasks.** I mentioned above that I have assigned one afternoon a week for errand running. That means that each week I look at my upcoming schedule and pick the best day. You could simplify this by deciding once that you will always block Thursday afternoons for errand running. I have found that keeping this block of time a bit flexible has worked for me, as long as I make sure to get it in. On the other hand, Monday is always my administrative day. That's when I schedule all my staff meetings and knock off a bunch of the simple emails and tasks to clear the decks for the upcoming week. That guaranteed day and certainty of structure has been a lifesaver. Choose the best method for yourself or for the particular type of task.

✧ **Create a daily structure for batched tasks.** While working with a client who is a financial planner, we created a plan for incorporating blocks of call time into his day to ensure that he would always have time to do all the follow-up calls necessary for maintaining relationships with his clients. This strategy can also be applied to emails and meetings, so that they aren't creating constant interruptions in your productive thinking or creative time.

✧ **Keep needed items for batched tasks together.** Create a Bills to Pay folder, a To Be Filed folder, a Calls to Make list, or an Errands to Run list. Having all the necessary items together when you're ready to get your batched tasks done will make life *much* easier. Consider each set of batched tasks as a candidate for an activity kit (see Chapter 17).

With just a little bit of planning and forethought, batching can save a tremendous amount of time in your day or week. Give it a try!

Next Actions

✓ Brainstorm a list of batchable tasks in your life. In addition to the common ones I listed above, you might think of many more tasks that are unique to your job or lifestyle.

✓ Make a plan. You might amend or update your life rhythm chart (see Chapter 15: Your Ideal Week Vision) with time slots for your batched tasks. If you do not have this chart, then think about your daily or weekly schedule and assign times for different types of batched tasks from your brainstormed list above.

- ✓ Test out your plan for a couple weeks. With two to three weeks of experience with batching your tasks, you will likely think of the minor changes that make batching even more effective. Perhaps you would prefer to run all of your errands on Wednesday evening because that's the night when the library and bank are open later; or maybe just after lunch (rather than just before lunch) is a better time for calls because people aren't hurrying to grab food and are more available. These kinds of insights are generally gained only through lived experience.
- ✓ Keep an eye out for methods or solutions that could make your batched tasks even easier. Perhaps a basket by the front door for items to be returned would make errands day easier because you can just grab the basket and head out the door. Or maybe keeping your grocery list on your smartphone will make it quicker for you to add new items on the fly and remember the list when you're at the store.

Resources

Dream Dinners. http://bit.ly/DreamDinnersInfo.

GroceryIQ. http://bit.ly/GroceryIQapp.

Morgenstern, Julie. *Time Management from the Inside Out: The Foolproof System for Taking Control of Your Schedule—and Your Life.* New York: Henry Holt/Owl Books, 2004.

—28—

Weeding Your Tasks

Whether you dream big or just have a very busy life, at times you may look at all the items on your master list and feel utterly overwhelmed. Looking over that list gives you a big-picture view, and sometimes the big picture indicates that you're trying to take on too much. That's when it's time to get serious and weed out your tasks.

Your Menu of Options

One day I was talking with a client about his task list, and he seemed to go on forever. He acknowledged that looking at the list frequently made him feel hopeless and overwhelmed. That is not how you want a task list to make you feel!

If you've been feeling like my client, let's start by simply reframing the situation.

In the past, you may have been taught to create a to-do list, then get everything done. That old mindset needs to be shifted when you begin using a master list because… it's not about getting it all done. I know. I'm shocking you, right?

When you open your master list think of it more like opening a menu of options. These are experiences that you could choose to have today. These are actions that you can choose to take, but you always have choice.

Now, some of them, if they aren't done, will have specific consequences. For instance, if you choose to not complete your taxes by the deadline, then there will be specific consequences that may encourage you to make it a priority. However, everything is a choice. What do you choose to do today?

Reframing the Feeling of "Overwhelm"

When one of my teachers, Niurka, started feeling overwhelmed by her projects, she decided that continuing to feel overwhelmed was disempowering her sense of action. So, she began to rewrite her mind's response. She decided that rather than saying to herself, "I'm overwhelmed" when those thoughts and feelings arose, she would think to herself, "I'm deeply engaged with my life and in high demand!"

How different do those ideas feel? To be "deeply engaged with life" is to be involved, active, moving. To be "in high demand" is to be popular, sought after, desirable. Both of these attractive qualities are far more empowering than feeling overwhelmed. Thus, simply by changing what she was saying to herself, she was able to regain energy and momentum. Shifting this type of thinking allows you to reclaim your feeling of control and yet again feel "at cause" in your life rather than being a victim of circumstance. This powerful reframe can be your first step out of a frustratingly disempowering state of "overwhelm."

Weeding as Part of the Process

If you fully implement the strategies and approaches described in this book, then these habits of productivity will become a way of life—and it's highly likely that you'll still have a master list on the day you die. Which is good news! The point is *not* to get your master list done. It won't go away, just like you'll still have a calendar and address book when you finally pass on too. It's simply the place where your actions live. And if your master list continues to be long even when you are in your golden years, you can take that as a wonderful sign that you've chosen to remain deeply engaged with life rather than fading away. So, try to think of your master list as a menu or guidebook of options instead of a journey to be completed.

When my husband and I travel, I love to pore over the guidebooks for our destination and consider all the possible adventures that we might create for ourselves while we're there. Some sights become definite "must-dos," while others I consider "cool if there's time and energy." Your master list is the same type of guidebook. Some items on it feel like "must-dos," while others might have been exciting at one time but no longer seem worth the time and energy. That's fine. That's normal. That's why occasionally weeding your tasks, projects, and goals is part of the process.

Ways to Weed

Here are a few ways to weed your master list and bring it back under control.

- **Demote some items from Active to On-Hold.** Some items on your master list might just need to be postponed. Narrowing your focus to a smaller number of projects and giving yourself permission to let other things wait might provide necessary emotional and mental breathing space.
- **Let some of your On-Hold Projects go.** There might be some projects in which you have just completely lost interest, focus, or momentum. Perhaps it sounded like a good idea when you captured the project, but you aren't excited about it anymore. That's okay. Just delete it. If it's meant to be, then it will likely occur to you later in your life, and you can choose to renew your commitment to it then.
- **Delegate and ask for help.** Are you trying to do too many things yourself? Maybe it's time to find other people who could help you complete tasks. Those people could be your partner, your kids, your co-workers, your staff members, your friends, or other professionals. As you consider your projects and tasks, the question is not only "Do I *need* to do this?" but "Do *I* need to do this?" If you need help with delegating effectively, take a look at Chapter 37: Delegation Plans.
- **Do a commitment audit.** Take a look at Chapter 5: Time for a Commitment Audit. It might be time to review all your current responsibilities and commitments and then begin saying no or wrapping some of them up. You might simply be spreading

yourself too thin, and the only way to resolve that problem is to remove the unnecessary activities and focus on the ones that align with your purpose and passion.

Reframing your thoughts and applying these four weeding options will help you to bring your master list back to a manageable size. It will also help you to feel even more energized as you decide what you want to do today.

Next Actions

- ✓ Check in with yourself as you review your master list. Is it beginning to feel overwhelming? That's okay. Take a breath, remind yourself that it's good to be deeply engaged with life and in high demand, and then apply the four weeding strategies above to your list and see how much you can postpone, release, or delegate.
- ✓ Make weeding a seasonal habit. Create space on your calendar to repeat this process quarterly.
- ✓ Challenge your assumptions about what *you* really need to do. If you can't think of alternative arrangements to get tasks accomplished, then ask your most resourceful friend to help you brainstorm. What other solutions can you figure out together?
- ✓ Stretch yourself by exploring simplicity. Give yourself permission to narrow your focus to the smallest number of projects needed to keep your life functioning. Often we only allow ourselves this level of narrow focus when we're in an emergency or under extreme pressure. But, surprisingly, the world doesn't end when we arrange a simple and streamlined birthday party for our child instead of a completely over-the-top, Pinterest-propelled extravaganza. Focus on what's truly important, and release the rest.

Resource

Babauta, Leo. "Zen Habits." http://bit.ly/ZenHabitsBlog.

Part 6

Ballast Overboard: Simplifying

—29—

Managing Interruptions and Distractions

Have you ever gotten to the end of your day and wondered, "What happened?!" I know I've had a few days like that in my life. Sometimes the off-kilter day was a matter of poor planning. Other times my energy simply didn't match the tasks that I had planned to do. We all have days when our creative juices simply aren't flowing, no matter how much we want to get that report done by next week.

Often, however, that "Where did my day go?" experience happens because we fail to check in with ourselves periodically to make sure that we are on track with the actions that we intended. We allow interruptions and distractions to win the day. It's so easy to let that happen because life today is riddled with interruptions and distractions. Email dings, the telephone rings, a text message pings, and life suddenly zings past us with little attention paid to the plans that we made for the day.

This was a persistent problem for my client, Matt, an accountant and tax planner. He would plan to work on a big project and then start his day by turning on his email "just to see if anything important has come in." Unfailingly, email would distract him for one to three hours of his prime thinking time. During that time, the phone would inevitably ring and interrupt the flow of his emailing. Often the phone call was a client or colleague with a question, and Matt would be off chasing this new issue. On other days, the call came from a client's lawyer, who "needed" Matt to prepare financial information to be presented in court in two days. Matt would drop everything he'd planned to do—i.e., his big project work—and take care of this unexpected "urgent" priority.

Frequently, Matt would get to lunchtime without even touching his big project. Instead, he would spend prime morning hours reacting to everything (and everyone) else.

So, Matt would leave for lunch in a bit of a daze and remind himself that he needed to get down to work on the big project after lunch. Some days he would do just that for an hour or so until the midafternoon slump hit, his energy dropped, and the big project felt even bigger and more challenging—thus increasing his resistance to working on it and justifying various types of procrastination.

Does this story sound familiar? Shift a few details, and probably most of us have experienced days like this, when a dash of procrastination, a sprinkle of interruptions, some poor energy management, and a dose of adrenalin turn that productive day we planned into a stew of frustration, exhaustion, and confusion—certainly not my favorite meal.

To help you avoid or minimize this experience, I'm going to give you some tools to address the two sides of this problem: 1) handling interruptions, distractions, and unplanned events, and 2) structuring in check-ins and course corrections.

Handling Interruptions

Interruptions are an unavoidable part of life. Telephones, emails, co-workers, and kids jockey for our attention and aim to pull it away from whatever we planned to focus on. First, it's important to acknowledge that interruptions dissipate our productive energy and thus are important to minimize. Second, it's important to recognize that you have a *choice* to be drawn off course or to maintain your focus.

You *choose* to answer the phone, to check your email when it dings, or to respond to that text right now. Which means that you can also choose when it will be most productive for you to do so. The difference between a top-performing individual and someone who will perpetually scrape by is his or her ability to accept and wield that power of choice.

Exercising the power of choice is a learned skill that you can strengthen over time. But first, you can start by limiting the opportunities for interruptions in your life. For example, if you're going to work on a big project, try any of the following:

- Turn off your phone's ringer
- Silence the new-email and text notifications on your smartphone and computer
- Put a DO NOT DISTURB sign on your office door or cubical entrance

These actions will remove tempting interruptions entirely, which can be great for periods of intense work or creative action. However, eventually you will want to work on building your choice reflexes more directly rather than just eliminating the outside influence. Here are a couple ways to accomplish this goal:

- Get comfortable screening your phone calls. Choose which calls you really *need* to take and which ones can wait for later. Let the caller leave a voice mail, and then call back if it's important.
- Build up your tolerance level for waiting to check email. If you check email as a knee-jerk response every time you turn on your smartphone or see an alert on your computer screen, then get used to seeing unread emails in your inbox and choosing to review and respond to them later.

Most of us (though unfortunately not all) are good about not interrupting meetings or quality time with friends and loved ones to attend to extraneous calls, texts, and emails. If this isn't you, consider this your wake-up call! Which is more important: that email, text, or call, or the person sitting in front of you? One of the fastest ways to damage a relationship is to imply that this person matters less than the alerts on your smartphone. People deserve your full attention if you've committed to spending the time with them, and the current epidemic of partial presence in relationships needs to be addressed, starting with ourselves. Be present!

Managing Distractions

Distractions, while similar to interruptions, are internally driven. When you're distracted, you have allowed your mind to wander to any shiny idea, object, or task that it wants rather than staying focused on the activity at hand. Sometimes distractions can be productive because your mind makes connections between ideas that perhaps were unclear before. However, more frequently distractions are simply your mind's way of playing a procrastination and avoidance game with you.

Don't get me wrong: I've procrastinated with the best of them, and I pulled plenty of all-nighters in college and grad school because I allowed various other things to pull me away from papers that I was supposed to be writing. However, I also know that one of the greatest assets of a top performer is his or her ability to turn on laser focus and dismiss the brain's attempts to distract them from a task.

Julie Morgenstern has emphasized the single best change most of us can make to avoid distractions: never check email in the morning. By its very nature, email is a reactive task that pulls you away from your productive plan. Give today's Inspired Action task precedence as the first thing you do each day, and don't even open your email until afterward. You may be surprised at how great that simple change can feel. (For more information about choosing your Inspired Action "One Thing" each day, see Chapter 50: Daily Planning.)

As with the above suggestions for handling interruptions, you can work to build up your strength of choice regarding when you need to focus intensely and when some daydreaming—or, as psychologist Eric Maisel calls it, productive obsession—might be acceptable or appropriate.

Distractions can be harder to deal with than external interruptions since, after all, you can't turn your brain on mute and expect to keep functioning. Nevertheless, managing distractions is a skill that can be learned and strengthened with exercise, so it's worth deciding to develop it for yourself.

Navigating the Unexpected or Unplanned

Sometimes the universe simply has a different agenda for you today. You are on course and in flow, but you keep coming across unexpected obstacles: massive traffic jams, additional steps that you didn't anticipate in your project planning, or major personal or global life events that steer you off course. If your child has an accident and goes to the hospital, your plan rightfully flies out the window. Similarly, major world events like 9/11 may understandably pull your attention away from the activities that you intended to accomplish.

In reality, there is little you can do about this type of interruption. It's important to give yourself space and time to handle the immediate situations or emotions that arise, and when you are ready and have some space, you can consider how to regroup and move forward. These are times for patience, adaptability, and emotional resiliency to take their place for the day.

Structuring Check-in and Course Corrections

Most days don't involve massive elements of the unexpected or unplanned. Instead, you'll probably have your typical share of interruptions and distractions. One of the best ways to minimize their counterproductive impact is to build in regular check-in structures for your day. Here are some ways that you could do that:

- Set an alarm on your cell phone or computer that goes off in the midmorning and midafternoon. Use the alarm as a reminder to ask yourself, "Am I done with today's Inspired Action task? Is what I'm doing right now the best use of my time and energy?"

- ✧ Use a mindfulness app that sounds a bell either each hour or at random, and ask the guiding questions above whenever it sounds.
- ✧ Plan a 5-to-10-minute meeting with yourself at the end of your lunch break to recalibrate your plan for the day based on the morning's events and to focus on the best activities for you that afternoon.

Can you think of other check-ins or daily course-correction techniques that could help you get yourself back on task during the day? Maybe you can attach your new check-in technique to an established pattern, such as your midmorning coffee break, to help you remember to do it.

Becoming skilled at handling interruptions and distractions is no longer optional for living an effective, productive, and happy life. Whatever you can do to make it easier to build that skill is probably worth the effort.

Next Actions

- ✓ Look at your calendar for the next few days and identify a time when you will really need focused, creative energy. Practice reducing interruptions by removing common sources of interruption during that time. (Don't forget to turn your phone back on or otherwise restore those sources when you're done.)
- ✓ Practice screening your calls for the next week. Every time your phone rings, consciously ask yourself, "Is this the best time to have this conversation? Do I *need* to take this call?"
- ✓ Turn off the new-email notifications on your machines. I could become a broken record on this topic, but no one needs to be alerted every time a new spam message comes into your inbox.
- ✓ Establish one check-in or daily course-correction technique and try to maintain it for two to three weeks. Then reflect on it at the end of the test period. Did you get more important tasks done than usual? Did you feel better about how you managed your time? Do you

want to make any universal adjustments to your planning or daily rhythms in order to avoid certain frequently encountered patterns? For instance, waiting to check your email until later in the morning, or prioritizing your Inspired Action task at the very beginning of your day.

✓ Strengthen your power of choice and focus through meditation. Learning to calm your mind not only can increase your productivity, but also can improve your overall health and well-being. Try sitting for just three minutes with your eyes closed. Focus on your inhales and exhales. Just three minutes of focus practice can strengthen that muscle significantly, and you can increase it slowly over time.

Resources

Buddhify 2.0. http://bit.ly/BuddhifyApp.

Chime app. http://bit.ly/ChimeApp.

Maisel, Eric, and Ann Maisel. *Brainstorm: Harnessing the Power of Productive Obsessions.* Novato, CA: New World Library, 2010.

Mindfulness Bell app. http://bit.ly/MindfulnessBell.

Morgenstern, Julie. *Never Check E-mail in the Morning: And Other Unexpected Strategies for Making Your Work Life Work.* New York: Fireside, 2004.

—30—

Eliminating Tolerations

You get up in the morning and hold the toilet lever down for an extra five seconds...just to make sure. In your bedroom, while getting dressed, you wrestle with the ferociously squeaking drawer of your old bureau just to get your underwear. On your way to the kitchen, you step over the pile of clothes in the hallway that you keep meaning to bag up and take to Goodwill. While making breakfast, you walk across the kitchen 15 times, knock over four objects, and dig in the back of a cabinet for three minutes just to find a mug to hold your coffee.

Does this sound at all like your life? For many of us, these little irritants become simply part of the background noise of our lives. However, the details matter, and broken, problematic, distracting, or inconvenient things that annoy you *every day* are causing you unnecessary pain. I call these minor annoyances tolerations because they are the silly, obnoxious things that we have learned to simply tolerate in our everyday lives. We just accept them without noticing how much they drain our energy.

Call It Quits with Tolerations

Well, the time has come to say, "NO MORE TOLERATIONS!" Start paying attention. How much of your day is implanted with these minor irritations? Seriously, think through your day and look for those minor inconveniences that you have gotten used to. It's time to stop tuning out, ignoring, and tolerating everything in your life.

Are the same things happening at work? It could be the old metal desk drawer that squeals when you open it, the copier that always seems to be out of paper and requires a walk down the hall to the office manager to get another ream, or those cheap pens that never seem to be able to write when you need to take a phone message. These are all examples of common workplace tolerations.

Some of the tolerations in your life might be so long-standing that it never even occurred to you to question them. For instance, I recently had a conversation with the assistant of one of my executive clients about her email-processing habits. In her role as an assistant, she received literally hundreds of messages each day. She filed away messages that contained certain types of information that she knew she'd need again, such as travel details for expense reports, but all other messages just stayed in her inbox. Every day her eyes fell upon thousands of messages, most of which were complete—they required no action or further thought. But still her mind spent time processing them each day, even if only for a split second. We made the simple modification of creating an Archive folder so that when she was done processing her messages, she could simply multi-select anything that didn't require action and drag it into that folder. One more processing step? Yes. But one that saves her the endless experience of separating completed items from actionable ones *every time she opens her inbox*.

Take Inventory

Take a look at your life and environment, and ask yourself the following questions:

- What is broken and needs to be fixed?
- How could I make everyday activities easier by moving things around or making needed supplies more easily available?
- What regularly causes me to say, "Ugh!" or to sigh in frustration?
- What makes annoying noises that send prickles up your neck? (This might include some children's toys. It's okay, the world won't end if Chloe can't find her obnoxiously beeping electronic robot. As my mother taught me, introduce something different, and she'll likely forget about the robot for a while.)

- ✧ What unfinished projects and tasks do I see reminders of daily? How can I prevent them from making my heart and energy drop?

Take control! If you want more peace in your daily life, then it's time to address these tolerations. Your energy is much too valuable, and there is no need to go through life in toleration mode when you could experience more contentment, pleasure, and joy.

Next Actions

- ✓ Take inventory of the tolerations in your life, both at work and at home. If you don't start recognizing them, it's hard to take action to resolve them. Create a list of the issues.
- ✓ For each of your tolerations, can you determine a possible resolution? Does something need to be replaced? Repaired? Removed? Is it time to reorganize? Decide what course of action will best get each issue resolved.
- ✓ Pick a couple easy ones, and do them—today! Hide Chloe's robot, WD-40 the desk drawer, pitch the cheap pens, and pick up a nice gel rollerball on your lunch break. It's time to begin conquering your tolerations and resume *living* your life.
- ✓ For the more complicated projects, identify a simple next action. Call the plumber to get a quote? Measure the dresser and research replacements? Enlist your office manager as a teammate to brainstorm ways to store extra paper near the copier?

—31—

Conquering Overload

"We are drowning in information and starving for knowledge."
—Rutherford D. Rogers

In our lives today, we are constantly barraged by information from every possible direction: TV, Internet, texts, Twitter, blogs, Facebook, email, magazines, newspapers, books, radio, podcasts, YouTube, and more. We could spend every hour of every day reading, watching, or listening to sources of information. The question is, does this information serve us?

Rogers: Ahead of His Time

Rutherford D. Rogers was a staff member at the New York Public Library in the mid-1950s, and even at that time he felt overwhelmed by information. Imagine his thoughts if he were to look at us now. What he recognized, and the key for all of us, is the importance of seeing the difference between information and knowledge. We would do well to take that idea even further to recognize the difference between information and wisdom. Both knowledge and wisdom require a key element that is increasingly less available in our lives: time for reflection. Knowledge and wisdom require the transformation of information into meaning, which can be created only when we allow our minds time to translate, reflect, and draw connections.

Part of the central message of this book is the need to bring more meaning into our everyday lives. To achieve that goal, we need time to turn our information into knowledge and, occasionally, wisdom. We need more time for reflection. Thus, we need to limit our information intake.

How to Limit Information Intake

The good news is that we do have some control over how information flows into our lives, and we can take steps to manage the pipeline's flow. Here are a few ideas to get you started.

Do a quality check. Pick a medium, and think about what information you regularly receive through it. As an example, how about TV? What do you find yourself watching on TV? Are all the shows equally valuable to your life? I'm not saying that you have to watch only PBS and documentaries. But do you truly enjoy watching that crime drama, or is it just filling space? One of the best tools for weeding out unnecessary TV from your life is a DVR. If you can record only the shows you're interested in and watch them when you're in the mood for TV, then you can take greater control over your TV information flow. (You can even save time—and avoid extraneous information—by skipping past the commercials!) You can do the same type of quality check on radio broadcasts, email lists, magazines, and any other medium. When you've taken a moment to reflect on their value in your life, you're ready for the next step.

- *Reduce the automated flow.* A lot of information cascades into our daily lives in the form of subscriptions: magazines, newspapers, email lists, blog feeds, and so on. What do you subscribe to? Are you getting solid value from the information these resources provide? If not, remove them from your world. Cancel the magazine and newspaper subscriptions. Unsubscribe from the email lists and blog feeds. Remove the Season Pass from your DVR. Did you know that you can add yourself to the National Do Not Mail List for junk snail-mail marketing? Go to http://bit.ly/JunkOptOut and add your name.

- *Unfollow and unfriend people.* I know, some people will be horrified, but social media is, at its core, an information-distribution tool. In the early days of Facebook and Twitter, I heard lots of complaints: "Why would I care about what my friend had for breakfast or the fact that she took her dog for a run?" The problem here isn't with the medium but rather with the channel to which you have it tuned. If your Twitter feed or Facebook friends list includes people who consistently add no value to your life and mind, then remove them. They haven't earned the right to be part of your limited-information lifestyle. You can begin by whittling down the unnecessary information flowing into your life in order to focus on what creates value. But even the flow of *useful* information needs to be appropriately managed so that you have the reflection time necessary to create knowledge and wisdom.

Here are some great ways to manage the flow.

- **Turn off the gadgets.** Notice whether most of your information sources are delivered through an electronic medium—TV, computer, radio, smartphone. The simplest and fastest way to limit the influx is simply to turn those gadgets off. I'm not saying you need to turn them off permanently. Believe me, I'm a gadget girl, not a Luddite. But if you want to create time away from the barrage of new information, then stepping away for even 15 minutes of silence can be powerful.
- **Treat your digital information as you would a morning newspaper.** Funnel your favorite blogs or social-media streams into a feed reader, and access all of your digital content in one place. Then turn off any notifications, badges, or alarms attached to getting new content. Read it when it works for you, not as a Pavlovian reflex.
- **Streamline your email.** This book has a whole chapter (Chapter 32) on how to do this. It's time to recognize that some email is like a newspaper or a magazine to be read at our convenience. Some email contains valuable personal or professional communication, and some is pure trash. I recommend creating systems to make sure that our attention to email is based on its value.

- ✧ **Set goals and reduce gradually.** If you are a major information addict, you might need to wean yourself from the high. If you tend to watch five hours of TV per day and wish it were no more than two, then limit it to four for the next month, three for the following month, and two after that. Same with Facebook: if you spend several hours a day wandering its streams, then identify your goal and reduce your time very slowly. Quitting information overload cold turkey is rather like jumping into a restrictive diet and may leave you feeling deprived and disconnected. If needed, use a timer or alarm on your phone to maintain your time awareness and avoid getting lost in the flow.

Next Actions

- ✓ Spend a week or so taking inventory. Become aware of the information inflows in your life, and start making a list of which sources to remove or limit. It will likely be different for each person. For me, I have completely stopped watching TV news shows because they brought very little value to my daily life. I can get most of that information online when I'm ready and interested to hear it. Use your power to decide what deserves your attention and time.
- ✓ Dedicate the needed time for your information-downsizing campaign. For the next month, spend 15 minutes a week removing the extraneous sources, whether that's weeding out your Facebook friends, adding yourself to the National Do Not Mail List, canceling your magazine subscriptions, or deleting shows from your DVR. Make *now* the time to take action.
- ✓ Get your support team on board. Let your friends, family, and coworkers know that you are doing some information downsizing. Give them your reasons, and ask them nicely to pause before sending you something to make sure it's really important for you to see or to have. It might take a bit of diplomacy, but perhaps your aunt who always forwards chain emails will be willing to take you off her distribution list.

Resources

LinkedIn Pulse app. http://bit.ly/LIPulse.

Feedly. http://bit.ly/FeedlyInfo.

Flipboard. http://bit.ly/FlipboardInfo.

The Early Edition 2 app. http://bit.ly/EarlyEdition2.

National Do Not Call Registry. http://bit.ly/DoNotCallReg.

National Do Not Mail List. http://bit.ly/JunkOptOut.

—32—

Streamlining Your Email

You get up in the morning, and one of the first things you see is a badge on your smartphone: that little number telling you how many messages have arrived since you went to sleep. If only every one of those messages were from your best friends, family members, or most valued clients. Out of the 40 new messages in your inbox, most likely only 1 of them is actually something worth reading or responding to.

Nevertheless, most of us go through a daily—or even hourly—clicking routine of selecting all the email messages to be sent to the trash. It's almost as if we hope to get exercise credit for having to click so many times to get rid of unnecessary stuff. But while filtering out the junk might occasionally get you irritated enough to raise your heart rate, I doubt that you can count it as aerobic exercise.

Let's analyze the costs of this daily processing routine:

- How many times a day do you cull email messages? Consider time spent both at home and at work. My guess is two to four times per day at least. How many minutes of your day does that take? Probably two to six minutes—and that might be a low estimate, depending on whether you tend to skim the items before you trash or file them.

- How many times do you get interrupted or distracted by new email, only to discover that it's largely trash? Perhaps four to eight times per day? And how long does it take you to get back on task? Probably anywhere from 2 to 15 minutes.

For years my mother has teased my stepfather that deleting emails is his favorite evening activity. In the evenings he regularly spends 30 minutes to 2 hours on his personal computer just weeding through various messages and lists to which he has subscribed. Sometimes she can lure him away from the computer to play cards with her. But generally speaking, after getting home from a full day at work, he spends a whole evening trying to catch up on his personal message backlog.

If you were calculating the numbers above, you would have discovered that you likely lose between 6 and 54 minutes per day to email distraction and elimination. Six minutes might not feel like much, but 54 probably does, and you are most likely somewhere in the middle. If you compound the figures weekly, the time costs are between 42 minutes and 7 hours a week. Would you be happy to regain one to seven hours per week of otherwise functional time?

A Simple Email System

It's time to invest in your future happiness and ability to focus. I'm an advocate of maintaining a minimal folder system because email programs have such great search capabilities now.

So, here are the basic folders I recommend to my clients:

- @Reply/Action
- @Read/Newsletters
- @Unsubscribe
- Archive (built in to Gmail and many other email programs)

Why the @ symbol? Because in most email programs, that keeps the folder near the top of your list of folders so that it's easy to find. Depending on your circumstances, a few more folders might be helpful:

- @Receipts—Particularly if you run a business and receive tax-deductible receipts via email
- Project Folders—If you have teams of people with whom you are working on specific projects (work-related projects, boards, volunteer committees, etc.), it can be helpful to maintain a folder for each of those projects to keep all relevant communica-

tions together. (It's unnecessary if you are just working with one person, because you can simply search for that person's name.)

With these folders in place, your inbox becomes a space purely for *new* messages ready to be processed into your folders. That's the key to Inbox Zero: no old emails living in your inbox.

Once you create these folders, try these email-processing steps for one week:

- Move anything that requires a response or further action to @Reply/Action.
- Take all the messages that you would normally trash and drag them into @Unsubscribe. (You could unsubscribe to each email source as it comes, but I'm a fan of batching similar actions together, so I would prefer to do all unsubscribing at the end of a week or delegate the task to my assistant.)
- Take all the e-zine or newsletter messages that you actually read or enjoy, and drag them into @Read/Newsletters. (Note: If you use Gmail, you could set up the smart tabs and drag them to your Forums tab to make it easier to filter out the newsletter lists from the juicy personal messages.)
- Send the rest of the messages that you're done reading or acting on to the Archive.

This is your new daily email processing routine, which I would recommend you do two to three times per day during your designated email time. (If you're opening your email more frequently than that, then it's time to break your addiction to your inbox and make sure you're working from your master list *intentionally* rather than *reactively* from your email inbox. (See Part 5: Your Helm and Rudder: Task-Management Essentials for instructions on how to get this system set up to support you.)

After you've finished processing the new messages that have arrived, then, with your remaining email time, open your @Reply/Action folder and focus on the messages in there. This strategy will keep you laser-focused on the high-value messages and ensure that you respond to people appropriately.

After sorting your email this way for one week, look ahead to your calendar for the following week and choose a block of time—at least one hour—for a bigger email-cleanup session. I suggest a time that's not your peak creative time but is good for getting little nitty-gritty actions addressed (for me that's an afternoon or evening).

When your designated time arrives, here's the plan:

1. Open your @Unsubscribe folder and go down the list. Look at the bottom of each message for a "Safe unsubscribe" link. Follow the necessary instructions to have your email address removed from each list, but *do not delete the messages* yet. Now, go down the list of messages again and set up a rule or filter to delete or archive the messages from that sender when they arrive. This double procedure covers you in two ways. Once you are "safe unsubscribed," any responsible and legitimate company will stop sending you messages. However, if that fails somehow, at least your email program will automatically shunt these messages away from your inbox.

2. Open your @Read/Newsletters folder. For each sender, create a rule in your email program that will send their messages to this folder automatically so that you don't have to manually click and drag each one to file it. Outlook has a Rules Wizard that will walk you through the process. Generally, the rule should say, "When a message arrives from [ACME Newsletter], move it to my @Read/Newsletters folder." For Gmail users: Gmail calls these rules "Filters," which you can find under the "More" button; they work in the same way.

You may want to repeat this filter-setup process once a month or, at minimum, once a quarter to catch any new lists that you've added. Set up the appropriate filters to handle those too.

There are several other great ways to use rules to streamline your email to fit your situation. Remember, the goal is to be able to find or see the information you need quickly and easily. So, target the high-volume senders first, and segment them into appropriate folders. Just be careful about going *too* rule crazy. If you send too many messages into subfolders without reviewing them, there might be negative consequences. For instance, if your rules prevent you from reading a company-wide email announcement that all the computers will be down for two days, you'll be stranded at work with a nonfunctional computer.

Backlog Bankruptcy

Do you have several thousand emails in your inbox? If the idea of processing your huge backlog seems daunting, here are a few additional steps to bring you up to speed with this simple system:

1. Move all your old emails into a @Backlog/To Process folder.
2. Choose a target horizon. Messages from one to two years ago are highly unlikely to be essential to your current daily operations. So, you could move anything older directly into the archive, where it will be out of your way but present if you want to search for something. I would recommend archiving anything older than six months, but use the horizon that makes you comfortable.
3. Set up and start using the simple email system above for all new messages as they come in, and focus primarily on building your habits with these messages.
4. Batch your backlog processing. Tackling the older stuff will be more manageable if you work in small batches moving backward toward your horizon. Maybe you process 50 old messag-

es each day, or you spend 15 minutes per day processing the backlog messages. Use whichever method feels right for you.

Next Actions

- ✓ Do you have more than one email account? Repeat the processes in this chapter for each one. It's your call whether you do them all simultaneously or space them out and attack one account per month.
- ✓ Be aware anytime you enter your email address into a field on the Internet. Do you see a prechecked box giving you permission to send "news and updates" from a certain company? Uncheck these boxes as much as possible.
- ✓ Don't give your email address to cashiers in stores unless you want to get spammed with their sales coupons. When they ask you for it, you can just politely say, "No, thank you, I would rather not provide it," and they will move on with your purchase.

Resources

Merlin Mann: Indie Writer, Speaker, and Broadcaster. http://bit.ly/InboxZeroVideo.

Morgenstern, Julie. *Never Check E-mail in the Morning: And Other Unexpected Strategies for Making Your Work Life Work.* New York: Fireside, 2004.

Trapani, Gina. *Upgrade Your Life: The Lifehacker Guide to Working Smarter, Faster, Better.* Hoboken, NJ: Wiley Technology Pub., 2008.

Unroll.me. http://bit.ly/UnrollMeInfo.

—33—

Automating Your Life

If time is your most valuable asset, and therefore freeing up your time is one of your primary goals, then a logical major objective would be to automate many parts of your life to happen either without your repetitive action or as easily as possible. There are three ways I know to automate life effectively: technology, delegation, and habit formation. Freeing and simplifying time is such an important goal that I have given each of these strategies its own chapter. Here we will focus on the first strategy: using technology to automate parts of your life.

Technology has much to contribute to making our lives easier. While computer crashes and data losses are sources of annoyance and frustration, we sometimes fail to recognize and honor everything that technology makes possible—even easy—these days. If you are an avowed Luddite and choose to steer clear of all 21st-century technological advances, then I wish you the best and suggest that you move on to the next chapter. But for everyone else…you're going to love this.

Nine Ways Technology Can Automate Your Life

I have pared down thousands of ways that technology can automate your life into eight of the best and most helpful. If you achieve all eight, you will most certainly free up a significant amount of time each week for more important—and pleasant—pursuits.

With Your Finances

1. **Automatic bill pay.** This practice makes some people anxious, but having your bills automatically deducted from your checking account or charged to your credit card is a big time saver.

Rather than having to remember and act on each of your bills on a monthly basis, you go about your life as each bill gets paid automatically and instantaneously—or all of them get consolidated onto your credit card bill and you just pay that one bill each month. This change alone can save you at least an hour each month.

2. **Savings transfers.** Similar to having bills automatically paid from your accounts, having money automatically squirreled away for the future is a great opportunity offered by most banks. Americans are generally very poor at saving money, but I believe that if more of us took advantage of automatic savings transfers, that would start to change. Choose an amount each week (or biweekly after your paycheck), and set up a recurring transfer that moves that money from your checking account to your savings account. Alternatively, many employers have the ability to split your direct deposit so that a portion of your paycheck goes straight into your savings account. It's a great way to save money without any additional effort or decision-making on your part. It could pay for your next vacation, your new house, or your children's education without you lifting an additional finger.

3. **Budget and spending notifications.** Today you have your choice of multiple computer programs that provide a greater awareness of your financial situation and spending habits. These programs, which require a minimal amount of time and effort to set up and maintain, help you track and categorize your spending. A very popular option is Mint.com, which collects all your financial transactions into your account and then categorizes them (often with a little guidance from you). In my opinion, one of Mint's best features is that you can have it send you email and text alerts when you start getting close to your budget cap for a particular category that month. These alerts help you manage decisions better. For instance, they will show you quite clearly that eating out, clothes shopping, and trips to

Starbucks make up a major part of your unconscious spending habits, which allows you to make more informed choices.

A second and somewhat lesser-known option is You Need a Budget (YNAB). This software uses the classic approach of envelope budgeting to split your paycheck money into virtual envelopes for each of your budget categories. You keep it up-to-date by spending just a few minutes each week to categorize transactions. Then, when you access your information via the smartphone app, you will always know how much you have to spend for your discretionary categories with very little hassle or effort.

With Your Calendars and Scheduling

4. **Shared electronic calendars.** This is one of the truly wonderful creations of the past several decades. Most companies could not function these days without shared electronic calendars, and now many households are benefiting from their wonders. The examples that I see most frequently are Google Calendar and Microsoft Office 365 with Outlook. If your company is already using Outlook, you're probably familiar with the ability to see your colleagues' availability and determine what time to set your meeting based on their free/busy information.

   Many homes and families, however, have not leveraged these tools to see what your spouse or kids have scheduled. Google Calendar, which is free and extremely versatile, might be a great solution for you. Each member of your family can have a unique Google Calendar account that is shared with the rest of the family. You can toggle on and off viewing each person's schedule to focus on your own schedule or the whole family's. Did you know that it's possible to sync your Google Calendar data with Outlook and vice versa? You can also sync it with your iPhone, iPad, Android, BlackBerry, and many other devices. In other words, it's now possible to see all of your work and family calendars in one place at one time so that you can make that next dentist appointment at a realistic time, rather than making your best guess and having to change it later.

5. **Online meeting-scheduling tools.** You may be familiar with the wonders of Google Calendar, but this next type of tool hasn't gained quite the same level of awareness. I have used three types of meeting-scheduling tools that have dramatically simplified communications in my business and personal life.

   The first tool is Doodle, which is very helpful when a group of people needs to find a common time to meet, or when you need to schedule a series of similar meetings with a large number of people and have to find out each person's availability. The facilitator/leader of the meeting creates an event and proposes a series of possible times for the meeting(s) to take place. Then she sends a link to everyone in the group, and each person goes to the link and votes for the time(s) when he or she could be available. Everyone involved gets to see which time the most people have in common and who can be available for each individual slot. I've also used it during our hiring processes to schedule candidates for interview slots.

   The other two are TimeTrade and Calendly, which allow you to create different types of activities, such as a 30-minute phone consultation or a 1-hour coaching call. Then you set up specific slots when you could be available to take those calls or meetings during an average week. Best of all, it syncs to your main calendar (Outlook, Google, or several others) to eliminate the times when you are unavailable and to offer only the slots that are free when your client or contact goes to the link you provide. These tools have been a huge scheduling simplification for my consulting work.

6. **Meeting-reminder alarms.** Most calendar programs have the ability to make a sound or send you a notification message when your meeting is about to start. Many people use this

function, but few use it effectively. Consider adjusting the time when your alarm goes off so that you'll have enough time to wrap up your current project, prepare for the next meeting, and travel to the meeting. For example, if you have a 12 PM lunch meeting with a client at a location 20 minutes away, why not set that alarm for 45 minutes before the meeting? Then you'll have five minutes to finish your current task, ten minutes to collect what you'll need and get out the door, and a ten-minute buffer for unexpected traffic and time to find parking. This secret alone can help people avoid chronic lateness.

7. **Timers.** If you are still using paper calendars, these last few paragraphs have probably been getting tiresome, but this strategy applies to you too. Most mobile phones have a clock timer app or function—even the old "dumb phones," as my colleague Amanda called hers. That timer can be a fantastic tool. Set it to remind you to change over the laundry. Set it when you're working on an unpleasant or difficult task to tell you when it's time to quit or to take a break. Set it to remind you when it's time to leave to pick up the kids. A simple alarm can keep you moving forward with your day and help you avoid falling down a rabbit hole, as I like to call it—getting absorbed in your current task to the detriment of all other activities, commitments, or bedtimes. It also can help you break down an unpleasant task into manageable segments that keep you making progress.

With Your Task Management

8. **Shared project/task systems.** While construction companies have appreciated for years the value of high-powered project-management software like Microsoft Project, the rest of us have much less experience in using collaborative project/task software. However, project management tools can bring increased visibility and thus easier communications to shared tasks for any project. I help a lot of executives and their assistants set up

functional task-management systems that show both parties what's on their plate and reports the status of any individual task. Outlook can be a completely functional tool for this need, but it's not my favorite. There are several SAAS (software as a service) solutions that I think do this job significantly better: Asana, Wunderlist, Trello, and Basecamp.

These tools put all your task information into one place, allow multiple people to access the lists, assign tasks to different people, and, most important, make it easy to add or view tasks from any Internet-enabled device. These days, cloud solutions are the only way to go for most teams, so that everyone can access the information and stay up-to-date on the fly.

9. **Task reminders.** Similar to calendar reminders, task reminders are a subfunction of most task-management software, and they can be a tremendous blessing. Your devices can remind you of tasks that need to be accomplished on a certain day, at a specific place and time. I love setting up my iPhone's Reminders software to help me remember to pick up the dry cleaning on the way home or to cue me into particular habitual tasks at specific times of day.

   Many people put individual tasks, such as "Do laundry," on their calendar as appointments and then set up reminders through their calendar program. Personally, I'm not a fan of that solution. I believe that it's important to manage calendar appointments and task information separately because filling your calendar with non-time-specific activities that frequently get bumped from one day to the next shifts your entire relationship with your calendar from one of specific commitments to one of multiple theories about what you *might* do—or *wish* you could do—today. This is not a strong position to work or live from. A separate task-reminder solution allows you to manage these activities differently.

These nine tools should be plenty to get you thinking about how technology can simplify your life in truly helpful and easy ways. The next step is to choose one tool and give it a try for a couple weeks. Play with it. See what it can do for you.

Next Actions

✓ If you have success in implementing one new technology tool, then try another. If it doesn't work immediately as planned, remember that there might be a minor learning curve, and you might have to develop some associated habits. For instance, most new calendar systems and task-management systems take a little time to get used to, but if you're not seeing some definite benefits after two to four weeks, then try a different solution.

✓ Talk to your friends, co-workers, and family about the technology tools that make their lives easier. You might get turned on to even more great tips and tricks that solve huge daily frustrations for you.

✓ For those of you looking for even more tech tools and solutions, we frequently post reviews of new technologies that we're playing with at our ChosenCourse.com/blog. So, take a look and subscribe to hear about new apps and software that we love because they simplify our lives.

Resources

Asana. http://bit.ly/AsanaTasks.

Basecamp. http://bit.ly/BasecampProjects.

Calendly. http://bit.ly/CalendlyInfo.

ChosenCourse.com/blog.

Doodle. http://bit.ly/DoodleInfo.

Lifehacker. http://bit.ly/LifeHackerInfo.

Mint.com. http://bit.ly/MintInfo.

TimeTrade. http://bit.ly/TimeTradeInfo.

Trello. http://bit.ly/TrelloInfo.

Trapani, Gina. *Upgrade Your Life: The Lifehacker Guide to Working Smarter, Faster, Better.* Hoboken, NJ: Wiley Technology Pub., 2008.

Wunderlist. http://bit.ly/WunderListTasks.

You Need a Budget (YNAB). http://bit.ly/YNABInfo.

Part 7

Your Crew: Leveraging Your Team

—34—

Leading by Example

In my early days as a professional organizer, I had an initial phone call with a woman who became one of my favorite clients. She struggled with ADD, and the clutter in her home had become a major hindrance. She had a full-time job, two kids, a husband, and houses in two countries. What I remember most from that first conversation was that she was determined to improve her organizing skills because she wanted to be able to model them for her kids, who were three and five years old. "How can my kids learn to be organized," she said, "if they grow up in chaos?"

This aspiration was one of her clear driving forces and a major "why" behind her dedication to our organizing work. I loved that she claimed responsibility for creating the future she wanted and thus focused on improving herself rather than the people around her.

The Only Way to Guarantee Change

There is only one person you can influence directly and with a guarantee: yourself. We too often spend our lives waiting for others to change: "If only my husband would..." "When my children finally learn...." "Why can't my co-workers...?" All intentional changes begin with you. As one of my teachers, Niurka, has said many times, our true power comes from taking full and complete responsibility for everything that shows up in our lives. She calls this living "at cause" rather than "in effect."

That doesn't mean you're always going to like what shows up—but rather than bemoaning undesirable situations, you have the power to get curious about them. How have I helped bring this into my life? What is the gift it has to offer me? What can I learn here? What can I do to create my next result even more intentionally? This approach is even more valuable as you think about communicating with people around you, as we will explore in the next chapter.

The key to becoming the leader of any team is to take complete responsibility for the results, and then start leading by example. If you want your life to be better organized, how can you improve your organization skills? If you want better communication in your life, how can you improve your communication skills? If you want more money to live your life, how can you improve your money-management skills?

The solution will always come back to you leading by example. And that doesn't mean beating others over the head with how you do things. As you work to improve in a given area, others around you will notice or feel the effects of your efforts. As Niurka says, "When you change, the world around you changes. You have that much power."

Asking Empowering Questions

The key to leading by example is to get curious and to ask good questions—of yourself. Is there an area in your life that you want to improve? If so, ask questions that will give you empowering answers:

- What could I do today to make a difference in this area?
- Who do I know that succeeds in this area brilliantly? How can I use that person as a model or resource for change in myself?
- How can I become an even stronger model for others in this area?

These types of questions will lead you toward the future you want to create. So, we will begin with Niurka's formula for asking empowering questions:

- **State questions in the positive/affirmative.** You want to ignite your passion to move *toward* something rather than pushing away from something. How much better does it feel to ask, "What can I do today to get even more healthy exercise?" instead of "What can I do to not be such a lazy bum today?" Your subconscious mind won't hear the *not* in that sentence; it will pay attention to being a "lazy bum" instead of grasping the outcome your aiming for. Another example: "What can I do to be well prepared for the big meeting?" instead of "How can I not procrastinate as I get ready for the big meeting?"

- **Start with *How, What,* or *Who.*** Most empowering questions begin with these words rather than with *Why*. While you know that I'm a fan of knowing your "why," *Why* questions can get you into a mire of self-pity and self-deprecation—"Why is this happening to me?" "Why do I always…?" Questions that begin with *How* and *What* are likely to lead you forward—to identify a process or action you can take: "What can I do today to improve my communication with my spouse?" "How can I make the healthiest choice in this moment?" *Who* questions help you identify others who can help you: "Who can help me improve my money-management skills?"
- **Create velocity using *even more, while,* or *right now.*** This subtle distinction can be exceptionally powerful. Notice the difference between saying, "How can I get focused on this project?" versus "How can I get even more focused on this project right now?" There's a sense of momentum, immediacy, and even urgency that calls your energy forward to find the answer quickly. Similarly, notice the difference between asking, "How can I be healthy and fit?" versus "How can I be even more healthy and fit while having fun?" I find the second question far more motivating. Don't you?

The more positive and empowering you become, the more magnetic and influential you become as a leader. You will draw people into your energy, and they will begin to emulate and learn from you, often without any direct effort on your part. Here lies the essence of leading by example. As Gandhi said, "Be the change you want to see in the world."

Next Actions

- ✓ Practice writing empowering questions. Think about an area of your life that you want to improve, and take a minute to write five to ten empowering questions that could lead you toward the desired outcome or improvement.
- ✓ Incorporate empowering questions into your daily practices. I often end my journal entries with an empowering question that leads my focus toward what I want to create or attract to myself. What if with your first sip of coffee you identified an empowering question to focus on for today?
- ✓ Use empowering questions to plan your meetings! For example, "What is the best and most powerful outcome that we could create from bringing this group together today?" What questions could you ask that might lead or inspire the most action on your important projects?
- ✓ Try empowering questions with your kids or your spouse: "What could we do to make our mornings even more joyful and easy?" "How can I bring even more passion to my relationship right now?"

Resource

Niurka. *Supreme Influence: Change Your Life with the Power of the Language You Use*. New York: Harmony Books, 2013.

—35—

Influence: Yourself and Others

Our success in life relies directly on the actions we take. Sometimes we need to influence either our own behavior or the behaviors of people around us in order to achieve our goals. Whether the behavior is a habit we want to form, a physical action, or a pattern of communication, we need a clear strategy that will lead us there.

Beginning with Yourself

As I learned from Niurka, influence begins with inward fluency—the complete alignment of our outward behavior with our internal highest intention and connection to our values and our Source. Inward fluency is visible when you are congruent and your thoughts, beliefs, values, and actions are all moving clearly toward your intended outcome. When you have complete congruency, you have power to create change in your life and, by extension, in the lives of everyone who encounters you.

Influence begins within ourselves. First, we must create inward fluency to guide and empower our decisions and actions. Then, with that power in place, we are ready to use intentional strategies for influencing others.

Some of the best thinking I've found on the topic of influence strategies comes from the book *Influencer: The New Science of Leading Change* by Joseph Grenny, Kerry Patterson, and others. They boil down behavior change to two key phases of planning: 1) identifying the "vital behavior" and 2) leveraging multiple sources of influence.

Identifying the Vital Behavior

Identifying the vital behavior involves determining the one key action or process that would make a difference in your results. Grenny, Patterson, and co-authors offer examples of these strategies in action: influencing the use of condoms in AIDS-ravaged countries, influencing the behavior of former convicts to reduce recidivism, and influencing any person to go to the gym more often. These strategies can be applied at many levels, both individually and across multiple networks of people.

Think about a problem that you are trying to influence, and ask yourself these questions: what is the issue that most often gets in the way, and what is the action that I or we could take to shift or resolve it? You might come up with a whole list of actions that you struggle with. That's okay. You might need to test more than one theory, but first review your list of possible actions/behaviors and get clear: Which ones are key? What one or two things, if shifted, might make all the difference? That is the vital behavior to focus your influence strategies towards.

Leveraging Multiple Influence Strategies

With your vital behavior identified, now you need to create strategies to bring about the necessary change or development of the vital behavior thoroughly and effectively. The authors of *Influencer* consider two factors of influence across three different levels. The two factors are motivation and ability. In other words, are you *motivated* and *able* to do the desired vital behavior? Depending on the change we aim to make, we frequently focus only on this personal level of behavior, but there can be tremendous power in expanding our awareness to include two other levels of both motivation and ability: social and structural.

The authors of *Influencer* summarize these six areas of influence and give them phases that help us get a handle on what each area means in action. Here are the six areas:

1. Personal Motivation: Make the Undesirable Desirable
2. Personal Ability: Surpass Your Limits
3. Social Motivation: Harness Peer Pressure
4. Social Ability: Find Strength in Numbers
5. Structural Motivation: Design Rewards & Demand Accountability
6. Structural Ability: Change the Environment

I like to think about these six elements as chips on an Othello board. Did you ever play that game as a child? The game consists of chips with a white side and a black side. You place the chips strategically on grid-style game board. The goal is to make sure there are more chips of your color than of your opponent's color by the end of the game. The six areas of influence are like strategies in the game of Othello. If you want to succeed at changing a behavior, then the more of these strategies you use to influence yourself (or someone else) in the direction of that behavior, the more likely you'll create the desired behavior.

The titles of the six influence areas give you a general sense of what's involved with each one, but to help you get creative and explore how you could apply this methodology in your life, I'm going to give you a list of possible strategies for each area. Then you can choose a customized group of strategies that hit as many of the six areas as possible in order to bring about your specific vital behavior. For simplicity, I will assume that the behavior you're influencing is your own. However, these strategies are also relevant to influencing the behavior of others, so feel free to replace any references to you with the appropriate people or group you're aiming to influence and extrapolate from there.

Personal Motivation: Make the Undesirable Desirable.

- Spend time connecting to your "why." Is this change important in your life? What will be possible when you accomplish it? Write down your "why" in a notebook or journal.
- Find a picture to represent your "why" or the ideal outcome of this behavior change, and post it in a place where you'll see it frequently.
- Visualize yourself with your goal achieved. How do you feel? What do you see? What can you touch, taste, smell, hear? Step into the achievement as if it were happening right now.

Personal Ability: Surpass Your Limits.

- Visualize yourself *doing* the vital behavior. Seed your imagined experience of it with feelings of how easy it is and how confident you feel doing it. Use the New Behavior Generator Audio to help integrate unfamiliar behaviors. Find the audio at InspiredActionBook.com/Resources.
- Ability is sometimes just about *remembering* to do something. Attach your new vital behavior to a well-established one. Use the existing behavior as a cue for the new routine. For instance, are you trying to remember to take your vitamins each day? Then plan to do it right after you brush your teeth in the morning (a habit that most of us accomplish fairly consistently). (For more habit-building strategies, see Chapter 14.)
- Post reminders of your new behavior around your home or workspace. They can be sticky notes, photographs, or any other visual cues that will jar you into action at the right time.
- Plan ahead: Think about the obstacles that might get in your way, and figure out how to avoid them or recover from them. For instance, imagine you're about to travel but don't want to disconnect with your commitment to exercising four times per

week. Can you create a workout routine to do on the road? How can you plan that time into your travel activities?

Social Motivation: Harness Peer Pressure.

- Tell someone about your intended vital behavior change. Enlist that person to hold you accountable to the action. It could be your spouse, co-worker, coach, friend, or child—whoever is in a position of interacting with you frequently enough for you to regularly report on your progress.
- Find people who have already mastered the behavior you want to bring about, and ask them what helped them succeed. Model their success in both approach and attitude.
- Post your actions and results to your social-media network. Facebook can be great here because, presumably, you have already created a community of family and friends who would be delighted to hear what you're up to and cheer on your progress. Make your goal and your consistent actions toward it visible to others. Depending on your goal, there are some specialized websites and apps that help you both track your success and share it with your networks.

Social Ability: Find Strength in Numbers

- Find a buddy who wants to improve the same area of his or her life, and take action together or in parallel, so that you know you're not alone in making the change.
- Take action in a group. Sign up for a class, group, or mastermind in which several people are equally committed to the behavior you aim to bring about. That's part of the power of our Inspired Action Mastermind Program. Using the group to increase your accountability for intentional change.
- Create a group. Send out an email or social-media message to your network to find others who want to create the same be-

havior. Use tools like Meetup to find or create a like-minded set of people beyond your immediate circle of friends and acquaintances.

Structural Motivation: Design Rewards and Demand Accountability

- Create a tracking system for recording your actions and your successes. It could be a calendar with days that you cross off, a spreadsheet to record actions/instances of your vital behavior, or a success journal in which you write about each event and your results. Habit-tracking apps, such as Streaks or Habit List, make this easy.
- Brainstorm a series of rewards for yourself. What could you earn if you consistently bring about your vital behavior for one week, two weeks, one month, and three months? Rewards can be items you buy, but also consider experiences or "me time."
- Identify your "stick" (as opposed to your "carrot"). Make taking action matter by assigning a specific negative consequence for not doing it. Donate $25 to your least favorite charity if you miss a day. Go alcohol-free next time you're out for a drink with your buddies. Make a deal with your partner that every time you miss your vital behavior, you owe him or her a specific action that wouldn't normally be your responsibility or part of your routine. For instance, if he usually takes out the trash, then you would take that over for a week or a month.

Structural Ability: Change the Environment

- Consider what tools or elements will make your behavior easier. What could you move around to make the action easier to accomplish? Could you create a kit of the necessary items that you can just grab and go? (See Chapter 17: Activity Kits.)

- Create a dedicated space for your vital behavior. Is there a specific location in your home, workspace, or regular world that could house or structure that activity? For example, if you want to meditate or read inspirational books regularly, you could choose a chair, a room, or a corner where you will always do it.
- Create a dedicated time for your vital behavior. Have an alarm that goes off to remind you that it's that time. Even better, set two alarms: a five-to-ten-minute warning alarm telling you to wrap up what you're doing, and then a "Now's the time" alarm that sets you in action.

Making It Happen

Choose the combination of strategies above that feels good to you. Remember: try to pick at least one strategy from each of the six areas to increase your likelihood of complete success. The more of those Othello chips you turn in your favor, the more you guarantee a win for yourself. To help you develop your plan, we've created a Vital Behavior Change worksheet (see resources below) that will help you get clear, focused, and moving forward on making this behavior a new part of your daily life.

Next Steps

- ✓ Identify one challenge that you frequently face, and get curious. What is the one vital behavior—the root that, if changed, would dramatically shift the outcome? Identify your vital behavior, and then create your personalized influence strategy starting with the options above.
- ✓ Are you trying to help someone else succeed? Invite him or her to do this process together. Identify the vital behavior, and then brainstorm a strategy that incorporates as many of the six influence areas as possible.

✓ Are you stuck? Shift techniques, or add more. Your best asset is curiosity. Have you identified the true vital behavior? Might a different approach to one of the six influence areas have a more effective impact?

Resources

Grenny, Joseph, Kerry Patterson, et al. *Influencer: The New Science of Leading Change.* New York: McGraw-Hill Education, 2013.

Habit List app. http://bit.ly/HabitList.

Inspired Action Mastermind Program. www.ChosenCourse.com/InspiredActionMasterMind.

Meetup. http://bit.ly/MeetupInfo.

New Behavior Generator Audio. www.InspiredActionBook.com/Resources.

Niurka. *Supreme Influence: Change Your Life with the Power of the Language You Use.* New York: Harmony Books, 2013.

Streaks app. http://bit.ly/StreaksApp.

Vital Behavior Change Worksheet. www.InspiredActionBook.com/Resources.

—36—

Locating Support-Team Leaks

As children, we are mesmerized by superheroes. They lead double lives and can achieve the impossible. As adults, even though we see the magic of the fantasy, we still seem to hold the belief that we want to be superheroes in our lives. The truth is that we cannot "do it all" by ourselves. We cannot leap tall buildings in a single bound; we cannot run at lightning speeds to accomplish all our tasks. We are human, and that is beautiful. What we *can* do is leverage our strengths and acknowledge our weaknesses.

The truth of being human is that our lives depend upon a collaborative team. Whether it's our family and friends or our accountant, plumber, house cleaner, and auto mechanic, we rely on the support and services of others to keep our lives moving forward. The need for some of these professionals, such as plumbers, becomes obvious rapidly: most of us don't know how to snake a drain, replace a toilet, or repair a water heater. However, sometimes we overlook the benefit of hiring someone to do the things that we could accomplish ourselves, such as house cleaning, lawn mowing, laundry, and bookkeeping. We agonize about the limited amount of time we spend with our families and loved ones, and yet we are willing to sacrifice whole days at a time to basic life-maintenance tasks that could be done easily by someone else.

The world's richest people all know that *time* is a far more valuable commodity than money. More money can be earned by providing greater value to the marketplace, but no one can earn more time. The minutes, hours, and days we are given here are all we have. Wouldn't you like to spend them on the activities that only *you* can do? Only you can be your child's parent. Only you can be your parent's child. Only you can bring the gifts of your life's purpose into this world.

How can you create a support team that will allow you to focus your time, effort, and attention on those uniquely *you* activities as fully as possible? That is the question this chapter aims to help you answer.

You might be saying, "Yeah, this all sounds great, but I'm not made of money. How can I afford to pay for a support team?" T. Harv Eker, author of *Secrets of the Millionaire Mind: Mastering the Inner Game of Wealth,* has a simple answer: The amount of money you make is directly related to the amount of value you provide to the marketplace. If you need more money, then it's time to start asking, "What additional value could I provide?"

Is there a service you could offer, a product you could create, or a book you could write that would help others in their lives or on their paths? If you run a business, how could you devote a greater amount of your time to marketing your business and creating new opportuntities rather than operating or working "in" your business so that you can serve more people and increase your revenue? Do you see where this is going? Money can be earned by asking the right questions—and then you are back to the question of who can help you free up time to provide this increased value.

Identifying Support-Team Leaks

Lacking support in different areas of your life is rather like having holes in your emotional bucket through which your personal energy is rapidly leaking. To help you figure out where you might benefit most from someone else's support, let's explore a series of questions.

Support at Home

What activities do you spend large amounts of time accomplishing at home and in your personal life? Here are some common ones:

- House cleaning
- Laundry
- Lawn care

- Cooking and washing dishes
- Grocery shopping
- Running errands
- Taking your kids to activities
- Maintenance or repair projects

Who could help you accomplish those activities? The answer might be a service provider (many professionals out there would be delighted to provide all of these services for you). Or the answer might be people in your personal network—family members or friends who would be delighted to support you more. (I know a lot of grandparents who would be overjoyed to spend more time with their grandkids, even if it just means going to and from karate practice.)

Another idea is batch some tasks, such as grocery shopping and cooking, and trade off responsibility for them with friends. It takes a very small amount of additional time to make a double batch of a meal compared to a single batch. Think of the time you could save if you only had to go grocery shopping every other week because you trade off with a friend or neighbor. After all, once you are already at the store, picking up two gallons of milk isn't much more work than picking up one.

It's important to get really clear on the potential benefit of additional support. How much time do you currently spend on the activity? How much time might you save by finding the right help? Could there be additional benefits? Could task sharing help you create closer connections with people you care about? Are you supporting someone else in providing his or her gifts and services to the world?

Support at Work

What work-related activities do you spend a lot of time accomplishing? Here are some common ones:

- Bookkeeping

- Data entry
- Scheduling appointments
- Making routine calls
- Copywriting
- Filing
- Processing incoming paperwork

Who could help you accomplish these activities? If you're a solo entrepreneur who makes more than $15 per hour, then every hour for which you hire someone to do an administrative task is one more hour that you could spend on marketing your business and bringing in more business and thus more revenue. The key is to reinvest a good portion of your recouped time in marketing, and the administrative help quickly pays for itself with new business you've attracted. For years I've used Craigslist, Guru.com, and Upwork to find exceptionally qualified team members, including administrative support, for my own company. Learning the skill of hiring and interviewing is a bit of an initial challenge, but once you're over that hill, I promise you'll never go back.

If you're an entrepreneur, corporate manager, or executive and you already have an assistant, now is your chance to reevaluate your assistant's duties and make sure you are using him or her effectively and fully. If you do not currently have administrative help, then perhaps you could explore the possibility with your boss. Even if it's not a dedicated person but someone you share with a couple colleagues to free time up for higher-level work, it might not be as hard a case to make as you think. And, as they say, if you don't ask, then the answer is always no.

If adding a new administrative staff member won't fly, then what about an intern? Some companies or industries frown upon unpaid internships, but it still costs significantly less to bring on an intern part-time than it does to hire a new employee. Internships can be a huge win-win. You get freed-up time from the work that the intern can easily be trained to accomplish, and the intern gets a valuable learning opportunity and a line item for his or her resume.

Support in Personal Growth & Self-Care

When you think about building a support team in this area, the consideration is less about freeing up time and more about *investing* time and money in activities that will help you to become more valuable and effective in all the rest of your hours. Investing in your own personal care and growth is about increasing your own value.

If you want to improve a set of skills, then now might be the time to find teachers, mentors, trainers, therapists, or coaches who could help you to grow in that way. Why do so many companies hire sales trainers to work with their employees? Because people aren't born with highly developed sales skills, but those skills are learnable—and they create significant value to the company. The same is true in our personal lives. Many of my clients and ignition-event attendees come because they are aware that improving their productivity skills will vastly improve the quality of both their personal and their work lives. That's probably why you bought this book, right? What skills do you need more support in order to master? Who could help you?

The sometimes overlooked members of your support team might be focused primarily on providing care for you and your body. Personal trainers, massage therapists, Reiki practitioners, nutritionists, health coaches, and similar professionals play an essential role in our physical energy management. As we discuss in Chapter 13, energy management is all about showing up each day as the best version of yourself. It's hard to be highly productive and effective when you're exhausted, poorly nourished, and physically out of shape. Thus, working with self-care professionals can be a hugely valuable investment of your time, money, and effort. So, how might adding one (or more) of these professionals to your support team help you to take even better care of yourself and allow you to show up more for the rest of your life?

Who's on Your Team?

Now, it's time to make a list of people you would like on your team. Consider the three sections above, and write your wish list of all the helpers who could improve your life. Everyone's list will be different; for example, you might be perfectly happy to go grocery shopping, but cooking might be a major challenge. For a brief time, while growing my business, I hired someone to do meal planning for me. I didn't mind grocery shopping, and the cooking specifically wasn't a problem, but figuring out healthy options that worked for me as a somewhat picky vegetarian was a real challenge. So, I found someone who could help me plan meals, and it made my life significantly easier. Eventually, I will add a personal chef to my support team.

This brings me to an important point: go ahead and make your dream list of support-team members. You may not be in a position to build your ideal support team right now, but this exercise is like a life-vision exercise: it shows where you want to go. If you haven't defined the destination, then it's impossible to choose a path to get there.

Additionally, I have found that one of the best surprise outcomes from creating this list is that it inspires creative solutions. As I suggested earlier, you don't have to fulfill all your needs by hiring a professional service provider. For example, let's say you want help with filing. Could your kids help? What about a neighborhood kid? Is there something that you could swap with a friend who needs support in a different area? Maybe your friend would be happy to do your filing for an hour a week in exchange for consulting with you over coffee about something in your area of expertise.

Creativity is king. If you don't immediately identify several possible options for a given support need, then I encourage you to invite help from family and friends. Have them create their own support-team lists, and see what tasks you can trade, batch, or accomplish in some other creative way. Sometimes, just by creating your list, new options, ideas, and opportunities will dramatically change your life for the better.

Next Actions

✓ If you need support, begin with your partner, spouse, or roommate! Perhaps a specific task has fallen to you by default, but you would happily swap it for something else that your partner has been doing but dislikes. At a minimum, he or she might be able to think of new alternatives for adding support to your team. Have a brainstorming session together: write down every possible way to get the support you want. Then pick one option to try for a few weeks or months. You can always try something else later if it doesn't work as planned.

✓ Never underestimate what your kids can be taught to do. They might be thrilled to do a particular task in exchange for an extra hour of video-game or TV time, or permission to have a sleepover with a friend next week. Kids develop important skills in earning and managing money by providing additional value to your household or business. I believe that everyone over the age of three can be responsible for contributing in some way to the whole family's chores. I've also heard of great systems that allow kids to provide additional value in the home and thus earn money rather than simply receiving an allowance.

✓ Invite a group of friends or neighbors to work on this exercise collaboratively. You might strengthen your relationships and make all your lives easier at the same time.

✓ Take action. You might have created a long list of desirable support-team members, and if you're feeling overwhelmed, then the best next step is simply to choose one. If you could enlist help in accomplishing one type of task, which one would make the greatest difference in your life? Sometimes the energy, emotional space, or freedom resulting from just that one change can be enough for the moment—or it can inspire you to begin working on a second type of task.

Resources

Craigslist. http://bit.ly/CraigslistInfo.

Guru.com. http://bit.ly/GuruInfo.

Chosen Course Ignition Events. www.ChosenCourse.com/IgnitionEvents.

Upwork. http://bit.ly/UpworkInfo.

—37—

Delegation Plans

For years parents have wondered why their "Go clean your room" requests have yielded unsatisfactory results. One executive I know was baffled that simply saying "well-lit" was not enough information for his team to execute an adequate lighting design at their new site. And I have heard many roommates and couples have lengthy "discussions" about what cleaning the bathroom or kitchen means.

All of these examples highlight the fact that good delegation and teamwork are predominantly about good communication. The less information you offer up front about a desired outcome, the more likely you will get an undesirable and unexpected result. Therefore, in order to delegate a task or project to someone else effectively, you need to take the time to think through the process of that task and provide your team (or family) member with adequate information or support. You need to answer questions like these:

- ✧ What are the specific attributes of a successful outcome?
- ✧ How much decision-making authority are you granting your team member as he completes the task or project?
- ✧ What resources might your team member need, and where or how can she get them?
- ✧ Can you document your preferred process so that it's repeatable?
- ✧ Could you teach, demonstrate, or supervise the first process for your supporter to give him a visual, verbal, or experiential taste of the steps and the ideal outcome?

These questions might seem to suggest micromanaging, and occasionally that can become be true. However, more likely the answers to these questions provide the necessary clear communication that will achieve the desired outcome of the delegated project or routine. One of the most common problems is turning delegation into abdication due to unclear communication. Whether the person you are delegating to is your co-worker, your spouse, or your child, the same questions will need to be answered. What follows is a delegation plan: a set of steps that will help you ensure a successful outcome for both delegator and supporter.

Step 1: Define the Outcome

What are the attributes of a successful outcome for the task you are delegating? Start by getting very clear on where you're going—define the sights, feelings, sounds, products, or other evidence that will confirm the achievement of your specific end result. Part of the challenge with delegating any task is that you probably have an internal representation of the successful outcome that might not be obvious to the person to whom you're delegating. For example, imagine that you say to your assistant, "Let's get a dog for the upcoming photo shoot." You likely have a particular image of that dog in your mind, right? Is it big or small? Fluffy or sleek? A particular breed? Now, without further guidance, what's the likelihood that your assistant is going to get a dog that fits your vision? Pretty small, huh? You were thinking of a golden retriever, but he showed up with a Chihuahua. Not quite the outcome you intended.

Step 2: Define the Authority Level Granted

One of the most commonly missed elements of good delegation is identifying and communicating the level of authority being granted to the supporter. It's very different to say, "Buy a new printer for the office" than to say, "Research possible printers for the office." Make sure you don't skip this part. Here are several options that indicate different levels of authority:

- "Research options and bring them to me."
- "Research options, bring them to me, and make a recommendation."
- "Research options and bring me your recommendation for my approval."
- "Research options, implement your best option, and then I'll evaluate it."
- "Research options, implement your best option, and then we'll evaluate it."

What level of authority will get you to the desired outcome both efficiently *and* successfully?

Step 3: Assign Steps and Plan Feedback Points

As you look at the list of steps related to the project you want to delegate, you might recognize that the project will be more successful if the responsibility ball gets tossed back and forth a bit, or if your supporter brings you in to consult about the status and next steps at strategic moments. Define these moments at the beginning so that the project can stay on track and your supporter can feel confident that he or she is moving forward successfully and not wasting time or energy on an unintended path. In your task-management system, you may want to use your Waiting Response list to track when the ball is in another's court and you are waiting to hear back from your supporter before you take your next step. (For more information about Waiting Response lists see Chapter 24: Your Master List.)

Step 4: Provide Full Information

If you're delegating a process that you've done before, such as cleaning the kitchen, then you might want to communicate specifics, best practices, or expectations that are stored in your head. For instance, is there a particular cleaning product that you use on the counters and a different one for the floor? That might be obvious to you, but not to someone else. Maybe you know that wooden items shouldn't go through the dishwasher, but they may not. Because these details are part of creating a successful outcome, it might be a good plan to either demonstrate or guide each step the first time you delegate a complex repetitive process. Communicate the answers to these questions:

- What happens during each step?
- What are the attributes of a successful outcome for each step?
- Why is each step necessary, or why do steps need to happen in a particular order?
- What guidelines or lessons learned will help your supporter learn from your past experiences?

Step 5: Confirm Expectations

What you said and what your supporter heard might be two different things. So, it's helpful to have your supporter confirm what she understands about the task, project, or process. To ensure your communication was effective, have a conversation with these three parts:

A. Confirm understanding: evidence of outcome, authority level granted, and process

B. Define progress format and time-line expectations

C. Get agreement and commitment

With this sequence of communication in place, you have a really good shot at getting the result you expect. Now it's time to get moving.

Step 6: Follow Up and Provide Guidance

Once the task or project starts, make sure that you're continuing to track the progress of the projects and providing appropriate opportunities for questions, feedback, and troubleshooting. In other words, be available; don't run the other way. Then, when the project is complete, make sure you celebrate its achievement and show gratitude and appreciation for your supporter's contribution. Catch supporters doing things *right,* and always remember to say a heartfelt thank-you for their efforts.

Next Actions

✓ Make a list of the projects or processes that really don't need *you* to do them. Brainstorm who could help you accomplish them. Maybe it's not a whole project, but a few simple steps in the middle. If you've already read Chapter 36: Locating Support-Team Leaks, then you might already have a delegation list.

✓ Choose one process, project, or frequent task and identify whom you could ask for help. When you make your request, arrange a convenient time to have the discussion outlined above. (It's best not to assume that your supporter will have time for this full discussion at the same time you ask for the help.)

✓ Remember to leave space for creativity and to be surprised. Sometimes your supporters will come up with solutions that are even better than what you had envisioned. As I say often, "Create the shape, and hold it loosely." Leave space for flow and delightful surprises that may surpass even your ideal visions.

✓ Don't give up. If someone's first attempt isn't 100 percent successful, then improve communication, provide feedback, and make sure that your supporter has the information and resources that will lead to success next time. Yes, communication takes time, but if you take an hour once to teach someone to do a process that usually takes an hour every week to do, then you are still regaining a ton of time in the long run.

Resource

Fisher, Roger, William Ury, and Bruce Patton. *Getting to Yes: Negotiating Agreement without Giving In.* New York: Penguin Books, 2011.

—38—

Communication: Team & Family Meetings

The people closest to you are your most important teammates. Depending on the different roles you play in life, these people might include your spouse and kids, your assistant and direct reports, or your immediate colleagues. Whoever your groups happen to include, they are your crew—for this leg of your voyage, at least. Ensuring that good, consistent communication happens with these folks is essential.

The weekly staff meeting is a familiar professional structure that can run the gamut from pleasurable to painful, depending on how it is run and how long it lasts. There is almost always room for improvement when it comes to staff meetings, and if you're in a position to make such changes for your team, then this might be a good moment to reflect on how to improve the experience.

However, far fewer people have integrated a similar style of consistent communication within their families. When my husband and I first moved in together, we quickly realized that it would benefit us to share information about our shared lives—calendar items, household tasks, financial details, relationship "air clearing"—and we could make this easier by creating a consistent structure for doing so. All these slices of communication lacked a natural home and tended to come up at times when one or the other of us was not in the best position to receive them, due to timing or energy levels.

So, we started having weekly family meetings to ensure that we could be full partners, empowered with the same information and able to take the appropriate actions to care for our shared life. This structure was very successful for us, and over our first few years together I discovered that we had become an example for several other couples around us. People began to ask me how we developed and handled these meetings, and that is what inspired me to include a chapter about successful family meetings here.

Start with the Purpose

Every meeting, at work or at home, needs to have a clear purpose. The purpose of our weekly family meetings is to create a sense of shared information, vision, and partnership that allows us to support each other throughout the week even more fully and intentionally.

Create a Structure

What sets of information would be valuable to share? What frequent questions need to be answered each week? The content of a family meeting can vary widely depending on the family, but here are a few common topics to get you started:

- **Upcoming calendar.** Review the upcoming week, as well as anything further out that might require advance planning or action, such as family vacations and summer camps. Who has driving duties on which days? When are evening commitments shared, and when are they separate?
- **Meal planning and preparation.** This topic is so often avoided, and yet such a perfect fit for this time. What's for dinner this week, and who's responsible for shopping for and preparing it?
- **Household finances.** Consider weekly spending as relates to the family budget. Also, review cash flow as it relates to upcoming bills or expenses.
- **Household tasks.** What little tasks or big projects need to be done around the house or in your personal lives? Who's going to take care of them, and when? Errands to run? Things to fix? Calls to make? Thank-you or birthday cards to send?

- **Clearing the air.** What issues from the past week need to be aired? Having the space to ask for help or to share a point of frustration, with love and caring, can keep relationships from exploding due to pent-up emotions.
- **Weekly gratitude.** Share something you're grateful for in the past week. Say thank you for your family or partner's support.

You might want to add other topics to your meetings. You might also want to develop and refine the information systems that you use for your family meetings: shared family calendar, meal-planning system, task-management system, and family financial reports. To create more clarity in those areas, take a look at Chapter 20: Making Calendars Work for You, Chapter 21: Task-Management Tools (a.k.a., To-Do Lists), and Chapter 33: Automating Your Life.

Get Family Buy-in

If you've never had the habit of family meetings in the past, then you might be wondering how to introduce it to your partner or kids. Consider whether you want to open the conversation individually or as a group. Either way, you'll want to focus on two things: 1) the attitude you project when making the request, and 2) the outcome/benefit that your family member(s) will receive by joining this effort. If someone came to you frustrated, whining, and making demands for your participation, would you say yes? How might your response be different if your family member said, "I've been thinking about how we can simplify all our last-minute communications and frustrations and support each other even better. I have an idea that I want to kick around with you. Could we find some time to talk more about it?"

During your introduction conversation, offer your intended purpose for suggesting this new habit, and give some examples of how weekly family meetings might make everyone's lives easier—for example, fewer "What's for dinner?" questions, the ability to influence dinner decisions more directly, less confusion about who's picking up Jimmy from soccer practice, more clarity about where your family's money is being spent, and the ability to make financial decisions proactively rather than reactively.

Consider a two-part meeting. You might want the kids involved in some parts of the discussion but not others. How might you structure the meeting so that your kids participate in their parts, and you and your partner have privacy for the adult sections of conversation?

Ask for your family's input on when to schedule the weekly meeting. I'm a big fan of just after breakfast on Sunday, since everyone's rested and fed. However, there might be a different time that's more natural for your family.

Finally, if you suggest giving family meetings a try for a month (as opposed to every week for the rest of your lives), then you're more likely to get a yes. Get the soft yes, give them a taste of the experience, and then work together to improve and refine it.

My own family meetings, and the systems we use within them, have undergone regular tweaks and transformations as better options and tools become available or as new needs arise. As I like to say, create the shape and hold it loosely. Allow space for it to shift and develop organically.

Next Actions

- ✓ Define the topics that you want to cover during your family meeting. Consider recent family miscommunications. What sets of information could you discuss on a regular basis to prevent those issues from happening again? What are the most frequently asked questions in your family, and how could you answer them in advance?
- ✓ Visualize a successful family meeting. Imagine yourself after your first meeting or perhaps even a few months into the future. What will it look like and feel like? What will tell you that this new habit is successful in your lives?
- ✓ Ask the opening question and arrange for an initial conversation to discuss the benefits and mutually create a vision for success. No time like the present to ask for what you want. Worst case scenario: Give

your partner this chapter to read and then explain why specifically you want to try this process.

Resources

Asana. http://bit.ly/AsanaTasks.

Google Calendar. http://bit.ly/GcalInfo.

Mint.com. http://bit.ly/MintInfo.

Mvelopes. http://bit.ly/Mvelopes.

Weekly whiteboard calendars (for events and meal planning).

You Need a Budget (YNAB). http://bit.ly/YNABInfo.

—39—

Choosing Your Influencers

Once, in a class on social media, the presenter said that if all you are getting in your Twitter or Facebook feed are updates on what people had for breakfast or FML(F*#$ my life) posts, then it's not a problem with the tool; it's a problem with the people you're following. If you don't like what you see, then change the channel. I remember laughing at the time and being grateful that my friends only very rarely post about their breakfast bagel.

Then a few years went by, and I began attending more personal- and professional-development events. I enjoyed the energy, got information that was immediately relevant to my life and business, and suddenly created a whole new network of positively motivated and passionate people. The people I have met span the globe from London to New Zealand and all across North America, and many of us have become Facebook friends to maintain our connection. When this first began to happen, it was like a positive thought revolution took place in my feed. I hadn't realized how wonderfully connected and motivating people could be until I began surrounding myself with people who were also filled with joy, curiosity, and ambition. The change was amazing.

We've all had the experience of emotional influence or contamination. Positive and negative emotions spread so easily. For example, you call a friend just to say hi and walk unexpectedly into a misery fest. Prior to that call you were feeling rather upbeat, even cheerful, but by the time the call is over all you feel is drained. We all have bad times, sure, and none of us want to be fair-weather friends who disappear during the tough times. Nevertheless, have you noticed that some people always seem to have tough times? They surround themselves with problems, manifest them, and focus on them to the point where nothing good ever seems to happen. Or, if good things do happen, then the response is, "Well, it won't last." Ugh!

Negative Nellies, newscasters, and drama queens (regardless of gender), these are beautiful human beings who are stuck in very disempowering patterns. The problem is that they will continue to be stuck until they are ready to make a different choice. And in the meantime, they will persistently drain and infect everyone around them.

Cultivate Lilies, Get Rid of Leeches

If you recognize negative patterns in the people around you, then you have a choice to make. As psychiatrist Ned Hallowell says, "Cultivate lilies and get rid of leeches." Invest in the positive relationships, grow your lilies in a beautiful field, and surround yourself with their wonderful fragrance.

Meanwhile, pull off the leeches and leave them back in their swamp where they prefer to wallow. It's your choice where to put your attention and energy. That can include turning off the TV news, which is full of negative storytelling. And if some people in your life are living in leech land, then now might be the time to gently create more distance. Call these people less often, fill your social time with other commitments (preferably with your lilies), and create some emotional space around yourself by reducing or eliminating their influence.

Of course there are some relationships in which it's much harder to create that space. Immediate family members and co-workers might be in full leech mode, and you don't have the option to simply walk away. Perhaps you can create some space by limiting encounters, but these people are part of your journey and are not going anywhere soon. In these circumstances you need a strategy to help protect and manage your own emotional energy well and wisely.

Grounded, Centered, and Safe

The key to navigating encounters with people in leech mode is to handle your own energy differently. In order to ride through their storm, you might need a little advance preparation. The good news is that this preparation can take just 30 seconds to 2 minutes and can be done anywhere. What follows is a brief visualization exercise that can help you to immediately ground and center your own energy in your body, making you less easily influenced by others' emotions or attitudes.

Find a quiet place, if possible, and take a few deep breaths. Imagine your body as the trunk of a great tree, with roots growing down from your feet and into the earth. Reaching down deep, spreading out wide, your roots are creating a strong and stable base beneath you. You can send any emotions or energy that's not serving you in this moment down into the earth, knowing that Momma Earth will transform anything you send. Pause, and feel the energy of the earth flowing around your roots. Draw it up with your roots and send it throughout your whole body, from the tips of your toes to the tips of your fingers to the tip of your nose and everywhere in between. Feel the earth energy grounding you and holding you solidly and lovingly rooted to Mother Earth.

Next, imagine your energy rising up from your core, through your body, and out the top of your head to grow your branches. The branches reach up tall and span out wide from the top of your head toward the sky. Growing in every direction, they reach toward the sun, the moon, and the stars, whose vibrant energy shines down on your branches. Drink it in through your leaves, draw it into your branches, and bring that vivid, vibrant energy down into your body. Move it from the top of your head all the way down your body, arms, and legs to the tips of your toes.

Pause for a moment, breathe, and feel yourself grounded in place, connected to the earth, and centered in space connected to the sky. Know that you can maintain this connection and carry it with you wherever you go. Finally, since we anticipate that you are about to encounter a challenge, imagine that a clear, constantly flowing waterfall surrounds you. This waterfall can act as a filter that captures any negativity or harmful intentions and washes them down immediately to Mother Earth, who can transform and recycle them. Thus, the waterfall creates a boundary of safety around you and washes away that which does not serve you while still allowing any good energy to pass through. Imagine it less as a wall and more as a filter programmed to serve your highest intentions. Then, within yourself, find a space of compassionate strength, a knowing that any person who has leechlike qualities is on his or her own journey, for which you can feel compassion. Simultaneously you can remain strong in your own grounded energy and secure in your personal space.

You can find a recording of this guided grounding meditation in our companion resources listed below.

A Grounding Practice

If you've done this visualization and find that you're still feeling emotionally triggered when certain people are around, then it's likely that a gift of learning is waiting for you there. Get curious. What are you trying to learn from this experience? What is the gift that will allow you to transform in this moment? If you're still feeling triggered, then there's still something there for you, and it will keep coming up until you're ready to learn the lesson, gather the gift, and release this pattern for yourself. When you do, find a space of gratitude to this person who has been a teacher for you, and your entire relationship with him or her may change. He or she may become a new ally, or at least lose the power to trigger that negative emotion in you in the future.

This visualization makes an excellent daily morning meditation. I've discovered that I have a greater ability to control my mental focus and create even more joy in my life when I feel grounded and centered, and you never know who you're going to encounter during the day. There's nothing like being prepared from the outset.

Next Actions

- ✓ Take a moment to reflect on the relationships and influencers in your life. Who are your lilies and leeches? With whom would you like to spend more time? Who might be appropriate to give some more space? Start by identifying which relationships you want to cultivate, and take action to spend more time on them. Simply focusing on what you want may allow what you don't want to drop away.
- ✓ Stop watching the TV news. This was one of my quickest leech-removing decisions. When I'm grounded and in the right mind space to learn about world events, then, very intentionally, I pull up an appropriate website, but filling my world with negative news while getting dressed in the morning was supremely disempowering for my day and even more troublesome to my dreams at night.
- ✓ Build a grounding habit. When in your day might it be helpful to get a bit more grounded? Early in the morning? When you first arrive at work? Before you walk into your home at night? Practicing grounding on a regular basis has many more benefits than simply handling challenging encounters with others. It can increase focus, decrease your own emotional volatility, and give you a greater sense of connection with the world around you. For more ideas about how to develop this practice as a habit, see Chapter 14: Habits: The Power of Patterns and Chapter 35: Influence: Yourself and Others.

Resource

Grounding Meditation. www.InspiredActionBook.com/Resources.

Part 8

The Journey: Everyday Meaning

—40—

Creating an Environment That Feeds You

It amazes me what an impact an attractive and functional environment can have on your daily productivity. Long ago I learned that when I have plenty of open space around me, and preferably a beautiful view to look at, then I am significantly more productive and much happier.

Recently, when I arrived at my hotel for a business retreat in San Diego, I decided to pay the slightly higher rate for a room with a beautiful view of the harbor and the city skyline. I knew that the moments I would spend happily glancing at the view would more than compensate me for the additional expense—particularly since I spent a fair amount of time in my room writing.

To create an environment that feeds you, consider these elements:

- **Function first!** Look around your workspace and consider the layout. Are the things you use frequently within easy reach? Do you end up running all over your office space to grab additional items? Do you have to do uncomfortable contortions to get certain tools or files? All of these inconveniences take a toll on your focus and your body, which in turn can reduce your effectiveness. Consider reorganizing your workstation to bring frequently accessed tools or paperwork closer.

- **What feeds you?** Think about what kinds of spaces make you feel best. I mentioned at the beginning that I need open space around me and beautiful views. Do you need photos of the people you love? Do you need lots of light? Do you prefer to be warm or cool? What makes you feel most happy, peaceful, or energized? How could you rearrange your work environment to bring those elements into the space? You might need to add lighting, move your desk, or even move your entire work environment to a different space. Unless you're a computer programmer who hates the glare of light on your screen, dark, enclosed spaces are rarely optimal work environments.

- **Add color.** Scientific studies show that the brain functions more creatively and effectively when exposed to colors. If all you can see around you is a drab taupe, then your brain is likely to want to check out completely. Add elements of color to your environment! There are many ways to get color into a workspace: colorful folders, artwork (whether on the walls or a small art object on your desk), photographs, and colorful desk accessories (paper trays, vertical file stands, pen cups, and so on). Obviously, you can also paint the walls or choose colorful furniture if you have the ability and desire for a more dramatic change.
- **Add life!** I am a strong proponent of having something *alive* near you when you're working. My mother probably inspired this habit in me, since during her years practicing as a psychologist she always keep a single red rose on her desk. I continued this practice by keeping fresh-cut flowers on my desk or plants in my office. For you, the living element might be a plant, or at least an open window that looks out onto natural beauty. At times, even my cat curling up next to me on my desk helps me to feel more awake and alive as I work (even if he tends to sleep right on the papers I need).

Small changes such as these might seem unimportant, but when you think about the amount of time you spend in certain spaces, the value of making those environments even richer and more inviting becomes obvious. Our lives are works of art to be crafted, both in the patterns of our actions and in the physical containers that hold and support those actions. Spending a little time to consider how to create ease, peace, and joy in the structural arrangement of your space might influence the emotional-state changes you need to become even more successful in your life.

Next Actions

- ✓ Identify three ways you could make your work environment more functional and pleasant. Take the necessary steps to make those changes happen this week. If they help, then consider implementing a few more!
- ✓ Buy yourself flowers, and place them at your desk. Choose your favorites, or, if you don't have a favorite, then I recommend getting something that is both colorful and fragrant since you'll enjoy not only the sight but also the smell of them. Stargazer lilies are my favorite.
- ✓ Consider a major change. Have additional lighting installed. Hire an interior decorator to make your workspace beautiful. Renovate a guest room in your home to create a stunning office space. Ask your manager if you can telecommute for part of the week so that you could flexibly work from a cafe, from the beach, or from your beautiful home office. Your productivity may increase dramatically with such investments of time, money, and effort, and the return on the investment can be astounding. For more on creating a flexible work schedule, see Chapter 9: Freedom: The Real Wealth.

Resources

Stoddard, Alexandra. *Living a Beautiful Life: 500 Ways to Add Elegance, Order, Beauty, and Joy to Every Day of Your Life.* New York: Random House, 1986.

Varone, Linda. *The Smarter Home Office: 8 Simple Steps to Increase Your Income, Inspiration, and Comfort.* Arlington, MA: Great Meadows Publishing, 2010.

—41—

Infusing Meaning into Your Daily Life

Many of us tend to live our daily lives on autopilot. We get up and go, go, go, until finally the day ends, and we fall over into bed and get too little sleep before starting it all over again. We do things just because they're "what you do"—when you're a parent, or when you have a career, or when you have friends, or when you don't want people to hold their noses as you walk past.

Most of us have lost touch with *our* reasons and intentions for our actions. Instead, the things we do are driven by other people's expectations of us. But meaning comes from intention; it comes from knowing our "why" behind the things that we do. If we look at our lives and feel unsatisfied, then one of the first things we can do to help shift that feeling is to pause, reflect, and reconnect with our "why."

Now, it is not a bad thing to prefer that people not have to hold their noses as you walk by. The rest of us definitely benefit from you taking a shower and doing your laundry. But is pleasing others—or avoiding dirty looks—the only reason to do these tasks? Could you also be doing those tasks from a place of intentional self-care? We can wash and care for our bodies for intrinsically meaningful reasons: because it feels good to do it or because we feel good about ourselves when we do it.

Everything we do, in one way or another, is about how we *choose to show up* in the world. It's about how to take action and bring our best selves to the party each day. Showing up as your best self requires that you be present to your actions and direct them intentionally. One of the most direct routes to increase your sense of presence in even the most simple and mundane daily activity is to reconnect with your reason—your "why" for doing it.

How to Reconnect with Meaning

Reflect on the last couple of days, or think forward if you prefer. Brainstorm a list of the activities and actions that occupied (or will occupy) your time, even the mundane and seemingly trivial ones. Look over your list, and pick one. It doesn't matter which one. As an example, we'll choose emptying the dishwasher. Ask yourself, "Why is it important for me to do this?"

The easy and obvious answers will probably come first. "Because I need to have clean dishes to eat from." "Because the dirty dishes are piling up in the sink, and I need space in the sink." These answers are certainly true, but they may not be powerfully motivating. Acknowledge those answers, and then dig deeper and ask yourself again, "Why is it important for me to do this?" Listen for new answers. "Because I like to have a peaceful environment in my home, and taking care of the dishes consistently helps me create that environment." That's a stronger reason, certainly. Perhaps you can dig even deeper, however: "I empty the dishwasher because my husband and I agreed that it was his job to fill the dishwasher and mine to empty it. Taking care of that responsibility is part of how I care for our relationship and our lives together." For me that's a much more powerful "why."

Do you see how this process works? Now emptying the dishwasher is connected both to my values and to caring for those who are important to me. That's a pretty strong reason to make it happen. So, pick an item on your list and start asking yourself, "Why?" If the first answer you get is less than compelling, then ask again and see what else arises.

If you keep asking and getting weak answers, or if you are just coming up blank, then you have two options. One, ask your friends and family. They may have perspective or insights that you haven't considered. Be careful, however, because a reason that is important to them won't necessarily be compelling to you, and this is certainly not an exercise in having your family convince you to do things you are not invested in.

The second option is to ask yourself, "Do I really need to be doing this?" Maybe the reasons or purpose for this activity in your life have passed or faded over time, and you are ready to release it and move in a different direction. That's okay! In fact, congratulations! You have just freed up time and space for new things to grow in your world.

Repeat this exercise with each of the activities or tasks on your list, and give yourself the opportunity to reconnect with the purpose. By the end, you should have a list of activities and "whys" that feel compelling and motivating. The actions you do should reflect who you are and how *you* choose to show up in the world. Keep digging for your "whys" until you feel that truth coming through.

Reevaluate and Reengage

If you gained insights about many of your common activities in the last exercise, now is your chance to allow those insights to redefine the actions themselves. You might begin by checking in with yourself. Following my example, if emptying the dishwasher is important because it's how I care for my relationship and the person I love, then have I been giving it the attention and frequency that it deserves? Honestly, maybe not. It's so easy to take those daily minor actions for granted, just as it's so easy to take the people nearest to us for granted.

Recognizing and honoring *why* the task of emptying the dishwasher is important to me allows me to decide how I would like to handle it differently. Can I make that activity part of one of my regular daily routines, such as getting up in the morning, making dinner, or tying things up before going to bed? With an action like this, it's about developing the habit. Now might be the time to take a look at Chapter 14: Habits: The Power of Patterns to help you create a reengagement plan.

The activity you chose from your list may not be a repetitive action like mine is. Perhaps it is a project that you've been working on for a while, but you've lost focus or started to procrastinate. If that's the case, after reconnecting with the "why" of that project, you might want to spend some time reflecting on how to restart or move forward more effectively with it. For more support in getting started, see Chapter 25: What Is a Next Action?

Whether you've chosen a habit or a project, this is your chance to create a new plan or approach to show up intentionally for this activity. The final step is about bringing all of *you* to the moment.

Act from Intention

You've clarified your reason, your "why," for this activity in your life. You've made a plan to help you execute the activity as thoughtfully and effectively as possible. Now it's time to make a practice of showing up fully present for it. This type of daily practice is a combination of two elements: 1) connecting to your intention or purpose, and 2) being wholly present to the fullness of the activity.

Here are some suggestions to help you do this:

- Simply pause for ten seconds before you start the activity. Breathe and reconnect with your "why" for doing it. Think of your strongest reason, breathe that intention into your heart, and then begin the activity with that sense of warmth and clarity.
- Turn the activity into a meditation. Clear your mind of other thoughts. Bring your attention to being fully here in this moment with this action. Be present. Feel deeply. You could even make your intentional "why" a mantra phrase to repeat and focus your mind during the activity.
- Set a timer for five or ten minutes if the activity will take a while. When the timer goes off, pause to reconnect with your "why." Reset the timer for another interval, and repeat until the task is done.

These types of practice may feel unusual for some people—particularly for those of us who have spent years on that superfast treadmill of life where stopping or slowing down felt either dangerous or wasteful. My question to you is, how has that way of being in the world made you feel? Do you feel clear, powerful, and engaged? Or do you feel frazzled, exhausted, and drained? The practices above might feel a bit odd or even hokey to you in the beginning. However, if it helps give you a stronger sense of purpose, power, and engagement in your life, then might that be worth a few moments of feeling hokey? Consider it an experiment. Try it out for three days, and see how you feel by the end. You might be surprised.

Next Actions

✓ Repeat the process described above for other activities on your brainstormed list. Perhaps you could even create a personal ritual of pausing before each new activity of your day to take a deep breath and connect with the "why" for the upcoming action.

✓ Share these exercises with a friend, co-worker, or partner. If you do them together, then you'll have someone to help you reflect on your reasons and to help you stay connected and accountable to your practice of presence on a regular basis.

✓ Daily meditation is a way to improve your practice of presence each day. Even just five minutes of being quiet and watching your breath can strengthen your ability to be fully present in other moments as well. If you've never meditated before, then start with three minutes in the morning and three minutes in the evening. Set a timer, sit or lie quietly, and just focus on your breathing. When thoughts float through your mind, acknowledge them, and then bring your attention back to your breath. After a couple weeks at three minutes, move up to six minutes. Just allow your meditation practice to grow in whatever way feels natural, aiming for baby steps and a comfortable and gradual increase. Eventually that habit of presence and breath will appear at other points in your day almost automatically.

Resources

Buddhify 2 App. http://bit.ly/BuddhifyApp.

Brother Lawrence of the Resurrection, E. M. Blaiklock, trans. *The Practice of the Presence of God.* Nashville: T. Nelson Publishers, 1982.

Chittister, Joan. *Wisdom Distilled from the Daily: Living the Rule of St. Benedict Today.* New York: HarperOne, 2009.

Thorp, Gary. *Sweeping Changes: Discovering the Joy of Zen in Everyday Tasks.* New York: Walker & Company, 2000.

—42—

AM and PM Self-Care Rituals

Have you had those days when it felt like you were sprinting from the moment you awakened until you dragged yourself to bed with your mind still whirling? Does it happen to you often? Now, what about the opposite? How easily can you remember a day when you felt like you flowed easily through your morning routine, had a both relaxing and productive day, and wrapped things up neatly before going to bed? Those days always feel so much better, don't they?

Your morning and evening routines are about setting yourself up for success. They can be magical times, both metaphorically and literally. When we put the right pieces in place during our AM and PM routines, we feel better about ourselves and our lives, and we are frequently better prepared to get "more" out of our day. As my friend Lisa frequently says, "The battle for the day is won or lost the night before." She has discovered, as I have, that how you end the previous day can dramatically affect how functional and productive you feel the following day.

No one's AM or PM routine looks quite the same, but there are common elements:

- ✧ Bathing, dressing, and preparing to go out into the world (or undressing and wiping away the world at the end of the day)
- ✧ Exercising
- ✧ Eating
- ✧ Connecting with and caring for family
- ✧ Meditation or spiritual practice
- ✧ Personal reflection or quiet time; journaling

- Connecting to the world by reading newspapers, blogs, or social media; watching TV
- Planning your activities and tasks for the day

Does your morning consist of some set of these activities? What else do you include? Do you *want* to include some of these elements but find it hard to create the habit? (See Chapter 14: Habits: The Power of Patterns.)

What about your evening routine, either postwork or before bed? I bet it includes many of these same activities—perhaps even the ones that you couldn't fit in to the morning because you wouldn't have been able to get to work at a reasonable time.

One of the most powerful shifts I have seen in my clients (and myself) happened when they approached their morning and evening routines not simply as "what has to happen to get out the door or go to bed," but rather as rituals of self-care. Most of the elements I've listed above are likely important parts of your life. When you do them consistently, you likely feel happy and feel good about yourself. When you miss or exclude them, you probably start to feel lousy.

I believe that the key to creating powerful AM and PM rituals comes from two elements: rhythm and intention. You probably already have some type of rhythm—a regular order and pace—to the actions you take in your morning and evening. But have you taken the time to think about why you do things in that order or whether there might be a benefit to changing it? For the items that you have yet to include in your daily patterns, have you considered where specifically the activity could fit in your daily rhythm so there would be an easy segue from a well-established activity into the new one? Rhythm is a powerful force, both to make habits easier and to give us a feeling of rightness as we flow from one activity to the next.

The second element, intention, involves the combination of intentional planning and increased presence during your routine activities. When brought to any specific activity, even the most simple or mundane, intentionality and presence can transform that activity into a ritual with purpose. Zen practitioner and author Gary Thorp addresses both the power and the simplicity of treating everyday activities as a spiritual practice in his book *Sweeping Changes: Discovering the Joy of Zen in Everyday Tasks*:

> *There are not many things in this world less mysterious than Zen practice. When you're washing the breakfast dishes, there is no need for you to think of Zen at all. Just stick your hands in the water. You don't have to study the mysterious intermingling of air and water or the relative value of energy transformation or the emptiness of the cups and saucers or the miraculously surprising adhesive qualities of marmalade. The simplicity of the situation is captured in the following saying: The Zen master asked his student, "Have you had your rice?"*
>
> *"Yes."*
>
> *"Then, wash your bowl."*

Turning your AM and PM routines into rituals isn't about making every action a metaphoric or grand exploration of the mysteries of the universe. It's about focusing your mind and entire being on where you are and what you are doing in this specific moment and doing that activity with a clear understanding or intention for its purpose in your day and life. We discussed this topic fully in the previous chapter (Chapter 41: Infusing Meaning into Your Daily Life).

Why do we bathe and brush our teeth? Perhaps it's so people don't run away scowling from us, but preferably it's because we want to take care of ourselves, our bodies—this vehicle that is carrying us through life. Same with exercise. For the gym rats and runners who get a high, I know there is an inherent motivation (and I'm slightly envious), but most of us work out because it makes us feel better about ourselves, or because we know that it's essential to staying healthy and living a long life with our family and friends. That is the intention; that is the "why" of the action.

Creating Your AM and PM Rituals

So, how do we apply this philosophy to our morning and evening rituals? Here's a process that can help you revisit your morning and evening routines and turn them into more pleasing and powerful rituals.

Download a copy of our Morning & Evening Ritual Design worksheet at www.InspiredActionBook.com/Resources, and grab a pencil (preferably).

Refining Your Rhythm

1. Walk through your current "standard" day. On the appropriate part of the worksheet, list the activities that you frequently include in your mornings *in the order you do them.* Then do the same for the evening.
2. Ask yourself, "What's missing?" Look at the list near the beginning of the chapter to help jog your memory. Are there items that you don't currently do but want to start including more frequently? Where would they fit best, morning or evening? Looking at your current routine, imagine when these new activities could fit in to your rhythm. Then write it in that spot.
3. Look at the order of your steps. How can you stitch them together into a more flowing ritual? Is there anything else you want to change about the order of the actions?
4. Determine the necessary timing to make the ritual comfortable and successful. How long will each step take? Add up all the steps and figure out when you would have to start to complete the full ritual.

Infusing Intention

1. What is the purpose of each step? Why are you doing it? What is your intention for including it in your ritual?

2. How could you help yourself become more present during each activity? What frequently interferes with that presence? Your smartphone? Computer? TV? Can you turn them off?
3. Close your eyes and visualize moving through your morning ritual as written. Can you feel a sense of flow from one activity to the next? Do the same with your evening ritual. Do the two create a sense of clear bookends for your day?

Making It Happen

All this lovely planning and envisioning will be for naught without some clear methods to help you implement your new rituals. Here are some suggestions:

- Post your Morning & Evening Ritual Worksheet in your bedroom, bathroom, or kitchen to remind you of your new routines.
- Set timers on your smartphone, tablet, computer, or microwave for the intended duration of each step to keep you on track and to serve as a reminder to bring your focus and attention back to being present in the next activity. That timer ding can help you do both!
- Pause between each step for one breath, and bring your attention back to presence before moving to the next step.
- To keep you on track, put up Post-its around your house with simple phrases like "Remember presence" to serve as brief visual reminders that you will encounter naturally during your ritual.
- Talk to your partner or family members about the new ritual you want to create. At minimum, ask for their support to change the experience of your mornings and evenings together. Or, even better, help them to create similar rituals for themselves.

Using a combination of these methods may help you move your ideas and good intentions into lived, sustainable action, and that's the goal! Pick which ones work for you and give them a try, or brainstorm some of your own. Find the methods that will help you create greater meaning in your life.

Next Steps

✓ If you are adding new steps to your AM or PM rituals, then it might be necessary to do some reorganizing to make sure you have everything you need at hand at the appropriate time. (Reorganizing might be helpful even if you aren't adding anything new to your routine, but simply have a somewhat disorganized home.) Ask yourself, "What tools, items, or spaces do I need to successfully complete my ritual?" Then take the time to gather the items and set them up. (For more help with organizing your space, read Chapter 16: Eight Steps to Organizing Success.)

✓ Create a shortened emergency version of your rituals to use as needed. What gets included, and what gets cut? Make sure that your emergency version doesn't become the standard. This is for that late night out with friends or that day with the early-morning meeting. If you travel a lot, you might want to consider how these rituals will change when you're on the road and create a travel version.

✓ You might also want to create a similar type of ritual for the end of the workday or for the after-school/dinner hour. A powerful routine at this part of the day can help ease the work-home transition. (See Chapter 43: Transition Rituals.)

Resources

Richardson, Cheryl. *The Art of Extreme Self-Care: Transform Your Life One Month at a Time.* Carlsbad, CA: Hay House, Inc., 2009.

Thorp, Gary. *Sweeping Changes: Discovering the Joy of Zen in Everyday Tasks.* New York: Walker & Company, 2000.

—43—

Transition Rituals

As I talked one day with a client of mine, she observed that she had the hardest time staying focused during transition times. When one project was finished, she found herself feeling confused or adrift until she identified the next big task. On the flip side, I have experienced the opposite problem: the adrenalin rush of zooming from one task to the next can keep me moving until finally I crash out both mentally and physically, completely drained of energy.

In a similar way, I've worked with several clients on their travel preparation and recovery patterns. One senior executive I consulted with traveled frequently for work, and he found that upon returning home he almost immediately felt swamped and exhausted. This situation was significantly impacting his sense of effectiveness and well-being.

All of these challenges are connected to how we handle our transition times. How might life change if we gave ourselves a real chance to make transitions, whether between tasks, between blocks of travel and homecomings, or even between life chapters? I believe we can ease these transition-time challenges by crafting intentional rituals that allow us to both rest and refocus. To understand better what this might look like, let's explore some ideas and examples.

Transitions between Tasks

Throughout every day we shift our attention from one action to another, sometimes every few minutes, sometimes at least every hour or so. We often make these shifts automatically, hopping from task to task as a bee does from flower to flower. But too often, in spite of all the research clearly discouraging it, we multitask. Thus, we weave a braid of activity in our lives in which there are rarely any clear beginnings or endings, just a continuous flow (perhaps "onslaught" would be more accurate) of activities.

There are three steps that we can take to address this exhausting problem.

1. **Choose one task and give it your full attention.** Most often you'll actually finish that one task much faster, leaving space to take on the next task as well. We have idealized the concept of multitasking as being a hugely advantageous skill, but too often it leads to low-quality work and a state of constant distraction. I often sigh internally when I'm interviewing new candidates for our company and they proudly tout their excellent multitasking abilities. I would rather hear that they have an excellent ability to focus on the task at hand and complete it with high standards.

   However, the shift from being a multitasker to a single-tasker is not easy for many people, since our minds have become used to the adrenalized overload. Slowing down that rush of activity to select one task and give it our full attention can feel like shifting from fifth gear to first. A better analogy, however, might be the difference between firing a round of bird shot versus firing a target rifle. Yes, the job gets done either way, but the first way wastes a lot of energy and resources, and the second way makes for much greater accuracy. So, give it a try, even for 15 minutes to start: just pick one task and stick with it until it's complete. Or, as Robert Kiyosaki says, "FOCUS = Follow One Course Until Successful."

2. **Pause between tasks.** This pause need not be lengthy. You can just take one deep breath and ask yourself, "Where will I *choose* to focus next?" The space of a breath gives your body a brief experience of rest and reset, which can immediately boost your mental and physical energy. However, if you've been at something for a while, this might be a good time to take a 5-to-15-minute break. Get up, stretch, walk around, look out a win-

dow, and look at anything green and growing. All of these actions can help your mind shift gears and prepare for the next activity.

3. **Craft a transition ritual.** Professional tennis players have a particular sequence of actions that they take between points to help them rest, lower their heart rate, and prepare for the next burst of energy. What if you created a brief transition ritual that allows you to close one action, rest powerfully, and intentionally select the next task of focus? Perhaps it could consist of three deep breaths, a neck and shoulder stretch, a glance at the clock to see how much time you have before your next scheduled activity, and a quick check of your task list to choose your next action. Such a ritual can accomplish two goals: 1) help slow down the incessant racing from one activity to the next, and 2) provide a structure to help with that sense of being lost or adrift between tasks.

Travel Transitions

Most of us have had the experience of preparing to leave for a trip and feeling exceptionally productive (and sometimes overwhelmed) the day before we depart. Unfortunately, we have also probably had the experience of coming back from a trip and feeling inundated by emails and thrown immediately into meetings and action, often igniting cascades of stress that potentially unravel the sense of relaxation that our vacation was intended to create.

Just as we did with transition times between tasks, we can address these challenges by blocking out transition time before and after a trip and crafting rituals to help us depart and return easily. If you are going on a trip for more than a couple days, consider blocking a transition day just before and just after your trip so that you can focus on your preparations and recovery. Schedule minimal outside meetings or calls on those days. One great tip is to set your "Out of Office" phone and email messages to say you are coming back one day later than you actually return. Then you are automatically helping set expectations to give you more rest and recovery time.

You could also create departure and reentry checklists that list all the common activities or actions that you need to take prior to leaving or immediately upon returning home. This will take some of the thinking out of those tiresome times and help you avoid forgetting things in the potential chaos.

Life Chapter Transitions

When we make major life changes, we often do not give ourselves adequate time to make the transition and then recover from it. Think about the times when you've made a major life change: moving homes, changing jobs, having kids, retiring, and so many others. Did you give yourself enough time to adjust to the shift? How long did it take for you to feel reestablished and grounded again? Too often we rush through or truncate these transitions so that we have no clear sense of a beginning, middle, and end to the experience. While these types of changes frequently take place over several months, we can still create the transition intentionally.

In recently speaking with a client who is in a job-hunting process, I was thrilled to hear her say that she would request to delay her start date by several weeks before beginning her new job. She realized that allowing her emotions and mind to unspool from the hugely stressful experiences of the past job would allow her to feel more stable, grounded, and prepared for the new one. She decided to take the time to make sure that any new arrangements needed for her daughter's care could be made gracefully, rather than in a rush.

Whether it's a matter of taking a few weeks or even months off, or just removing or halting all optional activities during transition times, the important first step is to realize that you have *choice*. Start by asking yourself these important questions:

- What could you do to make this life transition as graceful and easy as possible?

- ✧ How could you remain even more emotionally and mentally grounded each day as you explore these new life changes?
- ✧ Who could help or support you to create the best possible result for this new chapter of your life?

Consider asking other empowering questions to guide you on your path. (For more on formulating empowering questions, see Chapter 34: Leading by Example.)

Breathing Space

Usually the key to any type of transition, whether between tasks or between life chapters, is, quite simply, breathing space—giving yourself permission to pause, settle, and breathe your way from one moment to the next. Without that pause to breathe, it's easy to find ourselves hurtling through our day or through our life, when we could be living with even greater depth and intentionality. What could you do today to create more breathing space for yourself and others?

Next Actions

- ✓ Play with transitions for the rest of today. Start by simply becoming aware of when you complete a task. Take one deep breath before you start the next task. How does that feel? What other actions could you do in those moments of pause to make the transition to your next task more intentional or thoughtful? Perhaps brainstorm a list of options and try a few of them today and tomorrow.
- ✓ Create breathing space in your meeting schedule. Try planning meetings to end ten minutes before the hour. This habit gives you—and everyone else at the meeting—at least ten minutes of breathing space before the next commitment.
- ✓ Work with your kids to create a transition ritual for when they arrive home from school. How could you shape that important time as they shift from school to home to help them feel more settled and grounded? Even just three deep breaths might go a long way.

✓ Driving or commuting can be great transition time. What could you do during that time to allow your mind and emotions to rest? I became a huge fan of listening to fluffy audiobooks during my drive time. Dipping for a while into a fictional story allowed me to let go of whatever I had just been doing and arrive at my next adventure fresher and more mentally prepared. Perhaps for you it's something else—NPR, gentle music, or meditating while on the train. What might you try tomorrow?

Resources

Buddhify 2 App. http://bit.ly/BuddhifyApp.

Niurka. *Supreme Influence: Change Your Life with the Power of the Language You Use.* New York: Harmony Books, 2013.

Schwartz, Tony. *Be Excellent at Anything: The Four Keys to Transforming the Way We Work and Live.* New York: Free Press, 2010.

—44—

Leaving Space for Flow

Can you remember the last time when you had a completely unscheduled day? You may have had a few things that you wanted to attend to during the time, but they could happen at your own discretion and when the energy was flowing right for you. Some of our best work happens when we allow ourselves the space for flow and inspiration in our days. Our best work also improves when we manage our personal pace and ensure we have space to rest throughout our days.

The demands on our time and attention today are persistent and never-ending. There is always more information to listen to, read, or learn. We keep a long master list of actions that we want to do—and those are only the ones we've thought of and captured so far. And, of course, there are the people and relationships that need our attention, encouragement, and nurturing. There is, and always will be, more to add to your plate, but I'm going to make a somewhat shocking assertion: you still have control over the pace of your life. I know, you may be scoffing now: "Tell that to my boss" or "Tell that to my eight-year-old."

The fact is that the pace of our lives comes down to two specific elements:

1. How many things we say yes to
2. How much space we leave for flow in our daily schedules

Surprisingly enough, both of these elements are connected to or primarily dependent upon your own decisions. Now, to address the scoffing crowd, I will acknowledge that some of the things you sign up for are a package deal. For example, some careers are, by their nature, high adrenalin, time driven, and fast paced; action must happen immediately as it arises. Wall Street stock trading and ER medicine are two careers that come to mind. However, if that is your profession, then you likely knew about the unique lifestyle going in—and if that lifestyle isn't working for you now, then you have a big decision to make.

I'm sure that a few other careers are tense and high paced, but many of them feel that way because we make them so. We have created and bought in to the assumption that everything must be tense or fast paced. Why? Three reasons. First, many of us like to show that we know how to perform under pressure. Second, we want others to see us as the "go-to" guy who can take care of anyone's problems. Third, we simply like to be able to say yes to people when they ask us for things—even if what they ask for is virtually impossible.

In some companies this assumption is cultural and systemic. However, those companies often chew through their employees and have miserable retention rates because they have created an unsustainable lifestyle. If this describes the company you work for, then you have two options: 1) raise the issue to management and try to create and encourage systemic change, or 2) look for a new place to work. If you are a leader at such a company, then you have the same two options—with the added responsibility of recognizing that your willingness to push hard on this issue might benefit not only your own life and sanity, but also the lives of hundreds or thousands of your colleagues who are similarly struggling.

The core point is that the pace of your life depends largely on your own decisions: your decisions to stay or go in a particular career or job, your decisions to push for a positive change or live with a struggling status quo, and your decisions to say yes or no to that new project when your plate is already full.

When it comes to parenting, obviously, you signed up for the ride, and you can't look for an available exit. However, if you feel like you're zooming from baseball practice to ballet to tutoring to dinner to bed, then your kids probably feel the same way. The current generation of children is growing up with a persistent experience of being overscheduled. We want to give our children everything—all the opportunities and experiences that will provide them with the "well-rounded" life that will get them into a good college. All I can say is "Oy! Too much!"

You are the parent. The choices are yours to make, and part of parenting is creating appropriate limits. Whether it's limits on scoops of ice cream or on the number of after-school activities that can happen in a given season, it's both your opportunity and responsibility to care for your children's energy management as much as you care for your own.

Saying Yes to Less

This lesson of saying yes to less has been hard fought in my own life because there are so many exciting ideas and activities that spark my curiosity. Keeping my commitments reasonable is an ongoing practice that needs constant attention. The desires drawing me to pack my world with new projects, tasks, and other commitments are many: to learn new things that contribute to my self-growth, to have new experiences, to support and connect with the people I care for, to build new relationships in my life, and to support and encourage the organizations and communities that have nourished me.

The urge to say yes can also come from a sense of obligation, expectation, or fear of "letting people down." We use these reasons to justify saying yes yet again, but all of them—both the noble reasons and the disempowering ones—distract us from the essential question: what am I sacrificing by saying yes to this?

Time, energy, focus, and peace of mind are not infinite commodities. We have only so much of each of them during our journey through life. So, when you commit any or all of these resources to a new activity, you are inherently reducing your availability for your previous commitments. In other words, don't say yes lightly. Consider and evaluate the commitment you are making. How much of your time is the commitment going to require? How much mental, emotional, and physical energy will be required? What might you be sacrificing if you add this to your life? It's easy to consider only the benefits of saying yes while ignoring the possible costs, but the reality is that every new yes has *both:* benefits and costs.

My client Heather faced this exact challenge. For several years she had been the chairperson for the regional breast-cancer awareness gala. This charity was close to her heart because of family struggles with the disease. Year after year she had recommitted to the responsibility, and it was a big one: hundreds of people impacted, months of advance planning, and several weekly hours of work. Then an opportunity in her regular job arose: a huge promotion to chief of staff for one of the senior executives of this global corporation. This brought her into my world because I had been working directly with that executive for several months.

During our first meeting, Heather shared her concerns about what was on her plate: the much higher level of responsibility in this new role and her preexisting commitment to the gala. It became clear that while she was thrilled to accept this new position, she needed to make a graceful exit from her role as chairperson for the gala—a role that was too important to do poorly. So, after brainstorming options for next steps, she found her answer: to shift her gala responsibilities to someone whom she could mentor for a year before handing over the full position. Saying yes to the promotion meant saying no to chairing the gala, but Heather was able to recognize that decision relatively quickly and hand off the gala gently to create more space in her life.

Have you already said yes to too many things? If so, perhaps it's time to take some corrective actions. Two options can immediately improve your situation:

1. If the end is in sight, then focus and get it done. Close the open loop, finish the project, and hand off responsibility for any future tasks or projects to someone else.
2. Formally "decommit" from the responsibility. If it involves other people, then you will have to consult with them, ask permission, and take the necessary steps to transfer the work to someone else as Heather did.

Either way, it's time to clear the decks and create some more space for flow in your life.

Scheduling Space for Flow

Overcommitment clogs our minds and spirits, but it really starts showing up and hitting hard when it clogs our *days,* and we feel like we are in an all-out sprint from one urgent, mandatory action to the next, with no time to eat or breathe. When these happen only occasionally—like on the day before a vacation, when you close dozens of open loops—then they can feel good and productive. But when most of your days are filled with a sense of urgency, you've got a problem on your hands.

We *need* space and downtime in our days. Having that space allows us to respond appropriately, without panic or scrambling, to the unexpected or emergent issues that appear during each day. In addition, the space simply allows us to breathe and to be more present to each of the actions we take because we have had time to make transitions in focus (see Chapter 43: Transition Rituals). Either way, multiple strategies can help you protect your space for flow.

Here are a few suggestions:

- *Create a rhythm to your days.* Plug your meal and break times in to your schedule *first*. Then plan your meetings, tasks, and activities around the breaks. (See Chapters 14 and 15 for more ideas on life rhythm.)

- *Define your limits.* Find a pace that works for you. I rarely schedule more than three meetings or other time-sensitive activities in a day. That gives me space around those activities for smaller tasks (emailing, phone calls, and so on) or just eating, resting, and preparing for the next task. I know some of my executive consulting clients would never limit themselves to three meetings per day; just come up with a rhythm that works for you. If your meetings are short, then maybe you could have four to six 30-minute meetings per day. Then you'll book only three to four hours of your day, thus allowing sufficient space for breathing, thinking, and other creative work.

- *Schedule in-house days.* Choose one day every week or two when you don't leave your home or office for outside meetings and activities. Just removing travel time can bring a lot of space for flow back into your day.
- *Block out creative, retreat, or clear-the-decks days.* Perhaps there's a big project that's going to need a lot of your creative energy, or you need to do some big-think strategic work on an upcoming challenge or initiative. At times like these, block a whole day in your schedule to create the space for that creative or reflective work to flow. Similarly, if you start feeling behind or underwater, or you're just returning from a trip, then block out a day to get back up to speed. (Again, for any frighteningly fast-paced executives, try blocking at least a half day if a full day seems inconceivable.)

Appreciating Downtime

One of the most frightening aspects of life today is the widespread assumption that if we're resting, then we're not being productive. The presumption that we have two gears—on and off—is killing our lives and hearts one day at a time. Downtime *is* productive. It creates and recuperates the energy necessary for the next burst of activity. It is our low gear that prepares us to take the next hill. Many of us have a little chatterbox tape in our heads that berates us for sitting down when we could be doing something. It's time to rip out that tape and create a new recording.

If your chatterbox tape starts going off each time you pause to rest, then here's your magic strategy for shutting it up. First, take a deep breath and drop your shoulders. Then tell the chatterbox, "Thank you for sharing" and take another breath. If that doesn't quiet it down, pull out the big guns and repeat to yourself, "Taking care of *me* is my priority right now. I deserve a break, and I'll be ready for that after I'm done resting." Show your chatterbox mind who's boss!

If your chatterbox mind can't handle unstructured downtime, then set a timer. Perhaps start with three minutes and build it up over time. I recommend aiming for a 15-minute break for every 90 minutes of focused action. So, if you were just in a three-hour meeting, then you'll want a 30-minute break afterward.

Protect your downtime like a tiger until you can comfortably sink into it and float around on it as if you're floating on the pool raft from your last vacation.

Next Actions

✓ Get clear on your current commitments. If you've already created your master list (see Chapter 24), then pull it out and review it. If not, then brainstorm all the major projects and activities currently on your plate. What are the essential items on your list? What can wait for another time? Postponing action on some projects will increase your focus and power, and it might mean that you reach the finish line on some projects sooner rather than pushing forward haphazardly in 20 different directions.

✓ Create a daily structure that allows for flow and downtime. Block breaks, and especially meal times, into your calendar, and plan around them. If necessary, set alarms on your computer or smartphone to help you remember to wrap up and take your break as planned.

✓ Ask for help. Team up with a co-worker, friend, or family member and take a break or a walk together. Having a partner can help you guarantee that you get that time away from the grind. Just make sure that it is genuine downtime, not another excuse for a meeting!

✓ Practice breathing or try meditating during your downtime. Part of the goal is to increase your mental and emotional clarity, and few contribute more to that outcome than breathing and meditating.

Resources

Loehr, Jim, and Tony Schwartz. *The Power of Full Engagement: Managing Energy, Not Time, Is the Key to High Performance and Personal Renewal.* New York: Free Press, 2003.

Schwartz, Tony. *Be Excellent at Anything: The Four Keys to Transforming the Way We Work and Live.* New York: Free Press, 2010.

—45—

Tech-Free Time

My husband and I spent over eight days camping in Squamish Valley, British Columbia. No phones, no email, no Internet…nothing. For full-fledged members of the digital era, it felt odd! No quick Facebook posts, no way to look up an answer on Wikipedia, and no finding the name of that song on Shazam. For me the first day or so was an adjustment. For my geeky, digitally inclined husband, apparently the twitches lasted most of the week, and he eagerly dove for the Wi-Fi as soon as we returned to civilization.

Upon returning to the digital world, what did I discover in my email inbox? Over 400 new messages, of which about 320 were immediately trashed. In other words, perhaps ten messages each day were actually worth my time to read or respond to, and only around 15 of them actually required a response. Some were FYI messages, some were interesting opportunities for webinars that had passed, and a few were newsletters that I do find worth a read. My point? After being cut off from digital civilization for over a week, no one died and nothing groundbreakingly exciting was missed.

Now, don't mistake me—I'm a big fan of the instant-gratification connectivity of our digital era. I love my iPhone, which is rarely more than four feet away from me on most days. However, I have also recognized that its power to distract and interrupt me from being fully present to the people and activities of my life is a significant cost. Sometimes that cost is not worth paying, and that's when even people who are naturally digitally inclined need to get clear: our gadgets are tools, not toys. They help us to accomplish certain tasks more quickly and easily, but they are not the lifelines they masquerade to be.

Sometimes the best way to be present to your life is to decide not to be available to the 100,001 possible alternatives that you could be googling, texting, or Facebooking. So, unless you plan on moving to a mountainside in a remote region, a fully conscious and intentional adult will have to choose to turn off the gadget and "go quiet," as submarine commanders call it. And no, I don't just mean turn it on vibrate. We all know that we can all hear that theoretically silent buzz when it's in your pocket or on the conference table—and it's still distracting.

Choosing Tech-Free Times

The first question you might want to ask yourself is, when do I want to be technology-free? For example, it's a good idea to ditch the technology anytime you are meeting with other people for business or social events. I believe that the people directly in front of you deserve your full attention for the length of time you have scheduled to be with them. If you think something urgent or emergent might arise in the midst of a long business meeting, then make sure to ask for appropriate breaks so you can step away and check in. This suggestion goes for dinner parties, children's birthdays, recitals, games, church/synagogue/worship, and any other event whose purpose is to show people in your life that you care and are here to give them your attention or support.

Additional tech-free times might include times when you are doing certain focused activities, such as writing, exercising, meditating, preparing for a big presentation, and strategic planning. What are the times when interruptions or distractions cost you the most? These are great candidates for tech-free time.

You might also consider holidays as prime quiet times. Imagine Thanksgiving, Hanukkah, Christmas, Easter, or Independence Day without the digital interruptions...just being present to your loved ones. Or, whether you are religiously devout or not, what about a digital sabbath once a week? I initially learned about this concept from my conservative Jewish aunt and uncle who wouldn't touch anything electronic (even light switches) during the Sabbath, and it also has been explored by William Powers in his book *Hamlet's BlackBerry* How might your life be different if you took one day a week without distractions to be fully present to yourself and your loved ones?

Tech-free time could also include everyday family meals, when the goal is to spend time connecting with your family and learning about their days. After all, do you really *need* to check to make sure the newest draft of the report has been sent around? If this knee-jerk reaction sounds familiar to you, then perhaps this can be your wake-up call. Your life and relationships may be passing you by, and now you have a choice to make a change.

To start figuring out which times will be your tech-free times, think about the different categories of activities in your life: meetings, dinner parties, writing, children's games, holidays, family meals, and so on. Decide which activities you want to give your full, uninterrupted attention. Make this decision *once,* and live it for the next two weeks. Two weeks from today, you can take a moment to reevaluate your decision.

Defining the Parameters

Some of you might be having minor heart palpitations at the idea of being disconnected and unavailable for any period of time (my husband being one of them). This issue has gotten so common that scientists in Britain have conducted studies on nomophobia, the fear of being out of cell-phone contact.

If you suspect that you might have picked up this particular fear, then what if we wean you off gently? If turning the entire device off makes your heart tighten, then let's start by going full silent mode: turning off the vibrate function and leaving the device in your pocket or briefcase. Start by going without it for the duration of a meeting, perhaps 30 to 60 minutes. Then try increasing your phone-free time by intervals, perhaps adding on 15 minutes each week. Slowly and gently show yourself that the world won't collapse if you're unavailable for short spans of time. After all, even a weekend away is less than eight days camping in a glacial valley.

When you can start managing without your cell phone's instant connectivity, then you can begin thinking about how far you want to take your screen-free times. Perhaps the first phase is weaning away from incessant email and Facebook checking. Then you could move to a fully powered-off cell phone for periods. What if you turned off your Internet at home? Just shut off or unplug your router for a few hours or a day. Or perhaps you could eliminate TV and video games in favor of family game time? Or maybe you'll turn off *all* gadgets: cell phones, TVs, computers, tablets, and even Kindles.

If you weren't twitching before at the thought of just turning off your cell phone, then you might be now. My husband looked terribly pained the first time I suggested such screen-free time for us. I had to relent on the Kindle because reading was far too important an alternative to eliminate. My point is that you get to define your own parameters for your tech-free time, and if the people in your life balk at your ideal extreme of no screens at all, then scale back on the scope and work up to it. Thus far, I have been able to get my sweetheart to agree to screen-free holidays for eight days each year. We'll need more time to work toward my vision of having a screen-free sabbath each week.

The idea is to start somewhere. What times in your life could you go screen-free, and what exactly would that mean or include? You decide! After all, our gadgets are tools, not toys. We decide when the tool can stay in the bag.

Next Actions

✓ Choose your version of tech-free time. Select the types of time that you will include (meetings, social parties, family meals, holidays, and so on), and decide what that will mean (no email, no cell phones, no computers, no TVs, and so on). Define your goals and make an initial commitment, perhaps for a month. Allow me to suggest more than just a week; it will still feel strange for most people with only a week's adjustment time. Give yourself time to get out of the awkward period and into the peace that follows.

- ✓ Invite your family, friends, or co-workers to join you or to support you in your commitment. Explain your reasons and purpose for the shift and, if necessary, negotiate the parameters to make it possible for you to accomplish the goal together.
- ✓ After your first commitment period, reevaluate. How did it feel? Did you adjust? What would you want to do differently? Reflect, adjust, and decide if you want to recommit.
- ✓ Consider taking screen-free vacations. I will say that a full week of no digital distractions and interruptions can bring you to a powerful level of presence that can rarely be achieved in "regular" life. Going without TV, Internet, computers, and phones for a week teaches you a lot about yourself and your ability to be quiet and present to yourself.

Resources

Carr, Nicholas. *The Shallows: What the Internet Is Doing to Our Brains.* New York: W.W. Norton & Company, 2011.

Powers, William. *Hamlet's BlackBerry: A Practical Philosophy for Building a Good Life in the Digital Age.* New York: Harper, 2010.

Part 9

Course Correcting: Knowing Where You Are

—46—

Your Strategic Life Plan

I knew that I needed to get away. It's not that anything was particularly going wrong with my life. I had a career I enjoyed, was in a good relationship, and had a beautiful apartment overlooking a lake in a great neighborhood. Nothing was *wrong* per se, but I felt overwhelmed and confused. I had been losing focus and steam in my everyday life, and the activities that I normally jumped out of bed to do were beginning to feel like drudgery.

I knew that it was time to dig deep and really check in with myself and where I was going. It was time to adjust my strategic life plan and get my heart and focus back on course. At the time, I was living just outside Boston, and for years I had heard about a lovely little town on the North Shore called Rockport. I looked it up on a map and discovered that the town was about an hour from my home. Within 30 minutes, I had found a historic inn where I could get a room with a view of the ocean (and a hot tub), and I knew this was what I needed to do. So what that it was February and not quite the season for an ocean-side retreat!

It was the right decision—even with the biting February winds off the Atlantic. The retreat gave me time to rest and to review what was happening in my life. It allowed me to rediscover my passion and develop a plan for how to bring my life more into alignment with that passion every day. It was time for some big changes, but I knew that I could do them gradually over a few years rather than dramatically overnight.

What Is the Next Chapter of Your Strategic Life Plan?

I truly appreciate the metaphor that our lives are lived in chapters. A chapter is usually a set of years, like your time in college, the period when you worked at your first job, the time in your marriage before your kids, and your empty-nest but preretirement years. If we look back on our lives, usually the chapters become clear, and they are marked by significant transition events. Sometimes those events are foreseeable, but occasionally they are not. (After all, you didn't see that health crisis or layoff coming, did you?)

If you reflect on your life right now, where are you in your current chapter? At the beginning, somewhere in the middle, or coming to the end? Often, people pick up a book like this one at the beginning or the end of a chapter as they look to redefine their focus for the next chapter that they know is coming (or that they are determined to create).

Perhaps now is a time when you're ready to step back and take some time to ask yourself the really big questions. We began this book with an exploration of purpose and a guide to creating your life list and lifestyle list. If you have not yet read and worked through Parts 1 and 2 (Chapters 1 through 10), it might be a good idea to do so now. It will probably put the next exercises into context. In many ways, this final part returns to those beginnings to offer a system that helps you check in on your purpose, direction, and life list in a meaningful way throughout your life.

In Chapter 47: Yearly Planning, we will explore how to create an annual retreat that gives you time to refocus, plan, and commit to the upcoming year's goals and activities. The current chapter, however, is most appropriate for your "life chapter" transition moments—or any moment when you find yourself wanting to choose a clear course for your life. You might bundle this process into your annual retreat every few years, or it might arise naturally as an instinct to step away from daily life, reflect, and recalibrate. These are the times when you step back and do a purpose and passion check.

As a guide through this experience, allow me to offer some suggestions and questions that can help you to create a space in which to find your best answers.

Creating the Space

Reflection time is best when we give ourselves permission to truly step away from our current life routines, and that will require a little planning. Here are a few thoughts to help you get that planning started.

Block off a week. A week is my preference for these life-chapter reflection times, but it should be at minimum four days, to give yourself the time and space alone to do your inner work. I encourage a week or longer because in reality you're unlikely to be able to dig deep for the first one to two days, while you unwind from the everyday and open up to the reflective work at hand. If you want to make it two or three weeks, then go for it!

Consider going away from home. Often a change of location can lead to clarity and possibilities that we cannot see from our usual vantage point. It doesn't have to include getting on a plane and flying somewhere (although it might if you live in the Midwest and are craving a beautiful tropical beach.) As you saw in my story, I simply found a lovely inn within driving distance of my home. It was away from my usual stomping grounds but still within easy reach.

Take your reflection tools. Journal, capture book, master list, plenty of pens, inspirational reading, music that puts you into a reflective space, perhaps a sketchbook...take along any tools that can help you clarify and process your thoughts and feelings in this moment and bring into focus what you want to create in the next chapter.

Decide who could help you. While I often recommend experiencing these life-chapter retreats alone, you might feel strongly that you would benefit from having your partner or a close friend with you. Just make sure you're clear with him or her that the trip is intended not as a vacation but as a reflection retreat, and make sure he or she is on board with participating in your process. Another solution can be to put your close friend or family member on alert that you might need to call while you're away to process your thoughts and feelings. Then you can create brief pockets of togetherness and still have significant space alone.

What to Do When You Get There

I encourage you to listen to your instincts about how you will structure your time. Here are some ideas if you feel you need further guidance.

On arrival day. Take some time to get grounded in your space. Unpack your luggage, explore the space you have chosen, find a seat with a great view, and just breathe and observe the world.

Talk to the concierge, the front-desk clerk, or someone local about great local restaurants—since you will have to eat on this trip and having excellent nourishment and beautiful atmospheres will definitely support your reflection work. If you prefer, check Yelp and bookmark some good restaurant options.

When you're beginning to feel more grounded in this place, take a few moments to pause and *set your intention* for this experience. You can think it and send it out to the universe as energy, meditate on it, write it in your capture tool, or say it aloud. Make it a positive statement about *what you intend to have or create* while you're here. This moment essentially begins your ritual experience and starts your reflective ball rolling. While you might choose to do activities that are purely for the joy of the experience on this trip, you are making it clear to the universe that you are open and looking for insights about how to focus the next chapter of your life.

During the middle days. These are your good "work" and reflection days. Listen to your energy. Do you want to take a walk someplace beautiful? Read an inspirational book? Write in your journal? Brainstorm new items for your life list? You'll find a rhythm and a pattern that is innately yours. Just open yourself and trust that in each of those activities, the insights you need to move forward will arise.

When you're ready, it's time to write a vision for your life. What do you want to create for yourself? To help you get focused on your inner work, here is a set of questions to guide your reflections and develop your vision:

1. Do you have a purpose statement? If so, what is it? Does your purpose statement still feel like it fits? (Read Chapters 1 and 6 for help.) Is it time to redirect, refine, or focus more deeply on a particular area, or is it time to shift directions entirely?
2. What might be the major attributes, activities, or life milestones during the next three to five years of your life?
3. Which key elements of your current life chapter do you want to *continue* in the next one?
4. Do you have any dreams or experiences from any previous chapter that you are now ready to fulfill?
5. What are your major goals in each of these areas: finances, career, fun/recreation, health, relationships, personal life, and your life legacy? Aim for one to three goals in each area.
6. Are there experiences that you are now ready to leave behind to start this new chapter fresh and feeling empowered? What healing and forgiving needs to happen in order for you to leave them behind?
7. How could you live each day to its fullest and know that if this chapter were your last, you would have no regrets?

Answering these questions will give you a much clearer vision of the life that you want to create in the next few years. Having that vision will allow you to manifest it.

On your final day(s). Now would be a great time to write or update your strategic life plan. Just as businesses have strategic plans to guide their focus and development, I believe we all can have a plan to help guide our lives. Will it change? Might you go off course? Absolutely! Did you know that the *Apollo 11* astronauts on their way to the moon were "on course" only 3 percent of the time? They were making constant course corrections.

The point of having a plan is to define where you intend to go. You can *never* be on course if you don't have a defined destination. Living life without a plan is simply meandering rudderless. It means consistently wasting this beautiful opportunity to live, learn, and give to those around you.

Your strategic plan can focus on the intention, energy, and outcomes you want to create for the next three to five years—i.e., your next chapter. Look at the goals you identified in question 5 above. Can you choose or identify where your focus needs to be in year one, two, or three in order to accomplish each one? This is your chance to break big goals down into smaller milestones. While you might include visions of the horizons and years beyond, most of your attention should stay on this upcoming chapter. Make sure to slot items from your life list into your strategic plan as well. This is how you ensure that they *happen* instead of remaining a perpetual "maybe someday."

You can download a template to help you create your first strategic life plan on our website at www.InspiredActionBook.com/Resources.

When you have come to the end of your life-chapter retreat, make sure you spend a few moments in gratitude. Make a list of all the things in your life for which you are currently grateful. I challenge you to think of at least 100.

Next Actions

✓ Make your strategic life plan a lived daily experience and a focus tool. This is not something to bury in a drawer and forget. For some strategies to keep your goals active and alive, read (or reread) Chapter 10: Vision the Possibilities, Then Make Them Manifest.

✓ Share your strategic life plan with a close friend, family member, or partner. Ask him or her to help you bring your plan into action, or at least cheer you on as you do. If you have a life partner, then you might want to work together to create some goals on your plan so that you are moving forward collaboratively.

✓ Celebrate every goal you achieve! There's nothing like a good celebration to share your gratitude with the universe and prepare it to send you more of what you want.

Resources

Blanchard, Robert and Melinda. *Changing Your Course: The 5-Step Guide to Getting the Life You Want.* New York: Sterling, 2008.

Canfield, Jack, and Janet Switzer. *The Success Principles: How to Get from Where You Are to Where You Want to Be.* New York: HarperCollins, 2005.

Miller, Caroline Adams and Dr. Michael B. Frisch. *Creating Your Best Life: The Ultimate Life List Guide.* New York: Sterling, 2009.

Yelp. http://bit.ly/YelpInfo.

—47—

Yearly Planning

When was the last time you took a true vacation? Only in the past two centuries has the concept of a vacation from work evolved. It was a time when we stepped away from our regular routines for rest, reflection, and renewal. In some areas of the world and in some families here in North America, this lovely break still exists, but in far too many contemporary households the concept of a time away from the routine has been lost to the never-ending onslaught of work activities. Either that or it has been transmuted into a crazy-making adventure of running kids around theme parks or trying to "do France" in three days. Does this sound familiar?

Similar to the modern concept of a vacation is the more ancient idea of a retreat: a trip to the country house, to the healing spring to "take the waters," to the monastery. The retreat was a period of time away for renewal and reflection. Its goal was to bring a return of clarity, energy, and focus that would last beyond your return home. Today, when we think of a retreat, we usually think of time spent at spas and yoga centers, where we theoretically undergo physical and spiritual renewal through lots of wheatgrass smoothies and downward dogs. Don't misunderstand me—I'm a big fan of spas and am a yoga practitioner myself—but I propose that an annual retreat could be so much more.

Your yearly planning retreat can certainly be a wonderful time to renew your body and soul, but it also can be a chance to check in with yourself and plan your course for the upcoming year. One year from now, what do you want to have accomplished? What are you committed to achieving? Your yearly planning retreat is the best possible time for you to set your personal direction and to define the accomplishments that you will be working toward during the upcoming turn of seasons.

This might also be a great experience to have with a coach or facilitator. Some clients of mine choose to schedule a private intensive day to allow me to facilitate their annual retreats and help them move strongly forward. I *love* these days with my clients as we meet all over the world and envision what they choose to create for their lives.

As Bill Gates said, "Most people overestimate what they can do in one year and underestimate what they can do in ten years." I definitely agree and feel the truth of that, and still so much *can* be accomplished in a year. It is the turning of one cycle of seasons, and thus is an easily defined span of time to focus your attention upon—more so than the indefinite span of upcoming years or even your current life-chapter horizon. You can really zoom in: what will bring purpose and passion to your life this year?

As with all planning, and high-level plans in particular, you want to create a shape and hold it loosely. Opportunities and detours might arise midyear, and you'll need to respond to them. You can reevaluate your priorities and commitments during your seasonal reflection days as necessary. (See Chapter 48: Seasonal Planning for more about that process.) However, as is so often said, the difference between successful people and everyone else is having clear goals. Here is your chance to get clear on your goals for the upcoming year.

Goals vs. Future Accomplishments

I used the word goals in the previous paragraph because it is the most common term for a specific intention that you are currently working to achieve. But how would it feel to think of goals as "future accomplishments" instead? Switching the language to express presumed accomplishments rather than hopeful possibilities paints your future as a set of defined outcomes. It engages your energy differently. So, that is the language I will use from here forward.

Creating the Space for Your Yearly Retreat

Retreats are generally more creative when we step away, so here are some recommended planning steps:

Set aside a full day. Your yearly retreat might happen in the middle or near the end of your vacation time, or you might just take a long weekend away and give your yearly planning retreat a full day of that weekend. I think it's a good idea to get some physical and mental rest time prior to your planning day to help you decompress and be ready to think broadly and with a fresh, expansive mind about your intentions for the upcoming year. So, yes, a retreat is a great thing to do after a day at the spa or yoga retreat center. Those environments are certainly peaceful and restorative. But they aren't necessary. Perhaps you could just go away to a cabin in the woods, rent a room at a nearby B&B, or borrow a friend's vacation home or guest room. I do think there's a value to getting away from your normal environment and routines for long enough to allow you to think creatively about what you want and what is possible during the upcoming year.

Pack your tools. You'll want to take along the items that will help you to both think clearly and expansively: your strategic life plan, your life list and lifestyle list, your capture tool, your master list, plenty of pens, inspirational books, and music that supports creativity (I'm a fan of classical or instrumental-only, and baroque music is highly recommended creative work).

Shut off the world's distractions. This one day is very important to the next year of your life, so I encourage you to make it focused. That means no email, no phone calls, no Facebook…nothing that's going to interrupt or distract you. You could make it a completely tech-free time, but that depends on whether your resources (such as your master list) are in paper or digital systems. So, use your best instincts. This retreat is yours to create, so you'll want to protect it.

What to Do on the Day

When the day arrives here's how to get started:

Get expansive. Ideally, you're starting with a good night's sleep so that you can be as fresh as possible for this day. In the morning, I recommend beginning by gently and creatively opening your heart, mind, and awareness to what you want in your life. A morning walk, meditation, or journaling time might work well. This would be a great time to begin peppering yourself with empowering questions, as we discussed in Chapter 34: Leading by Example. Here are some possibilities:

- What could I create this year that would catapult me into the next level in my career?
- How could I bring even more joy into my relationships with my family, friends, and co-workers?
- Who is a model of success for the next phase of my life?
- What project could I undertake that would bring me the most meaning and fulfillment in the upcoming year?

Empowering questions will prime your mind for the creative process of your retreat day.

Review your resources. Review your life vision, strategic life plan, life list, lifestyle list, and/or master list. What rises to the top of your awareness? What are you feeling a desire to focus on most this year? Which project or future accomplishment could you commit yourself to that would move your life forward this year?

Ecology check. If you were to achieve the outcomes that are at the top of your awareness, how would they impact you? How would they impact the people around you? Do these outcomes align with the highest possible intention and benefit for yourself, your family, your community, and the planet? We are powerful creators, and this is your chance to ensure that you are pausing to be careful what you wish for.

Get focused and specific. Could you commit to one to three accomplishments? Anything more than that, and you'll get scattered focus—

and scattered results. Identify the accomplishments you want to focus on this year, and make them powerful! Have you ever heard of SMART goals? Specific, measurable, achievable, relevant, and timely are the classic attributes of goals. I have gone on record saying to pitch them, which I still stand by. However, there are two aspects of them with which I do agree: specific and measurable.

Think about the difference between these two possible accomplishments:

I want to be healthy and fit this year.

I will weigh 130 pounds, attend three zumba classes each week, and complete my first half-marathon.

The language of the second one is a big improvement, right? It tells you the exact outcomes you intend to create in order to meet your definition of "healthy and fit."

Additionally, when phrasing your future accomplishments, focus on what you're moving toward in your life, rather than what you want to move away from. Rather than making the outcome about *losing* 40 pounds, frame it as a state of happily weighing whatever your ideal weight would be. This pulls you toward the joyous feeling of being healthy rather than away from the pain of carrying weight you don't want. What you focus on expands, so focus on positive, desirable outcomes rather than pain and problems.

Final visualization. Once you've written your specific, measurable one-year accomplishments, it's time to charge them up with energy and transform them into what I call "Vivid Future Accomplishments" (VFAs). Find a quiet place, close your eyes, and step into your life after your accomplishment has been achieved—just over one year from now. What do you see? What do you hear? What do you feel? What's happening in your life at this point? Imagine it vividly. Breathe it into your bones. Know it is already done in the world of creation, and this year you will simply manifest the accomplishment you are envisioning. Visit www.InspiredActionBook.com/Resources for more about VFAs, visit.

Wrapping Up

Lock in the energy of your outcomes. How will you feel when they are fully manifested and embodied? Anchor that energy into your body and soul. Then, end your day, knowing that you have done important work to create the future you want. Send your intention out into the universe. Know that it is already done, and now you are just walking the path to manifest it even more clearly in your daily life. Charge your future accomplishments with the certainty that whatever your set your mind and heart to create can be achieved in alignment with the highest good for yourself and others.

Next Actions

- ✓ Pick a date for your annual retreat, and block it off in your calendar. What feels like the natural beginning and end to your personal year? It might be January, it might be September, or it might be sometime in the spring. There is no right answer. You don't have to wait until that month to do your first yearly retreat. Just scale your accomplishments to be realistic for whatever partial portion of the year remains. Begin thinking about your upcoming retreat. It's never too early to start asking empowering questions and getting curious about what you could choose to create in the next year. Make it part of your daily or weekly reflection time. Talk about it with friends who can share your positive and creative attitude toward life and encourage you.
- ✓ Talk with your spouse or partner either before or after your yearly retreat. Enlist his or her support, whether that means cheering you on, sharing your vision, or actively working with you to achieve it. Having a partner on your journey can be a huge benefit, both to support you during challenging times and to help celebrate your successes.

Resources

Niurka. *Supreme Influence: Change Your Life with the Power of the Language You Use*. New York: Harmony Books, 2013.

Vivid Future Accomplishments. www.InspiredActionBook.com/Resources.

—48—

Seasonal Planning

Have you had that moment in which weeks and months have flown by, and suddenly you realize that it's June and the year is half over? Where did that time go? And how is it possible that you've barely even started on the big goal that you set for yourself this year?

Somewhere between your annual retreat and your weekly focused planning, it is helpful to have strategic check-ins on your goals and intentions for the year. Once I was talking with a professional speaker about this topic, and he asked for advice on whether he should review his strategic goals weekly, monthly, or quarterly. Although I think it would be admirable to focus on your higher-level goals on a weekly basis, I believe it would distract from the project- and task-level focus that you really need to keep things moving. I find the same to be true of doing a check-in monthly. It's astounding how quickly a month can zoom by, and taking the several hours necessary to do a strategic check-in once a month seems a bit excessive to me.

However, setting aside a half day (a whole day might be even better) roughly once per quarter to review the past few months of activity and to bring your life into focus for the next few months can make for a wonderful ritual. I find that this quarterly strategic check-in often matches the shifting of the seasons for me. Think of it this way: how much do your energy and focus shift as the seasons change? Kids' sports schedules shift, and projects that you had energy for in the summer might be impossible to focus on during the winter, or vice versa. While our lives today are more removed from these cycles than were the lives of our ancestors, there is still both a practical and an emotional value in embracing such check-ins as one season closes and the next begins.

I often plan my quarterly reviews to take place around the equinoxes and solstices, thereby honoring the close of one season and the beginning of the next with my seasonal planning ritual. This chapter aims to give you a sense of what such a day might look like and how to make the most of it.

Timing

I find that many people are attached to the standard calendar: January through March is the first quarter, April through June is the second, and so on. If that's you, great. If not, then embrace the fact that your quarterly check-ins and annual retreats can be on whatever schedule feels right for you.

Perhaps your family always takes a vacation in August, and it's easy for you to get a day or two of reflection to yourself for your annual planning retreat at that time. If so, then your first quarterly check-in might be in November. As I said, mine are tied roughly to the solstices and equinoxes and take place in March, June, September, and December. Spring (March to May) becomes my first quarter because it's when my energy is highest, and it's easier for me to get into a growing and expanding mood.

When planning for your seasonal retreats, block off at least a half day (three to four hours) to yourself. I prefer a full day, but whatever your schedule allows can work. I also recommend either scheduling your retreats directly into your calendar once a year, thus committing the time up front, or at least writing a reminder at the beginning of the months when your check-ins are due to schedule the day during that month.

Picking a Location

One of the most important aspects of both yearly and quarterly planning rituals is the benefit of doing them somewhere away from your usual routine. These are times where you are trying to zoom out from your everyday life and consider the bigger picture. For decades, corporations have reaped the benefit of taking executives away from the office to retreat locations to do their "big think" work more effectively.

Pick a location that is convenient to home but far enough outside your everyday activities to feel refreshing and novel to you. Here are some possible suggestions that might help you brainstorm options in your own area:

Natural Environments	Urban Locations
State or national park	Café
Beach	Library
Arboretum	Restaurant
Campground	Spa/retreat center
Conservatory	Museum
Lake	University campus
Garden	Friend's house/apartment

Listen to your instincts, and go for whatever area feels most attractive, but do consider a few possible logistical needs: bathrooms, food, and power/Internet for your technological tools. You might design a day that incorporates a couple locations. My quarterly planning days often start in nature somewhere, move to a café for some food and writing time, and wrap up back in nature as I settle in to my decisions and envisioning process.

What to Take with You

While this question partially depends on the locations you choose (for example, don't forget your sunscreen if you're going to be outside for while), there are a few things that you'll definitely want:

- Your strategic life plan
- Your year plan

- Your life list and lifestyle list
- Your master list
- Your capture tool and pen/pencil (if required)
- Your calendar

These are probably the most important items to allow you to effectively review where you are and where you want to be going.

What to Do When You Get There

Your seasonal-planning ritual aims to accomplish two goals:

1. Reflect on your progress for the past quarter
2. Plan your Big Rocks for the next quarter

What is a Big Rock? You may have heard of this concept from Stephen Covey's classic metaphor involving how to fit everything in to your life. You can find the video listed in the resources below, but the point is that you have to put the big, important stuff into the "container" of your life first and then fill the cracks and crannies of time with all the little things that arise, rather than the other way around, because the important things will get crowded out otherwise. The important commitments are the Big Rocks, and the other stuff makes up the pebbles, sand, and water that take up the rest of the space in your days. So, using this concept, seasonal planning is your chance to figure out what the Big Rocks are for you these days. Here is another way to think about it: what milestones are important to work on now so that you will achieve your yearly goals?

There are several possible ways to go about reflecting and planning during a seasonal check-in. One option is to break the reflective experience into three sets of questions in the categories of purpose, passion, and productivity.

Aligning with your purpose.

- Is your attention where you want it to be? What are your Big Rocks for this quarter?
- Are you working on projects that connect to your purpose and bring meaning to your life?
- Do you see and feel your purpose manifesting in your everyday life?
- What projects on your life list or master list might you bring forward in order to increase your daily or weekly experience of deeper meaning?

Igniting and feeding your passion.

- Is your energy where you want it to be?
- Have you integrated enough of all the areas of your life this past quarter? What could you do differently next season?
- What items from your life list might be important active projects for you this quarter?
- Are you integrating both work/purpose and fun/joy into your life?

Focusing and structuring your productivity.

- How have your systems been working for you? Do any of them need attention or tweaking?
- Are you taking care of your energy management and incorporating enough rest or recuperative time and self-care?
- What activities could you plan into your daily or weekly life to nourish you?
- What habits would be valuable to intentionally build in the upcoming season?

Asking these questions will allow you to both take your temperature on your current status and illuminate some areas that could use attention in the near future. It's likely that you will identify new projects or goals, some of which might get incorporated into next season's plans, but others of which can be captured on your life list or master list as On-Hold Projects for the future.

If simply reflecting on the questions above feels ambiguous, then try this process:

1. **Rest, relax, and recuperate.** Take a bit of time to do something pleasant that will allow your mind, heart, body, and spirit to settle in to a new place. Take a walk, go for a bike ride, curl up and read something inspirational, or just sit somewhere and look at something beautiful—anything that might nourish you.
2. **Do a self-check in.** How are you feeling about life, what you are doing, and where are you going? Ask yourself the questions above, and write or make notes about any issues, questions, or ideas that come up.
3. **Review what has had your focus.** Look over your year plan and your master list, both Active Projects and On-Hold projects, and notice any patterns or insights that arise. Have you focused predominantly on one area of your life? If so, that may be fine, but now is your chance to change that if necessary. Have you ignored or neglected any of your goals for the year? What projects might need to be created to get those goals moving?
4. **Make plans for the next three months.** What projects need to be brought to the fore? What can be completed, eliminated, or downgraded to On-Hold to address any concerns that came up in steps 2 and 3?

Does this process sound doable? This seasonal planning ritual is your chance to make a strategic readjustment to your life during the course of the year, as well as an excuse to just take some time away from the daily grind to rest, reflect, and open your creative mind. For me, it has become a favorite time that I look forward to every three months.

Next Actions

- ✓ Schedule a seasonal planning ritual for each of the next three quarters and an annual retreat for next year.
- ✓ A few weeks before your seasonal planning day, begin thinking about where you'll go and how you'll structure your time. Take a few moments to brainstorm elements for your planning experience. You might capture your ideas in your capture tool to help you plan.
- ✓ Try doing seasonal planning in parallel with a partner or friend. While most of us need time alone to reflect deeply, you can either plan a meeting for the following week with your friend or design a day that includes time apart and time together to discuss your insights and plans.
- ✓ Explore the possibility of creating themes for each quarter. Appropriate quarterly themes might be growth, reflection, exploration, teamwork, and renewal. Sometimes having a central idea, spirit, or word to focus on for each period helps you make in-the-moment decisions about whether a particular project is appropriate for you to work on now or should be reserved for later.
- ✓ After your seasonal planning day, share your insights or results with your network. Post progress updates on your blog or on Facebook. Support from your friends and family can help keep you moving forward.

Resources

Covey, Stephen. "Big Rocks." http://bit.ly/CoveyBigRocks.

Richardson, Cheryl. *The Art of Extreme Self-Care: Transform Your Life One Month at a Time.* Carlsbad, CA: Hay House, Inc., 2009.

Stoddard, Alexandra. *Time Alive: Celebrate Your Life Every Day.* New York: Collins, 2005.

Stoddard, Alexandra. *Living a Beautiful Life: 500 Ways to Add Elegance, Order, Beauty, and Joy to Every Day of Your Life.* New York: Random House, 1986.

—49—

Weekly Planning

Planning our time and activities is something that we all do in order to make sure that we get important tasks done and show up in the right places at the right times. For many people, this planning process happens fairly naturally when they glance over their schedule or to-do list. However, many of those same people are constantly frustrated by showing up to meetings unprepared, forgetting about errands that needed to be accomplished before the party this weekend, or trying to slam three weeks' worth of work into the last week before the deadline. Has this ever been you?

If so, then this chapter—indeed, all of Part 9—is for you. I have been this person in the past, and I have worked with others around these challenges for years. Almost universally, the solution to these crunch times and embarrassing moments involves better and more consistent planning.

A weekly planning ritual can save you untold frustrations, heartaches, and stressful days. A half hour per week of planning might help you lower your blood pressure, reduce your stress level, and even save you from a heart attack. (Did you know that several studies have shown that a higher number of heart attacks occur on Mondays, as people head back into work frustrated, disengaged, and overwhelmed?) Proactive planning will certainly help you feel more in control, on target, and ready for each day.

The "Why" of Weekly Planning

The purpose of a weekly planning ritual is to keep your task management system and your mind focused on the actions and projects that are immediately relevant to your current success. It also allows you to decide strategically what you are *not* going to worry about this week. This weekly process is the linchpin of keeping you productive and on-target for your daily life. Moreover, a frequent reason why productivity systems unravel is a lack of commitment to developing this weekly planning habit.

Planning is a maintenance part of life, kind of like doing laundry. If you only do it once a month, then you'll have a huge mountain to sort through, a bunch of loads to process, and an entire day of work on your hands. If you do it once a week, then it becomes more manageable. Adding in a daily planning element can help you make it *much* easier. (See Chapter 50: Daily Planning.)

During the weekly ritual, the focus is at both a project level and a task level. You are reviewing your entire master list, bringing it up-to-date based on recent events, and making strategic choices about where you are going to focus your attention in the upcoming week. In other words, you are maintaining your task-management system to allow it to continue functioning effectively for you and create a sense of natural flow.

Choosing a Regular Weekly Time

There is no universal right answer to when a weekly planning ritual should happens. It depends on your preferences and your life circumstances. However, here are some of the most popular choices and the rationales behind them to help you consider what feels right for you:

Friday morning or afternoon. You've gotten to the end of your workweek (if you're like most folks), and this is your chance to review the week's events, to integrate all the new information, and to decide what you are going to focus on next week. This allows to you start Monday morning fresh, knowing exactly where to focus your attention.

Sunday morning or evening. Some people prefer to use the end of their weekend to settle in and get ready for the new week. Perhaps by Friday afternoon you are too tired to think straight, but after a couple days of rest you are ready to bring yourself up-to-date and make plans. Some couples make this a mutual planning time and incorporate a family meeting to have conversations about plans or finances that might affect immediate decision-making or to review joint schedules and get on the same page about how to support each other through the week. (For more information, see Chapter 38: Communication: Team & Family Meetings.)

Monday morning. If you are slow to get moving on Mondays, then you might like to use your weekly planning ritual as a way to gear up for the week. Ideally, you are rested from the weekend at this time.

If none of these options feel right, then find your own right time. Perhaps Wednesday afternoons are quiet in your office and thus are a perfect time to settle in and make new plans. Whatever works for you! The most important thing is to choose one time and make a habit of it. Knowing that you will spend that time planning will allow you *not* to think about it at other times and trust that you'll get up-to-date on your system then. My best suggestion is to mark it right on your calendar so that you'll be disinclined to give up your planning time to other commitments.

How Much Time Will It Take?

If you stay current weekly, then your planning time will likely take an hour or less. However, the more weeks you skip, the longer it will take to get your systems back up-to-date and to make the needed plans and decisions.

What You Will Need

For your weekly planning ritual, you'll want to have the following items available:

- Your master list (See Chapter 24)
- Your daily task list tool (via your smartphone, index cards, or other task-management tool)
- Your calendar

- Your capture tool (See Chapter 19)
- Your email inbox (via your computer, laptop, or smartphone)
- Your paperwork action items folder

Weekly Planning Ritual Steps

Here are the main steps of an effective weekly planning ritual.

1. **Capture new projects.** Add all new projects that have arisen in your world—personal, work, and otherwise. Review your capture tool, calendar, and email inbox for cues about these new commitments. You can also walk around your space, both at home and in your office, to see if any new projects appear upon this visual inspection of your domains.
2. **Determine next actions.** Review your Active Projects on your master list and identify next steps. Based on what you accomplished this week, what must happen next to move each project forward? Any projects that have no further steps can be removed or marked as completed. Are there any projects that need to be demoted to On-Hold Projects given your current commitments and workload?
3. **Choose upcoming tasks.** Which tasks are going to be most important and relevant for the next week? This is a subset of tasks from your master list that you want on the immediate horizon. For paper systems, you might write these on a separate page for this week. For digital systems, hopefully there's a way to segment or mark these tasks as "Upcoming," "This Week," or a similar category.

Optional additional steps include the following:

1. **Start planning for new projects.** For new projects (see step 2), figure out the immediate next action (at least) or capture the major steps if appropriate or possible. Doing this type of plan-

ning once a week allows you to avoid thinking about it constantly during the week when you should be taking action (thus batching the planning task). It also allows you to consider the individual project in relationship to the whole group of Active Projects currently on your plate. Thus, you might see tasks that can be done together (for instance, two things that require you to talk to your co-worker) or determine why you would choose to make one next action a priority over another when you consider them together.

2. **Review your On-Hold Projects and your life list for items to upgrade.** Do you want to upgrade any of these items to active? A project might get upgraded because the deadline or event is coming up and it's time to start getting busy. Or, it might be that a recent event has made this project more relevant or useful in your current life than it was previously.

One member of my staff makes this weekly planning ritual a treat for herself on Sunday evenings by pouring a glass of wine, lighting a couple candles, putting on some soft music, and pulling out her planning materials. There's nothing like a little ambiance to make a necessary maintenance task enjoyable.

Next Actions

✓ Choose a good time during the week for your weekly planning ritual. Write it into your calendar for the next four weeks as a trial. After that time you can check in with yourself to evaluate (and potentially shift) the timing.

✓ Brainstorm ways to add ambiance to your ritual. Will you do it at a favorite café over a latte? Will you and your partner crack open a bottle of wine and plan together? What could make this weekly activity something to look forward to?

- ✓ Try implementing the above five steps during this week's scheduled planning time. How long did it take? Did you get distracted or start actually *doing* things rather than just planning? What would you change next time?
- ✓ Talk to your partner or a friend about doing your planning ritual together. Sometimes adding a social element and an accountability partner can improve the result and make the experience more fun.
- ✓ Have a staff member plan with you, or hire a productivity expert or professional organizer to help you implement your planning process consistently and regularly.

Resources

Allen, David. *Getting Things Done: The Art of Stress-Free Productivity.* New York: Viking, 2001.

Allen, David. GTD Methodology Guides. http://bit.ly/GTDGuides.

O'Connor, Anahad. "The Claim: Heart Attacks Are More Common on Mondays." New York Times, 2006. http://bit.ly/MondayHeartAttacks.

—50—

Daily Planning

What does a good day look like for you? If you are like many people, a good day includes getting done what you had planned and feeling good about the actions and decisions you took that day. Therefore, part of the recipe for a good day starts with making a good plan, and yet this is where most of us begin to go awry. Our day is doomed before we've even started because we've created either a completely unrealistic plan or no plan at all.

Perhaps you remember Elizabeth, the young entrepreneur whom I described in Chapter 29. She was overwhelmed with all the projects and activities involved in building her company, and she would consistently get to the end of her day feeling frustrated and incomplete because she hadn't finished even a third of the items on her long task list for the day.

When Elizabeth and I began to work together and discussed this problem, I pointed out to her that she wasn't really creating daily to-do lists. Instead, she was creating *dream lists* for all the things that she *wished* she could accomplish. She was setting unrealistic expectations for herself and her day. Thus, rather than feeling great about being two or three steps closer to her goals and putting in consistent, intentional, productive work all day, she felt constantly frustrated that she hadn't done more.

I asked her, as I ask you now, how is this pattern helpful? The key to shifting the tendency to create dream lists is to create a better daily planning ritual. We will explore how to create such a ritual for yourself, but it boils down to this: choose *one* thing—your Inspired Action. Your Inspired Action is a 5-to-30-minute task that you intentionally *commit* to completing today before you finish work or go to sleep. What is the *one* thing that, if completed, will help you feel great about what you accomplish today? What is one specific *task* (not project) that will help you move forward toward your goals?

The Power of Your Inspired Action

I have seen the magic of this "choose one thing" practice with many of my clients. It puts *your* priorities first. *You* choose what's most important for you each day. By choosing you create a sense of both intentionality and control in each day. When practiced regularly it also establishes a new pattern of behavior by which you consistently choose what's most important to you and get it done...over and over again. Develop this habit with consistency, and you create evidence for your internal belief that you are someone who "gets stuff done."

Any project, any dream, any goal is accomplished one step or task at a time. Do you want to write a book, build a company, or take a trip around the world? What would happen if you did *one* task that would move you forward toward that goal each day? Obviously, doing more than one will get you there faster, but even with just one step each day, you *will* get there.

Focusing on only one item might feel ludicrous. "After all," you might think, "I've got *all day*; surely I can get a bunch more things done than just that!" Yes, you probably can, but if you remember creating your life rhythm map back in Chapter 15, you know that "all day" probably equates to three to six hours of actual work time. And in your usual day, how many of those three to six hours are usually dedicated to responding to others, participating in appointments or meetings, or quickly addressing the issues that arise naturally in the course of the day? I'm going to guess anywhere from 40 to 60 percent of that time—which yields much less time for your own tasks. That's why we need to get laser-focused and set realistic expectations.

Whatever your actual amount of available time, the real point is to create a consistent practice of intentionality and accomplishment in your life. You will go further and do more in your life if you create a belief that you consistently succeed at the goals you set for yourself, rather than perceiving that you never quite measure up or reach the intended outcome. This concept is the true secret behind the Inspired Action. You are developing your belief in your own intentions and achievements by making your daily tasks consistently achievable.

In all likelihood, you will knock out your Inspired Action in your first hour of work. That's great. Then it's time to move on to your Three Bonuses. Your three bonuses are the next three tasks that, provided you have the appropriate time and energy, are your next priorities. Some days you will have a packed schedule and only be able to get your Inspired Action done or maybe one bonus too. That's okay! We all have highly scheduled days. You'll also have days when you get through your Inspired Action and *all three* bonuses, and those are days when you celebrate! That's a good day. Take a break, have a dance party, take a walk. Then you can decide if you want to look again at your master list and choose something else to knock out because you're on a roll. If you do, then recognize it's a *choice* to keep going because you're on fire. You can also choose to say, "My work for today is done." Then switch gears and rest, relax, and enjoy taking care of yourself and your family.

The key to this perspective is that your *commitment* is to your Inspired Action, and everything else is gravy. If you start shifting out of this mentality, then you will have slid right back into creating hopeless dream lists.

How Do I Choose My Inspired Action?

The real challenge for most of us is deciding what your one thing should be, and this is where a good daily planning ritual can be a real asset. Start by choosing a time of day for your daily planning ritual. Generally I prefer the end of the previous workday as a time to wrap everything up and leave me ready to go as soon as the next day starts. However, first thing in the morning works for many people too because it allows them to check in on their energy that day and plan accordingly. Decide what feels best for you, and try it out for a few weeks.

Let's talk you through choosing your Inspired Action for tomorrow (or, if you want to choose one for today, then go for it!). Here are the steps:

1. **Bring your task management system up-to-date.** Review and update your master list with anything new that's popped up. (Hopefully, you've already created this valuable tool, as discussed in Chapters 23 and 24.) Make sure that you're looking at a full picture of your options so that you can pick the best one. Check your email, calendar, or paper action items for new projects to be integrated into your system. Then glance over the whole list, your menu of options, or at least your "Upcoming" items, as discussed in Chapter 49: Weekly Planning.
2. **Check what's already been scheduled.** How much time or energy will you have tomorrow? Look at your calendar and locate your blocks of work time between your current commitments. Will you be in your office? Are you working from home? Are you going to be on the road between appointments, with some free time that you could leverage?
3. **Choose one task.** Drill down to a specific Next Action, something that will take 5 to 30 minutes to complete. Select a task that will a) fit the time and resources available, and b) move you forward on an active project that is important to you now. If it will take more than 15 to 30 minutes, then it's probably a project, not a task. (For more about identifying Next Actions, see Chapter 25: What Is a Next Action?)
4. **Check in and commit.** If you get this one task done tomorrow, will that feel like a win for the day? You want to make sure that your Inspired Action feels important and valuable to you. No one else can define this for you. Can you commit to getting it done? This isn't a "want to" or a "might do." This is the one thing that you are fully committing to make happen.
5. **Put it where you'll see it.** Create your daily to-do list, and write your Inspired Action at the top and your Three Bonuses

beneath it. Write it on a Post-it note, an index card, the whiteboard in your office, or wherever you can keep it front and center in your mind.

6. **Make sure you'll have what you need.** Collect any resources you'll need to be effective and to complete your Inspired Action: files, contact information, your laptop, and so on.

Common Daily Planning Pitfalls

Here are some of the most common mistakes I see with daily planning:

Getting distracted in the middle of your daily planning ritual. I suggested starting by reviewing your emails and calendar for additional items that need to be incorporated into your master list. However, this is not the time to shoot off that email to your co-worker about next week's meeting or to start brainstorming guests you are going to invite to your parents' 50th anniversary party. As long as the meeting and anniversary party appear where they should on your calendar and master list, then that's all you should care about right now.

Starting major project or goal planning. Project planning takes a while, and it can short-circuit you from your immediate, task-focused decisions into a higher level of exploration than is currently constructive. Save project planning for your weekly or seasonal planning rituals, or add it as a task to your master list and give it the appropriate dedicated time.

Slipping from choosing your Inspired Action and Three Bonuses to creating dream lists...again. You might *wish* that you could get six things done tomorrow, but in reality you're paving the road to disappointment. Pick your Inspired Action and your Three Bonuses, and get to work.

Failing to prepare appropriately for the following day. If your Inspired Action for tomorrow requires that you have a particular folder with you, then make sure you have what you need with you. That forethought will set you up for success.

What If It Doesn't Get Done?

Recently one of my new clients failed to complete her Inspired Action, and she went into a disempowering tailspin. That's not helpful, so let's start by getting clear on why this might have happened.

You forgot about it. Can you build in more reminders throughout the day to cue you about your Inspired Action? Phone alarms? Sticky notes?

You remembered it, but you procrastinated. How can you structure in time to do the task as early in the day as possible? As Brian Tracy says, eat the frog. It's only 30 minutes! Look at your calendar for tomorrow, decide exactly when you can dedicate that time, and then set a timer if necessary. Sometimes resistance looms its frightening head, but the reality is that starting is the hardest part. Once you get started with *any* task it gets easier.

A higher-priority item arose. That might happen sometimes. Emergencies, surprises, or unexpected opportunities happen to all of us. What's important is whether you made an *intentional choice* to renegotiate your Inspired Action for the day in order to do something else. Did you choose and recommit, or did you just get swept away in the moment? Provided you made an intentional change based on new information in the moment, you're golden. It's when you just let the day sweep away your choices and priorities that you've entered a danger zone that you'll want to exit the next day.

Bottom line: know your options, make your choices intentionally, set realistic expectations for what you can do each day, and celebrate often.

The most important aspect of a daily planning ritual is developing the consistent habit. Your entire perspective on your life and abilities can change with this one simple habit. You create a rhythm of decision, action, and completion that proves how *anything* can be accomplished.

Next Actions

- ✓ Choose your preferred time for your daily planning ritual, and put it on your calendar. If desired, make it a recurring appointment with an alarm that goes off, or set alarms on your cell phone to remind you ten minutes before that time, and again when the time arrives.
- ✓ Bring your master list up-to-date with new tasks and projects each day. This daily habit only works if you are looking at the whole picture and making thoughtful and considered decisions in relationship to everything that is currently on your plate.
- ✓ Try out the six steps above for this week, and see how it feels. Do you feel clearer about what you are doing and better about what you're getting accomplished? You will likely realize how many other tasks are also getting done each day, but for once these background tasks are not distracting you from accomplishing your Inspired Action—your most important item.

Resources

Allen, David. *Getting Things Done: The Art of Stress-Free Productivity.* New York: Viking, 2001.

Babauta, Leo. *Zen to Done: The Ultimate Simple Productivity System.* CreateSpace Independent Publishing Platform: 2008.

Inspired Action Mastermind Program. www.ChosenCourse.com/InspiredActionMastermind.

Complete Resource List

Add-on Resources

Available at www.InspiredActionBook.com/Resources:

- ✧ Dowsing for Purpose Worksheet
- ✧ Change Bridge Worksheet
- ✧ New Behavior Generator Visualization
- ✧ Chosen Course Excellence Assessment
- ✧ Life Rhythm Map Templates
- ✧ Vital Behavior Change Worksheet
- ✧ Grounding Meditation
- ✧ Vivid Future Accomplishments

Books & Articles

Achor, Shawn. *The Happiness Advantage: The Seven Principles of Positive Psychology That Fuel Success and Performance at Work.* New York: Broadway Books, 2010.

Allen, David. *Getting Things Done: The Art of Stress-Free Productivity.* New York: Viking, 2001.

Assaraf, John, and Murray Smith. *The Answer: Grow Any Business, Achieve Financial Freedom, and Live an Extraordinary Life.* New York: Atria Books, 2008.

Babauta, Leo. *Zen to Done: The Ultimate Simple Productivity System.* CreateSpace Independent Publishing Platform: 2008.

Blanchard, Robert and Melinda. *Changing Your Course: The 5-Step Guide to Getting the Life You Want.* New York: Sterling, 2008.

Brother Lawrence of the Resurrection, E. M. Blaiklock, trans. *The Practice of the Presence of God.* Nashville: T. Nelson Publishers, 1982.

Canfield, Jack, and Janet Switzer. *The Success Principles: How to Get from Where You Are to Where You Want to Be.* New York: HarperCollins, 2005.

Carr, Nicholas. *The Shallows: What the Internet Is Doing to Our Brains.* New York: W.W. Norton & Company, 2011.

Chittister, Joan. *Wisdom Distilled from the Daily: Living the Rule of St. Benedict Today.* New York: HarperOne, 2009.

Covey, Stephen R. *The 8th Habit: From Effectiveness to Greatness.* New York: Free Press, 2005.

Csikszentmihalyi, Mihaly. *Flow: The Psychology of Optimal Experience.* New York: Harper & Row, 1990.

Duhigg, Charles. *The Power of Habit: Why We Do What We Do in Life and Business.* New York: Random House, 2014.

Editors of Life. *LIFE Heaven on Earth: The World's Must-See Destinations.* New York: Life, 2011.

Ferriss, Timothy. *The 4-Hour Workweek: Escape 9-5, Live Anywhere, and Join the New Rich.* New York: Harmony, 2009.

Fiore, Neil A. *The Now Habit: A Strategic Program for Overcoming Procrastination and Enjoying Guilt-Free Play.* New York: Tarcher/Penguin, 2007.

Fisher, Roger, William Ury, and Bruce Patton. *Getting to Yes: Negotiating Agreement without Giving In.* New York: Penguin Books, 2011.

Frankl, Victor E. *Man's Search for Meaning.* Boston: Beacon Press, 2006.

Gawande, Atul. *The Checklist Manifesto: How to Get Things Right.* New York: Metropolitan Books, 2010.

Grenny, Joseph, Kerry Patterson, et al. *Influencer: The New Science of Leading Change.* New York: McGraw-Hill Education, 2013.

Kelley, Tim. True Purpose: 12 Strategies for Discovering the Difference You Are Meant to Make. Berkeley, CA: Transcendent Solutions Press, 2009.

Kolberg, Judith, and Kathleen Nadeau. *ADD-Friendly Ways to Organize Your Life.* New York: Brunner-Routledge, 2002.

Leider, Richard J. *The Power of Purpose: Find Meaning, Live Longer, Better.* San Francisco: Berrett-Koehler Publishers, 2010.

Loehr, Jim, and Tony Schwartz. T*he Power of Full Engagement: Managing Energy, Not Time, Is the Key to High Performance and Personal Renewal.* New York: Free Press, 2003.

Maisel, Eric, and Ann Maisel. *Brainstorm: Harnessing the Power of Productive Obsessions.* Novato, CA: New World Library, 2010.

Man, John, et al. *The New Traveler's Atlas: A Global Guide to the Places You Must See in Your Lifetime.* New York: Barron's Educational Series, 2007.

Miller, Caroline Adams and Dr. Michael B. Frisch. *Creating Your Best Life: The Ultimate Life List Guide.* New York: Sterling, 2009.

Morgenstern, Julie. *Never Check E-mail in the Morning: And Other Unexpected Strategies for Making Your Work Life Work.* New York: Fireside, 2004.

Morgenstern, Julie. *Organizing from the Inside Out: The Foolproof System for Organizing Your Home, Your Office and Your Life.* New York: Holt Paperbacks, 2nd Edition, 2004.

Morgenstern, Julie. *Time Management from the Inside Out: The Foolproof System for Taking Control of Your Schedule—and Your Life.* New York: Henry Holt/Owl Books, 2004.

Niurka. *Supreme Influence: Change Your Life with the Power of the Language You Use.* New York: Harmony Books, 2013.

O'Connor, Anahad. "The Claim: Heart Attacks Are More Common on Mondays." New York Times, 2006. http://bit.ly/MondayHeartAttacks

Powers, William. *Hamlet's BlackBerry: A Practical Philosophy for Building a Good Life in the Digital Age.* New York: Harper, 2010.

Pressfield, Steven. T*urning Pro: Tap Your Inner Power and Create Your Life's Work.* New York: Black Irish Entertainment LLC, 2012.

Pressfield, Steven. *The War of Art: Break Through the Blocks and Win Your Inner Creative Battles.* New York: Black Irish Entertainment LLC, 2002.

Richardson, Cheryl. *The Art of Extreme Self-Care: Transform Your Life One Month at a Time.* Carlsbad, CA: Hay House, Inc., 2009.

Schwartz, Tony. *Be Excellent at Anything: The Four Keys to Transforming the Way We Work and Live.* New York: Free Press, 2010.

Stoddard, Alexandra. *Living a Beautiful Life: 500 Ways to Add Elegance, Order, Beauty, and Joy to Every Day of Your Life.* New York: Random House, 1986.

Stoddard, Alexandra. *Time Alive: Celebrate Your Life Every Day.* New York: Collins, 2005.

Thorp, *Gary. Sweeping Changes: Discovering the Joy of Zen in Everyday Tasks.* New York: Walker & Company, 2000.

Trapani, Gina. *Upgrade Your Life: The Lifehacker Guide to Working Smarter, Faster, Better.* Hoboken, NJ: Wiley Technology Pub. 2008.

Varone, Linda. *The Smarter Home Office: 8 Simple Steps to Increase Your Income, Inspiration, and Comfort.* Arlington, MA: Great Meadows Publishing, 2010.

Waddill, Kathy. *The Organizing Sourcebook: Nine Strategies for Simplifying Your Life.* Chicago: Contemporary Books, 2001.

Websites & Software

Asana. http://bit.ly/AsanaTasks

Allen, David. GTD Methodology Guides. http://bit.ly/GTDGuides.

Babauta, Leo. "Zen Habits." http://bit.ly/ZenHabitsBlog.

Basecamp. http://bit.ly/BasecampProjects.

Bloom*– Mindbloom. http://bit.ly/bloomApp.

Buddhify 2.0. http://bit.ly/BuddhifyApp.

Calendly. http://bit.ly/CalendlyInfo.

Chime app. http://bit.ly/ChimeApp.

Chosen Course Blog. http://www.ChosenCourse.com/blog.

Chosen Course Ignition Events.
http://www.ChosenCourse.com/IgnitionEvents.

Collage apps for smartphone/tablet.
Search the App Store and you'll find plenty of options.

Covey, Stephen. "Big Rocks." http://bit.ly/CoveyBigRocks.

Craigslist. http://bit.ly/CraigslistInfo.

Doodle. http://bit.ly/DoodleInfo.

Dream Dinners. http://bit.ly/DreamDinnersInfo.

Dropbox. http://bit.ly/DropboxDigitalStorage.

The Early Edition 2 app. http://bit.ly/EarlyEdition2.

Evernote. http://bit.ly/EvernoteDigitalNotes.

Feedly. http://bit.ly/FeedlyInfo.

Flipboard. http://bit.ly/FlipboardInfo.

Google Calendar. http://bit.ly/GcalInfo.

Grocery IQ. http://bit.ly/GroceryIQapp.

Guru.com. http://bit.ly/GuruInfo.

Habit List app. http://bit.ly/HabitList.

iCal. http://bit.ly/iCalInfo.

iCloud Reminders. Built-in with the Apple iOS operating system.

Institute for Challenging Disorganization (ICD). http://bit.ly/ChallengingDisorg.

Inspired Action Mastermind Program. http://www.ChosenCourse.com/InspiredActionMasterMind.

Levenger. http://bit.ly/LevengerCirca.

Lifehacker. http://bit.ly/LifeHackerInfo.

LinkedIn Pulse app. http://bit.ly/LIPulse.

Living Peace Professional Organizing. http://bit.ly/LivingPeaceOrg.

Markel, Adam. 2013. Peak Potentials Training Programs. http://bit.ly/NewPeaks.

Meetup. http://bit.ly/MeetupInfo.

Merlin Mann: Indie Writer, Speaker, and Broadcaster. http://bit.ly/InboxZeroVideo.

Microsoft Outlook. http://bit.ly/OutlookTime.

Mindfulness Bell app. http://bit.ly/MindfulnessBell.

Mint.com. http://bit.ly/MintInfo.

National Association of Professional Organizers (NAPO). http://bit.ly/NAPOInfo.

National Do Not Call Registry. http://bit.ly/DoNotCallReg.

National Do Not Mail List. http://bit.ly/JunkOptOut.

"Overcoming Paper Clutter: BARFT Your Papers." http://bit.ly/BARFTVideo.

Pinterest. http://bit.ly/PinInfo.

Remember The Milk. http://bit.ly/RTMTasks.

Real Simple: Life Made Easier. http://bit.ly/RealSimpleInfo.

Streaks app. http://bit.ly/StreaksApp.

TimeTrade. http://bit.ly/TimeTradeInfo.

ToDoist Plugin for Microsoft Outlook. http://bit.ly/TodoistOutlook.

Trello. http://bit.ly/TrelloInfo.

Unroll.me. http://bit.ly/UnrollMeInfo.

Upwork. http://bit.ly/UpworkInfo.

Vistaprint. http://bit.ly/VistaprintInfo.

Wunderlist. http://bit.ly/WunderListTasks.

Yelp. http://bit.ly/YelpInfo.

You Need a Budget (YNAB). http://bit.ly/YNABInfo.

DVDs & Films

The Bucket List. DVD. Directed by Rob Reiner. Starring Jack Nicholson and Morgan Freeman. Warner Bros., 2008.

Last Holiday. DVD. Directed by Wayne Wang. Starring Queen Latifah and LL Cool J. Paramount, 2006.

Index

L

M

N

S

T

U

V

W

About the Author

Erin Elizabeth Wells is The Intentionality Expert and founder of Chosen Course, a professional productivity consulting and training firm. Erin works with high achievers including corporate leaders, entrepreneurs, and influencers to improve their productivity, focus, and effectiveness in their work and daily life. Her approach focuses on creating *productivity with purpose* for her clients connecting to the WHY of our action rather than simply doing more faster.

Erin is a graduate of Harvard Divinity School with a Masters of Divinity (M.Div.) degree, and she holds the designation of Certified Professional Organizer (CPO®). In 2014, Erin received her certification as a practitioner of Neuro-Linguistic Programming (NLP), which provides many additional skills to support habit formation and behavior change, which are key elements of productivity.

Erin lives with her husband and two cats near the ocean on the north shore of Massachusetts. She loves to explore the world, take long walks, read historical novels, and taste new wines and craft beers.

Connect with Erin more at www.ChosenCourse.com or via email at Info@ChosenCourse.com.

Your Next Steps with
Inspired Action

Visit www.ChosenCourse.com

A 10-Week Online Program to take your implementation of Inspired Action further.

Private Full-Day Intensive Sessions with Erin Elizabeth Wells to create your vision and strategy for the future.

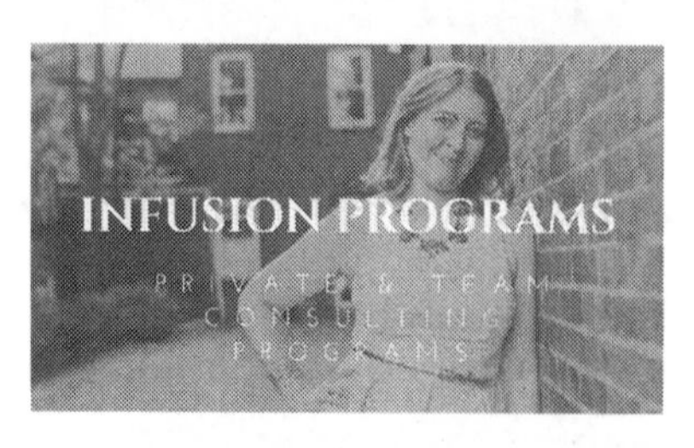

Long-Term Private and Team Consulting Programs with Erin Elizabeth Wells to implement the mindset, tools, and habits to improve your life.

Webinars, Speaking, and Training Programs for your community or organization to ignite Inspired Action in your group or company.

Take your Inspired Action implementation further today.